50% OFF Kapla School Entrance Exam Course!

By Mometrix

Dear Customer,

We consider it an honor and a privilege that you chose our Kaplan Nursing School Entrance Exam Study Guide. As a way of showing our appreciation and to help us better serve you, we are offering **50% off our online Kaplan Nursing School Entrance Exam Prep Course.** Many Kaplan Entrance Exam courses are needlessly expensive and don't deliver enough value. With our course, you get access to the best Kaplan Nursing School Entrance Exam prep material, and you only pay half price.

We have structured our online course to perfectly complement your printed study guide. The Kaplan Entrance Exam Online Course contains **in-depth lessons** that cover all the most important topics, **80+ video reviews** that explain difficult concepts, and over **1,850 practice questions** to ensure you feel prepared.

Online Kaplan Nursing School Entrance Exam Prep Course

Topics Included:
- Reading
  - Main Ideas and Supporting Details
  - Purpose and Tone
  - Fact and Opinion
- Writing
  - Eight Parts of Speech
  - Clauses and Phrases
  - Punctuation
- Mathematics
  - Numbers and Operations
  - Factoring
  - Expressions and Equations
- Science
  - Cell Structure and Support
  - DNA and RNA
  - The Systems of the Body

Course Features:
- Kaplan Nursing School Entrance Exam Study Guide
  - Get content that complements our best-selling study guide.
- Full-Length Practice Tests
  - With over 1,850 practice questions, you can test yourself again and again.
- Mobile Friendly
  - If you need to study on the go, the course is easily accessible from your mobile device.

To receive this discount, visit us at mometrix.com/university/kaplan or simply scan this QR code with your smartphone. At the checkout page, enter the discount code: **kap50off**

If you have any questions or concerns, please contact us at support@mometrix.com.

Kaplan Nursing School

Entrance Exam Study Guide 2022-2023

Prep Secrets

3 Full-Length Practice Tests

Step-by-Step Video Tutorials

3rd Edition

Copyright © 2022 by Mometrix Media LLC

All rights reserved. This product, or parts thereof, may not be reproduced, stored in a retrieval system, or transmitted in any form or by any means—electronic, mechanical, photocopy, recording, scanning, or other—except for brief quotations in critical reviews or articles, without the prior written permission of the publisher.

Written and edited by Matthew Bowling

Printed in the United States of America

This paper meets the requirements of ANSI/NISO Z39.48-1992 (Permanence of Paper).

Mometrix offers volume discount pricing to institutions. For more information or a price quote, please contact our sales department at sales@mometrix.com or 888-248-1219.

Mometrix Media LLC is not affiliated with or endorsed by any official testing organization. All organizational and test names are trademarks of their respective owners.

ISBN 13: 978-1-5167-2028-6
ISBN 10: 1-5167-2028-8

Dear Future Exam Success Story

First of all, **THANK YOU** for purchasing Mometrix study materials!

Second, congratulations! You are one of the few determined test-takers who are committed to doing whatever it takes to excel on your exam. **You have come to the right place.** We developed these study materials with one goal in mind: to deliver you the information you need in a format that's concise and easy to use.

In addition to optimizing your guide for the content of the test, we've outlined our recommended steps for breaking down the preparation process into small, attainable goals so you can make sure you stay on track.

We've also analyzed the entire test-taking process, identifying the most common pitfalls and showing how you can overcome them and be ready for any curveball the test throws you.

Standardized testing is one of the biggest obstacles on your road to success, which only increases the importance of doing well in the high-pressure, high-stakes environment of test day. Your results on this test could have a significant impact on your future, and this guide provides the information and practical advice to help you achieve your full potential on test day.

Your success is our success

We would love to hear from you! If you would like to share the story of your exam success or if you have any questions or comments in regard to our products, please contact us at **800-673-8175** or **support@mometrix.com**.

Thanks again for your business and we wish you continued success!

Sincerely,
The Mometrix Test Preparation Team

TABLE OF CONTENTS

INTRODUCTION _____ 1
SECRET KEY #1 – PLAN BIG, STUDY SMALL _____ 2
SECRET KEY #2 – MAKE YOUR STUDYING COUNT _____ 3
SECRET KEY #3 – PRACTICE THE RIGHT WAY _____ 4
SECRET KEY #4 – PACE YOURSELF _____ 6
SECRET KEY #5 – HAVE A PLAN FOR GUESSING _____ 7
TEST-TAKING STRATEGIES _____ 10
READING COMPREHENSION _____ 15
   MAIN IDEAS, SUPPORTING DETAILS, AND CONTEXT _____ 15
   PURPOSE AND TONE _____ 19
   FACT AND OPINION, LOGICAL INFERENCES, AND SUMMARIZING _____ 20
   VOCABULARY _____ 23
WRITING _____ 31
   FOUNDATIONS OF GRAMMAR _____ 31
   AGREEMENT AND SENTENCE STRUCTURE _____ 39
   PUNCTUATION _____ 55
   COMMON ERRORS _____ 61
MATHEMATICS _____ 65
   NUMBERS _____ 65
   OPERATIONS _____ 69
   FACTORING _____ 74
   RATIONAL NUMBERS _____ 75
   PROPORTIONS AND RATIOS _____ 88
   EXPRESSIONS AND EQUATIONS _____ 93
   UNITS OF MEASUREMENT _____ 101
SCIENCE _____ 105
   MACROMOLECULES _____ 105
   DNA _____ 107
   RNA _____ 109
   MENDEL'S LAWS _____ 109
   NON-MENDELIAN CONCEPTS _____ 111
   GENERAL ANATOMY AND PHYSIOLOGY _____ 112
   RESPIRATORY SYSTEM _____ 120
   CARDIOVASCULAR SYSTEM _____ 123
   GASTROINTESTINAL SYSTEM _____ 129
   NERVOUS SYSTEM _____ 133
   MUSCULAR SYSTEM _____ 134
   REPRODUCTIVE SYSTEM _____ 137
   INTEGUMENTARY SYSTEM _____ 140
   ENDOCRINE SYSTEM _____ 143

iii

Urinary System 147
Immune System 149
Skeletal System 151

KNAT Practice Test #1 155
Reading Comprehension 155
Writing 162
Mathematics 168
Science 173

Answer Key and Explanations for Test #1 176
Reading Comprehension 176
Writing 180
Mathematics 182
Science 188

KNAT Practice Test #2 191
Reading Comprehension 191
Writing 196
Mathematics 203
Science 208

Answer Key and Explanations for Test #2 211
Reading Comprehension 211
Writing 213
Mathematics 216
Science 221

KNAT Practice Test #3 222
Reading Comprehension 222
Writing 228
Mathematics 234
Science 238

Answer Key and Explanations for Test #3 241
Reading Comprehension 241
Writing 246
Mathematics 248
Science 254

How to Overcome Test Anxiety 256
Causes of Test Anxiety 256
Elements of Test Anxiety 257
Effects of Test Anxiety 257
Physical Steps for Beating Test Anxiety 258
Mental Steps for Beating Test Anxiety 259
Study Strategy 260
Test Tips 262
Important Qualification 263

Tell Us Your Story 264

Additional Bonus Material 265

Introduction

Thank you for purchasing this resource! You have made the choice to prepare yourself for a test that could have a huge impact on your future, and this guide is designed to help you be fully ready for test day. Obviously, it's important to have a solid understanding of the test material, but you also need to be prepared for the unique environment and stressors of the test, so that you can perform to the best of your abilities.

For this purpose, the first section that appears in this guide is the **Secret Keys**. We've devoted countless hours to meticulously researching what works and what doesn't, and we've boiled down our findings to the five most impactful steps you can take to improve your performance on the test. We start at the beginning with study planning and move through the preparation process, all the way to the testing strategies that will help you get the most out of what you know when you're finally sitting in front of the test.

We recommend that you start preparing for your test as far in advance as possible. However, if you've bought this guide as a last-minute study resource and only have a few days before your test, we recommend that you skip over the first two Secret Keys since they address a long-term study plan.

If you struggle with **test anxiety**, we strongly encourage you to check out our recommendations for how you can overcome it. Test anxiety is a formidable foe, but it can be beaten, and we want to make sure you have the tools you need to defeat it.

Secret Key #1 – Plan Big, Study Small

There's a lot riding on your performance. If you want to ace this test, you're going to need to keep your skills sharp and the material fresh in your mind. You need a plan that lets you review everything you need to know while still fitting in your schedule. We'll break this strategy down into three categories.

Information Organization

Start with the information you already have: the official test outline. From this, you can make a complete list of all the concepts you need to cover before the test. Organize these concepts into groups that can be studied together, and create a list of any related vocabulary you need to learn so you can brush up on any difficult terms. You'll want to keep this vocabulary list handy once you actually start studying since you may need to add to it along the way.

Time Management

Once you have your set of study concepts, decide how to spread them out over the time you have left before the test. Break your study plan into small, clear goals so you have a manageable task for each day and know exactly what you're doing. Then just focus on one small step at a time. When you manage your time this way, you don't need to spend hours at a time studying. Studying a small block of content for a short period each day helps you retain information better and avoid stressing over how much you have left to do. You can relax knowing that you have a plan to cover everything in time. In order for this strategy to be effective though, you have to start studying early and stick to your schedule. Avoid the exhaustion and futility that comes from last-minute cramming!

Study Environment

The environment you study in has a big impact on your learning. Studying in a coffee shop, while probably more enjoyable, is not likely to be as fruitful as studying in a quiet room. It's important to keep distractions to a minimum. You're only planning to study for a short block of time, so make the most of it. Don't pause to check your phone or get up to find a snack. It's also important to **avoid multitasking**. Research has consistently shown that multitasking will make your studying dramatically less effective. Your study area should also be comfortable and well-lit so you don't have the distraction of straining your eyes or sitting on an uncomfortable chair.

The time of day you study is also important. You want to be rested and alert. Don't wait until just before bedtime. Study when you'll be most likely to comprehend and remember. Even better, if you know what time of day your test will be, set that time aside for study. That way your brain will be used to working on that subject at that specific time and you'll have a better chance of recalling information.

Finally, it can be helpful to team up with others who are studying for the same test. Your actual studying should be done in as isolated an environment as possible, but the work of organizing the information and setting up the study plan can be divided up. In between study sessions, you can discuss with your teammates the concepts that you're all studying and quiz each other on the details. Just be sure that your teammates are as serious about the test as you are. If you find that your study time is being replaced with social time, you might need to find a new team.

Secret Key #2 – Make Your Studying Count

You're devoting a lot of time and effort to preparing for this test, so you want to be absolutely certain it will pay off. This means doing more than just reading the content and hoping you can remember it on test day. It's important to make every minute of study count. There are two main areas you can focus on to make your studying count.

Retention

It doesn't matter how much time you study if you can't remember the material. You need to make sure you are retaining the concepts. To check your retention of the information you're learning, try recalling it at later times with minimal prompting. Try carrying around flashcards and glance at one or two from time to time or ask a friend who's also studying for the test to quiz you.

To enhance your retention, look for ways to put the information into practice so that you can apply it rather than simply recalling it. If you're using the information in practical ways, it will be much easier to remember. Similarly, it helps to solidify a concept in your mind if you're not only reading it to yourself but also explaining it to someone else. Ask a friend to let you teach them about a concept you're a little shaky on (or speak aloud to an imaginary audience if necessary). As you try to summarize, define, give examples, and answer your friend's questions, you'll understand the concepts better and they will stay with you longer. Finally, step back for a big picture view and ask yourself how each piece of information fits with the whole subject. When you link the different concepts together and see them working together as a whole, it's easier to remember the individual components.

Finally, practice showing your work on any multi-step problems, even if you're just studying. Writing out each step you take to solve a problem will help solidify the process in your mind, and you'll be more likely to remember it during the test.

Modality

Modality simply refers to the means or method by which you study. Choosing a study modality that fits your own individual learning style is crucial. No two people learn best in exactly the same way, so it's important to know your strengths and use them to your advantage.

For example, if you learn best by visualization, focus on visualizing a concept in your mind and draw an image or a diagram. Try color-coding your notes, illustrating them, or creating symbols that will trigger your mind to recall a learned concept. If you learn best by hearing or discussing information, find a study partner who learns the same way or read aloud to yourself. Think about how to put the information in your own words. Imagine that you are giving a lecture on the topic and record yourself so you can listen to it later.

For any learning style, flashcards can be helpful. Organize the information so you can take advantage of spare moments to review. Underline key words or phrases. Use different colors for different categories. Mnemonic devices (such as creating a short list in which every item starts with the same letter) can also help with retention. Find what works best for you and use it to store the information in your mind most effectively and easily.

Secret Key #3 – Practice the Right Way

Your success on test day depends not only on how many hours you put into preparing, but also on whether you prepared the right way. It's good to check along the way to see if your studying is paying off. One of the most effective ways to do this is by taking practice tests to evaluate your progress. Practice tests are useful because they show exactly where you need to improve. Every time you take a practice test, pay special attention to these three groups of questions:

- The questions you got wrong
- The questions you had to guess on, even if you guessed right
- The questions you found difficult or slow to work through

This will show you exactly what your weak areas are, and where you need to devote more study time. Ask yourself why each of these questions gave you trouble. Was it because you didn't understand the material? Was it because you didn't remember the vocabulary? Do you need more repetitions on this type of question to build speed and confidence? Dig into those questions and figure out how you can strengthen your weak areas as you go back to review the material.

Additionally, many practice tests have a section explaining the answer choices. It can be tempting to read the explanation and think that you now have a good understanding of the concept. However, an explanation likely only covers part of the question's broader context. Even if the explanation makes perfect sense, **go back and investigate** every concept related to the question until you're positive you have a thorough understanding.

As you go along, keep in mind that the practice test is just that: practice. Memorizing these questions and answers will not be very helpful on the actual test because it is unlikely to have any of the same exact questions. If you only know the right answers to the sample questions, you won't be prepared for the real thing. **Study the concepts** until you understand them fully, and then you'll be able to answer any question that shows up on the test.

It's important to wait on the practice tests until you're ready. If you take a test on your first day of study, you may be overwhelmed by the amount of material covered and how much you need to learn. Work up to it gradually.

On test day, you'll need to be prepared for answering questions, managing your time, and using the test-taking strategies you've learned. It's a lot to balance, like a mental marathon that will have a big impact on your future. Like training for a marathon, you'll need to start slowly and work your way up. When test day arrives, you'll be ready.

Start with the strategies you've read in the first two Secret Keys—plan your course and study in the way that works best for you. If you have time, consider using multiple study resources to get different approaches to the same concepts. It can be helpful to see difficult concepts from more than one angle. Then find a good source for practice tests. Many times, the test website will suggest potential study resources or provide sample tests.

Practice Test Strategy

If you're able to find at least three practice tests, we recommend this strategy:

Untimed and Open-Book Practice

Take the first test with no time constraints and with your notes and study guide handy. Take your time and focus on applying the strategies you've learned.

Timed and Open-Book Practice

Take the second practice test open-book as well, but set a timer and practice pacing yourself to finish in time.

Timed and Closed-Book Practice

Take any other practice tests as if it were test day. Set a timer and put away your study materials. Sit at a table or desk in a quiet room, imagine yourself at the testing center, and answer questions as quickly and accurately as possible.

Keep repeating timed and closed-book tests on a regular basis until you run out of practice tests or it's time for the actual test. Your mind will be ready for the schedule and stress of test day, and you'll be able to focus on recalling the material you've learned.

Secret Key #4 – Pace Yourself

Once you're fully prepared for the material on the test, your biggest challenge on test day will be managing your time. Just knowing that the clock is ticking can make you panic even if you have plenty of time left. Work on pacing yourself so you can build confidence against the time constraints of the exam. Pacing is a difficult skill to master, especially in a high-pressure environment, so **practice is vital**.

Set time expectations for your pace based on how much time is available. For example, if a section has 60 questions and the time limit is 30 minutes, you know you have to average 30 seconds or less per question in order to answer them all. Although 30 seconds is the hard limit, set 25 seconds per question as your goal, so you reserve extra time to spend on harder questions. When you budget extra time for the harder questions, you no longer have any reason to stress when those questions take longer to answer.

Don't let this time expectation distract you from working through the test at a calm, steady pace, but keep it in mind so you don't spend too much time on any one question. Recognize that taking extra time on one question you don't understand may keep you from answering two that you do understand later in the test. If your time limit for a question is up and you're still not sure of the answer, mark it and move on, and come back to it later if the time and the test format allow. If the testing format doesn't allow you to return to earlier questions, just make an educated guess; then put it out of your mind and move on.

On the easier questions, be careful not to rush. It may seem wise to hurry through them so you have more time for the challenging ones, but it's not worth missing one if you know the concept and just didn't take the time to read the question fully. Work efficiently but make sure you understand the question and have looked at all of the answer choices, since more than one may seem right at first.

Even if you're paying attention to the time, you may find yourself a little behind at some point. You should speed up to get back on track, but do so wisely. Don't panic; just take a few seconds less on each question until you're caught up. Don't guess without thinking, but do look through the answer choices and eliminate any you know are wrong. If you can get down to two choices, it is often worthwhile to guess from those. Once you've chosen an answer, move on and don't dwell on any that you skipped or had to hurry through. If a question was taking too long, chances are it was one of the harder ones, so you weren't as likely to get it right anyway.

On the other hand, if you find yourself getting ahead of schedule, it may be beneficial to slow down a little. The more quickly you work, the more likely you are to make a careless mistake that will affect your score. You've budgeted time for each question, so don't be afraid to spend that time. Practice an efficient but careful pace to get the most out of the time you have.

Secret Key #5 – Have a Plan for Guessing

When you're taking the test, you may find yourself stuck on a question. Some of the answer choices seem better than others, but you don't see the one answer choice that is obviously correct. What do you do?

The scenario described above is very common, yet most test takers have not effectively prepared for it. Developing and practicing a plan for guessing may be one of the single most effective uses of your time as you get ready for the exam.

In developing your plan for guessing, there are three questions to address:

- When should you start the guessing process?
- How should you narrow down the choices?
- Which answer should you choose?

When to Start the Guessing Process

Unless your plan for guessing is to select C every time (which, despite its merits, is not what we recommend), you need to leave yourself enough time to apply your answer elimination strategies. Since you have a limited amount of time for each question, that means that if you're going to give yourself the best shot at guessing correctly, you have to decide quickly whether or not you will guess.

Of course, the best-case scenario is that you don't have to guess at all, so first, see if you can answer the question based on your knowledge of the subject and basic reasoning skills. Focus on the key words in the question and try to jog your memory of related topics. Give yourself a chance to bring the knowledge to mind, but once you realize that you don't have (or you can't access) the knowledge you need to answer the question, it's time to start the guessing process.

It's almost always better to start the guessing process too early than too late. It only takes a few seconds to remember something and answer the question from knowledge. Carefully eliminating wrong answer choices takes longer. Plus, going through the process of eliminating answer choices can actually help jog your memory.

Summary: Start the guessing process as soon as you decide that you can't answer the question based on your knowledge.

How to Narrow Down the Choices

The next chapter in this book (**Test-Taking Strategies**) includes a wide range of strategies for how to approach questions and how to look for answer choices to eliminate. You will definitely want to read those carefully, practice them, and figure out which ones work best for you. Here though, we're going to address a mindset rather than a particular strategy.

Your odds of guessing an answer correctly depend on how many options you are choosing from.

Number of options left	5	4	3	2	1
Odds of guessing correctly	20%	25%	33%	50%	100%

You can see from this chart just how valuable it is to be able to eliminate incorrect answers and make an educated guess, but there are two things that many test takers do that cause them to miss out on the benefits of guessing:

- Accidentally eliminating the correct answer
- Selecting an answer based on an impression

We'll look at the first one here, and the second one in the next section.

To avoid accidentally eliminating the correct answer, we recommend a thought exercise called **the $5 challenge**. In this challenge, you only eliminate an answer choice from contention if you are willing to bet $5 on it being wrong. Why $5? Five dollars is a small but not insignificant amount of money. It's an amount you could afford to lose but wouldn't want to throw away. And while losing $5 once might not hurt too much, doing it twenty times will set you back $100. In the same way, each small decision you make—eliminating a choice here, guessing on a question there—won't by itself impact your score very much, but when you put them all together, they can make a big difference. By holding each answer choice elimination decision to a higher standard, you can reduce the risk of accidentally eliminating the correct answer.

The $5 challenge can also be applied in a positive sense: If you are willing to bet $5 that an answer choice *is* correct, go ahead and mark it as correct.

Summary: Only eliminate an answer choice if you are willing to bet $5 that it is wrong.

Which Answer to Choose

You're taking the test. You've run into a hard question and decided you'll have to guess. You've eliminated all the answer choices you're willing to bet $5 on. Now you have to pick an answer. Why do we even need to talk about this? Why can't you just pick whichever one you feel like when the time comes?

The answer to these questions is that if you don't come into the test with a plan, you'll rely on your impression to select an answer choice, and if you do that, you risk falling into a trap. The test writers know that everyone who takes their test will be guessing on some of the questions, so they intentionally write wrong answer choices to seem plausible. You still have to pick an answer though, and if the wrong answer choices are designed to look right, how can you ever be sure that you're not falling for their trap? The best solution we've found to this dilemma is to take the decision out of your hands entirely. Here is the process we recommend:

Once you've eliminated any choices that you are confident (willing to bet $5) are wrong, select the first remaining choice as your answer.

Whether you choose to select the first remaining choice, the second, or the last, the important thing is that you use some preselected standard. Using this approach guarantees that you will not be enticed into selecting an answer choice that looks right, because you are not basing your decision on how the answer choices look.

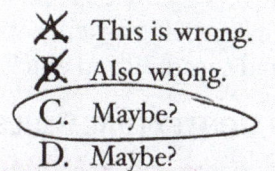

This is not meant to make you question your knowledge. Instead, it is to help you recognize the difference between your knowledge and your impressions. There's a huge difference between thinking an answer is right because of what you know, and thinking an answer is right because it looks or sounds like it should be right.

Summary: To ensure that your selection is appropriately random, make a predetermined selection from among all answer choices you have not eliminated.

Test-Taking Strategies

This section contains a list of test-taking strategies that you may find helpful as you work through the test. By taking what you know and applying logical thought, you can maximize your chances of answering any question correctly!

It is very important to realize that every question is different and every person is different: no single strategy will work on every question, and no single strategy will work for every person. That's why we've included all of them here, so you can try them out and determine which ones work best for different types of questions and which ones work best for you.

Question Strategies

⊘ READ CAREFULLY

Read the question and the answer choices carefully. Don't miss the question because you misread the terms. You have plenty of time to read each question thoroughly and make sure you understand what is being asked. Yet a happy medium must be attained, so don't waste too much time. You must read carefully and efficiently.

⊘ CONTEXTUAL CLUES

Look for contextual clues. If the question includes a word you are not familiar with, look at the immediate context for some indication of what the word might mean. Contextual clues can often give you all the information you need to decipher the meaning of an unfamiliar word. Even if you can't determine the meaning, you may be able to narrow down the possibilities enough to make a solid guess at the answer to the question.

⊘ PREFIXES

If you're having trouble with a word in the question or answer choices, try dissecting it. Take advantage of every clue that the word might include. Prefixes and suffixes can be a huge help. Usually, they allow you to determine a basic meaning. *Pre-* means before, *post-* means after, *pro-* is positive, *de-* is negative. From prefixes and suffixes, you can get an idea of the general meaning of the word and try to put it into context.

⊘ HEDGE WORDS

Watch out for critical hedge words, such as *likely, may, can, sometimes, often, almost, mostly, usually, generally, rarely,* and *sometimes*. Question writers insert these hedge phrases to cover every possibility. Often an answer choice will be wrong simply because it leaves no room for exception. Be on guard for answer choices that have definitive words such as *exactly* and *always*.

⊘ SWITCHBACK WORDS

Stay alert for *switchbacks*. These are the words and phrases frequently used to alert you to shifts in thought. The most common switchback words are *but, although,* and *however*. Others include *nevertheless, on the other hand, even though, while, in spite of, despite,* and *regardless of*. Switchback words are important to catch because they can change the direction of the question or an answer choice.

Face Value

When in doubt, use common sense. Accept the situation in the problem at face value. Don't read too much into it. These problems will not require you to make wild assumptions. If you have to go beyond creativity and warp time or space in order to have an answer choice fit the question, then you should move on and consider the other answer choices. These are normal problems rooted in reality. The applicable relationship or explanation may not be readily apparent, but it is there for you to figure out. Use your common sense to interpret anything that isn't clear.

Answer Choice Strategies

Answer Selection

The most thorough way to pick an answer choice is to identify and eliminate wrong answers until only one is left, then confirm it is the correct answer. Sometimes an answer choice may immediately seem right, but be careful. The test writers will usually put more than one reasonable answer choice on each question, so take a second to read all of them and make sure that the other choices are not equally obvious. As long as you have time left, it is better to read every answer choice than to pick the first one that looks right without checking the others.

Answer Choice Families

An answer choice family consists of two (in rare cases, three) answer choices that are very similar in construction and cannot all be true at the same time. If you see two answer choices that are direct opposites or parallels, one of them is usually the correct answer. For instance, if one answer choice says that quantity *x* increases and another either says that quantity *x* decreases (opposite) or says that quantity *y* increases (parallel), then those answer choices would fall into the same family. An answer choice that doesn't match the construction of the answer choice family is more likely to be incorrect. Most questions will not have answer choice families, but when they do appear, you should be prepared to recognize them.

Eliminate Answers

Eliminate answer choices as soon as you realize they are wrong, but make sure you consider all possibilities. If you are eliminating answer choices and realize that the last one you are left with is also wrong, don't panic. Start over and consider each choice again. There may be something you missed the first time that you will realize on the second pass.

Avoid Fact Traps

Don't be distracted by an answer choice that is factually true but doesn't answer the question. You are looking for the choice that answers the question. Stay focused on what the question is asking for so you don't accidentally pick an answer that is true but incorrect. Always go back to the question and make sure the answer choice you've selected actually answers the question and is not merely a true statement.

Extreme Statements

In general, you should avoid answers that put forth extreme actions as standard practice or proclaim controversial ideas as established fact. An answer choice that states the "process should be used in certain situations, if..." is much more likely to be correct than one that states the "process should be discontinued completely." The first is a calm rational statement and doesn't even make a definitive, uncompromising stance, using a hedge word *if* to provide wiggle room, whereas the second choice is far more extreme.

✓ Benchmark

As you read through the answer choices and you come across one that seems to answer the question well, mentally select that answer choice. This is not your final answer, but it's the one that will help you evaluate the other answer choices. The one that you selected is your benchmark or standard for judging each of the other answer choices. Every other answer choice must be compared to your benchmark. That choice is correct until proven otherwise by another answer choice beating it. If you find a better answer, then that one becomes your new benchmark. Once you've decided that no other choice answers the question as well as your benchmark, you have your final answer.

✓ Predict the Answer

Before you even start looking at the answer choices, it is often best to try to predict the answer. When you come up with the answer on your own, it is easier to avoid distractions and traps because you will know exactly what to look for. The right answer choice is unlikely to be word-for-word what you came up with, but it should be a close match. Even if you are confident that you have the right answer, you should still take the time to read each option before moving on.

General Strategies

✓ Tough Questions

If you are stumped on a problem or it appears too hard or too difficult, don't waste time. Move on! Remember though, if you can quickly check for obviously incorrect answer choices, your chances of guessing correctly are greatly improved. Before you completely give up, at least try to knock out a couple of possible answers. Eliminate what you can and then guess at the remaining answer choices before moving on.

✓ Check Your Work

Since you will probably not know every term listed and the answer to every question, it is important that you get credit for the ones that you do know. Don't miss any questions through careless mistakes. If at all possible, try to take a second to look back over your answer selection and make sure you've selected the correct answer choice and haven't made a costly careless mistake (such as marking an answer choice that you didn't mean to mark). This quick double check should more than pay for itself in caught mistakes for the time it costs.

✓ Pace Yourself

It's easy to be overwhelmed when you're looking at a page full of questions; your mind is confused and full of random thoughts, and the clock is ticking down faster than you would like. Calm down and maintain the pace that you have set for yourself. Especially as you get down to the last few minutes of the test, don't let the small numbers on the clock make you panic. As long as you are on track by monitoring your pace, you are guaranteed to have time for each question.

✓ Don't Rush

It is very easy to make errors when you are in a hurry. Maintaining a fast pace in answering questions is pointless if it makes you miss questions that you would have gotten right otherwise. Test writers like to include distracting information and wrong answers that seem right. Taking a little extra time to avoid careless mistakes can make all the difference in your test score. Find a pace that allows you to be confident in the answers that you select.

⊘ Keep Moving

Panicking will not help you pass the test, so do your best to stay calm and keep moving. Taking deep breaths and going through the answer elimination steps you practiced can help to break through a stress barrier and keep your pace.

Final Notes

The combination of a solid foundation of content knowledge and the confidence that comes from practicing your plan for applying that knowledge is the key to maximizing your performance on test day. As your foundation of content knowledge is built up and strengthened, you'll find that the strategies included in this chapter become more and more effective in helping you quickly sift through the distractions and traps of the test to isolate the correct answer.

Now that you're preparing to move forward into the test content chapters of this book, be sure to keep your goal in mind. As you read, think about how you will be able to apply this information on the test. If you've already seen sample questions for the test and you have an idea of the question format and style, try to come up with questions of your own that you can answer based on what you're reading. This will give you valuable practice applying your knowledge in the same ways you can expect to on test day.

Good luck and good studying!

Reading Comprehension

The reading comprehension portion of the exam requires the student to answer questions based on a passage that he or she has read. These questions are related to comprehension of reading and measure the student's ability to comprehend meaning, identify the main idea, find meaning of words in context, make logical inferences, etc.

Main Ideas, Supporting Details, and Context

PREPARATION

One of the best techniques for increasing reading comprehension is to **read** as much and as often as possible. Expand your literary horizons by reading a variety of publications. Read things like fiction stories, medical journals, comic books, and newspapers. This forces your mind to encounter new words and concepts. Keep reading materials in places where you will have idle time, such as the bathroom and your car. When you are waiting in line at the bank or pumping gas, you can thumb through a news magazine or read a chapter of a book. Tuck a book or pamphlet into your purse or pocket and read while standing in line at the grocery store. If you are using the Internet to decide which movie to see, read some reviews for each movie.

UNDERSTANDING A PASSAGE

One of the most important skills in reading comprehension is the identification of **topics** and **main ideas.** There is a subtle difference between these two features. The topic is the **subject** of a text (i.e., what the text is all about). The main idea, on the other hand, is the **most important point** being made by the author. The topic is usually expressed in a few words at the most while the main idea often needs a full sentence to be completely defined. As an example, a short passage might have the topic of penguins and the main idea could be written as *Penguins are different from other birds in many ways*. In most nonfiction writing, the topic and the main idea will be stated directly and often appear in a sentence at the very beginning or end of the text. When being tested on an understanding of the author's topic, you may be able to skim the passage for the general idea, by reading only the first sentence of each paragraph. A body paragraph's first sentence is often—but not always—the main topic sentence which gives you a summary of the content in the paragraph. However, there are cases in which the reader must figure out an **unstated** topic or main idea. In these instances, you must read every sentence of the text and try to come up with an overarching idea that is supported by each of those sentences.

Note: A **thesis statement** should not be confused with the main idea of the passage. While the main idea gives a brief, general summary of a text, the thesis statement provides a specific perspective on an issue that the author supports with evidence.

> **Review Video: Topics and Main Ideas**
> Visit mometrix.com/academy and enter code: 407801

Supporting details provide evidence and backing for the main point. In order to show that a main idea is correct, or valid, authors add details that prove their point. All texts contain details, but they are only classified as supporting details when they serve to reinforce some larger point. Supporting details are most commonly found in informative and persuasive texts. In some cases, they will be clearly indicated with terms like *for example* or *for instance*, or they will be enumerated with terms like *first*, *second*, and *last*. However, you need to be prepared for texts that do not contain those indicators. As a reader, you should consider whether the author's supporting details really back up his or her main point. Supporting details can be factual and correct, yet they may not be relevant to the author's point. Conversely, supporting details can seem pertinent, but they can be ineffective because they are based on opinion or assertions that cannot be proven.

> **Review Video: Supporting Details**
> Visit mometrix.com/academy and enter code: 396297

An example of a **main idea** is: *Giraffes live in the Serengeti of Africa*. A **supporting detail** about giraffes could be: *A giraffe in this region benefits from a long neck by reaching twigs and leaves on tall trees.* The main idea expresses that the text is about giraffes in general. The supporting detail gives a specific fact about how the giraffes eat.

THE MEANING OF WORDS

The **denotative** meaning of a word is the literal meaning. The **connotative** meaning goes beyond the denotative meaning to include the emotional reaction that a word may invoke. The connotative meaning often takes the denotative meaning a step further due to associations which the reader makes with the denotative meaning. Readers can differentiate between the denotative and connotative meanings by first recognizing how authors use each meaning. Most nonfiction, for example, is fact-based, and nonfiction authors rarely use flowery, figurative language. The reader can assume that the writer is using the denotative meaning of words. In fiction, the author may use the connotative meaning. Readers can determine whether the author is using the denotative or connotative meaning of a word by implementing context clues.

> **Review Video: Connotation and Denotation**
> Visit mometrix.com/academy and enter code: 310092

Readers of all levels will encounter words that they either have never seen or have only encountered on a limited basis. The best way to define a word in **context** is to look for nearby words that can assist in learning the meaning of the word. For instance, unfamiliar nouns are often accompanied by examples that provide a definition. Consider the following sentence: *Dave arrived at the party in hilarious garb: a leopard-print shirt, buckskin trousers, and high heels.* If a reader was unfamiliar with the meaning of garb, he or she could read the examples (i.e., a leopard-print shirt, buckskin trousers, and high heels) and quickly determine that the word means *clothing*. Examples will not always be this obvious. Consider this sentence: *Parsley, lemon, and flowers were just a few of items he used as garnishes.* Here, the word *garnishes* is exemplified by parsley, lemon, and flowers. Readers who have eaten in a few restaurants will probably be able to identify a garnish as something used to decorate a plate.

> **Review Video: Context Clues**
> Visit mometrix.com/academy and enter code: 613660

In addition to looking at the context of a passage, readers can use **contrasts** to define an unfamiliar word in context. In many sentences, the author will not describe the unfamiliar word directly; instead, he or she will describe the opposite of the unfamiliar word. Thus, you are provided with some information that will bring you closer to defining the word. Consider the following example: *Despite his intelligence, Hector's low brow and bad posture made him look obtuse.* The author writes that Hector's appearance does not convey intelligence. Therefore, *obtuse* must mean unintelligent. Here is another example: *Despite the horrible weather, we were beatific about our trip to Alaska.* The word *despite* indicates that the speaker's feelings were at odds with the weather. Since the weather is described as *horrible*, then *beatific* must mean something positive.

In some cases, there will be very few contextual clues to help a reader define the meaning of an unfamiliar word. When this happens, one strategy that readers may employ is **substitution**. A good reader will brainstorm some possible synonyms for the given word, and he or she will substitute these words into the sentence. If the sentence and the surrounding passage continue to make sense, then the substitution has revealed at least some information about the unfamiliar word. Consider the sentence: *Frank's admonition rang in her ears as she climbed the mountain.* A reader unfamiliar with *admonition* might come up with some substitutions like *vow, promise, advice, complaint,* or *compliment*. All of these words make general sense of the sentence though their meanings are diverse. The process has suggested; however, that an admonition is some sort of message. The substitution strategy is rarely able to pinpoint a precise definition, but this process can be effective as a last resort.

Occasionally, you will be able to define an unfamiliar word by looking at the **descriptive words** in the context. Consider the following sentence: *Fred dragged the recalcitrant boy kicking and screaming up the stairs.* The words *dragged, kicking,* and *screaming* all suggest that the boy does not want to go up the stairs. The reader may assume that *recalcitrant* means something like unwilling or protesting. In this example, an unfamiliar adjective was identified.

Additionally, using description to define an unfamiliar noun is a common practice compared to unfamiliar adjectives, as in this sentence: *Don's wrinkled frown and constantly shaking fist identified him as a curmudgeon of the first order.* Don is described as having a *wrinkled frown and constantly shaking fist* suggesting that a *curmudgeon* must be a grumpy person. Contrasts do not always provide detailed information about the unfamiliar word, but they at least give the reader some clues.

When a word has more than one meaning, readers can have difficulty with determining how the word is being used in a given sentence. For instance, the verb *cleave*, can mean either *join* or *separate*. When readers come upon this word, they will have to select the definition that makes the most sense. Consider the following sentence: *Hermione's knife cleaved the bread cleanly*. Since, a knife cannot join bread together, the word must indicate separation. A slightly more difficult example would be the sentence: *The birds cleaved together as they flew from the oak tree.* Immediately, the presence of the word *together* should suggest that in this sentence *cleave* is being used to mean *join*. Discovering the intent of a word with **multiple meanings** requires the same tricks as defining an unknown word: look for contextual clues and evaluate the substituted words.

When you understand how words relate to each other, you will discover more in a passage. This is explained by understanding **synonyms** (e.g., words that mean the same thing) and **antonyms** (e.g., words that mean the opposite of one another). As an example, *dry* and *arid* are synonyms, and *dry* and *wet* are antonyms. There are many pairs of words in English that can be considered synonyms, despite having slightly different definitions. For instance, the words *friendly* and *collegial* can both be used to describe a warm interpersonal relationship, and one would be correct to call them **synonyms**. However, *collegial* (kin to *colleague*) is often used in reference to professional or academic relationships, and *friendly* has no such connotation. If the difference between two words is too great, then they should not be called synonyms. *Hot* and *warm* are not synonyms because their meanings are too distinct. A good way to determine whether two words are synonyms is to substitute one word for the other word and verify that the meaning of the sentence has not changed. Substituting *warm* for *hot* in a sentence would convey a different meaning. Although warm and hot may seem close in meaning, warm generally means that the temperature is moderate, and hot generally means that the temperature is excessively high.

Antonyms are words with opposite meanings. *Light* and *dark*, *up* and *down*, *right* and *left*, *good* and *bad*: these are all sets of antonyms. Be careful to distinguish between antonyms and pairs of words that are simply different. *Black* and *gray*, for instance, are not antonyms because gray is not the opposite of black. *Black* and *white*, on the other hand, are antonyms. Not every word has an antonym. For instance, many nouns do not: What would be the antonym of chair? During your exam, the questions related to antonyms are more likely to concern adjectives. You will recall that adjectives are words that describe a noun. Some common adjectives include *purple*, *fast*, *skinny*, and *sweet*. From those four adjectives, *purple* is the item that lacks a group of obvious antonyms.

> **Review Video: What Are Synonyms and Antonyms?**
> Visit mometrix.com/academy and enter code: 105612

Authors often use analogies to add meaning to their passages. An **analogy** is a comparison of two things. The words in the analogy are connected by a certain, often undetermined relationship. Look at this analogy: *moo is to cow as quack is to duck*. This analogy compares the sound that a cow makes with the sound that a duck makes. Even if the word *quack* was not given, one could figure out the correct word to complete the analogy based on the relationship between the words *moo* and *cow*.

Purpose and Tone

PURPOSES FOR WRITING

In order to be an effective reader, one must pay attention to the author's **position** and purpose. Even those texts that seem objective and impartial, like textbooks, have a position and **bias**. Readers need to take these positions into account when considering the author's message. When an author uses emotional language or clearly favors one side of an argument, his or her position is clear. However, the author's position may be evident not only in what he or she writes, but also in what he or she doesn't write. In a normal setting, a reader would want to review some other texts on the same topic in order to develop a view of the author's position. If this was not possible, then you would want to acquire some background about the author. However, since you are in the middle of an exam and the only source of information is the text, you should look for language and argumentation that seems to indicate a particular stance on the subject.

> **Review Video: Author's Position**
> Visit mometrix.com/academy and enter code: 827954

Usually, identifying the **purpose** of an author is easier than identifying his or her position. In most cases, the author has no interest in hiding his or her purpose. A text that is meant to **entertain**, for instance, should be written to please the reader. Most narratives, or stories, are written to entertain, though they may also inform or persuade. **Informative** texts are easy to identify, while the most difficult purpose of a text to identify is **persuasion** because the author has an interest in making this purpose hard to detect. When a reader discovers that the author is trying to persuade, he or she should be skeptical of the argument. For this reason, persuasive texts often try to establish an entertaining **tone** and hope to amuse the reader into agreement. On the other hand, an informative tone may be implemented to create an appearance of authority and objectivity.

An author's purpose is evident often in the **organization** of the text (e.g., section headings in bold font points to an informative text). However, you may not have such organization available to you in your exam. Instead, if the author makes his or her main idea clear from the beginning, then the likely purpose of the text is to inform. If the author begins by making a claim and provides various arguments to support that claim, then the purpose is probably to persuade. If the author tells a story or seems to want the attention of the reader more than to push a particular point or deliver information, then his or her purpose is most likely to entertain. As a reader, you must judge authors on how well they accomplish their purpose. In other words, you need to consider the type of passage (e.g., technical, persuasive, etc.) that the author has written and whether the author has followed the requirements of the passage type.

> **Review Video: Understanding the Author's Intent**
> Visit mometrix.com/academy and enter code: 511819

Fact and Opinion, Logical Inferences, and Summarizing

FACTS AND OPINIONS

Critical thinking skills are mastered through understanding various types of writing and the different purposes of authors in writing their passages. Every author writes for a purpose. When you understand their purpose and how they accomplish their goal, you will be able to analyze their writing and determine whether or not you agree with their conclusions.

Readers must always be conscious of the distinction between fact and opinion. A **fact** can be subjected to analysis and can be either proved or disproved. An **opinion**, on the other hand, is the author's personal thoughts or feelings which may not be alterable by research or evidence. If the author writes that the distance from New York to Boston is about two hundred miles, then he or she is stating a fact. If an author writes that New York is too crowded, then he or she is giving an opinion because there is no objective standard for overpopulation.

An opinion may be indicated by words like *believe*, *think*, or *feel*. Readers must be aware that an opinion may be supported by facts. For instance, the author might give the population density of New York as a reason for an overcrowded population. An opinion supported by fact tends to be more convincing. On the other hand, when authors support their opinions with other opinions, readers should not be persuaded by the argument to any degree.

When you have an argumentative passage, you need to be sure that facts are presented to the reader from **reliable sources**. An opinion is what the author thinks about a given topic. An opinion is not common knowledge or proven by expert sources, instead the information is the personal beliefs and thoughts of the author.

To distinguish between fact and opinion, a reader needs to consider the type of **source** that is presenting information, the **information** that backs-up a claim, and the author's **motivation** to have a certain point-of-view on a given topic. For example, if a panel of scientists has conducted multiple studies on the effectiveness of taking a certain vitamin, then the results are more likely to be factual than a company that is selling a vitamin and claims that taking the vitamin can produce positive effects. The company is motivated to sell their product, and the scientists are using the scientific method to prove a theory. Remember: if you find sentences that contain phrases such as "I think..." then the statement is an opinion.

> **Review Video: Fact or Opinion**
> Visit mometrix.com/academy and enter code: 870899

EVALUATING A PASSAGE

When reading informational texts, there is importance in understanding the logical conclusion of the author's ideas. **Identifying a logical conclusion** can help you determine whether you agree with the writer or not. Coming to this conclusion is much like making an inference: the approach requires you to combine the information given by the text with what you already know in order to make a logical conclusion. If the author intended the reader to draw a certain conclusion, then you can expect the author's argumentation and detail to be leading in that direction. One way to approach the task of drawing conclusions is to make brief notes of all the points made by the author. When the notes are arranged on paper, they may clarify the logical conclusion. Another way to approach conclusions is to consider whether the reasoning of the author raises any pertinent questions. Sometimes you will be able to draw several conclusions from a passage. On occasion these will be conclusions that were never imagined by the author. Therefore, be aware that these conclusions must be supported directly by the text.

> **Review Video: How to Support a Conclusion**
> Visit mometrix.com/academy and enter code: 281653

The term **text evidence** refers to information that supports a main point or minor points and can help lead the reader to a conclusion. Information used as text evidence is precise, descriptive, and factual. A main point is often followed by supporting details that provide evidence to back up a claim. For example, a passage may include the claim that winter occurs during opposite months in the Northern and Southern hemispheres. Text evidence based on this claim may include countries where winter occurs in opposite months along with reasons that winter occurs at different times of the year in separate hemispheres (due to the tilt of the Earth as it rotates around the sun).

> **Review Video: Textual Evidence**
> Visit mometrix.com/academy and enter code: 486236

Drawing conclusions from information implied within a passage requires confidence on the part of the reader. **Implications** are things that the author does not state directly, but readers can assume based on what the author does say. Consider the following passage: *I stepped outside and opened my umbrella. By the time I got to work, the cuffs of my pants were soaked*. The author never states that it is raining, but this fact is clearly implied. Conclusions based on implication must be well supported by the text. In order to draw a solid conclusion, readers should have multiple pieces of evidence. If readers have only one piece, they must be assured that there is no other possible explanation than their conclusion. A good reader will be able to draw many conclusions from information implied by the text which will be a great help in the exam.

When reading a good passage, readers are moved to engage actively in the text. One part of being an active reader involves making predictions. A **prediction** is a guess about what will happen next. Readers constantly make predictions based on what they have read and what they already know. Consider the following sentence: *Staring at the computer screen in shock, Kim blindly reached over for the brimming glass of water on the shelf to her side*. The sentence suggests that Kim is agitated, and that she is not looking at the glass that she is going to pick up. So, a reader might predict that Kim is going to knock over the glass. Of course, not every prediction will be accurate: perhaps Kim will pick the glass up cleanly. Nevertheless, the author has certainly created the expectation that the water might be spilled. Predictions are always subject to revision as the reader acquires more information.

Test-taking tip: To respond to questions requiring future predictions, your answers should be based on evidence of past or present behavior.

> **Review Video: Predictive Reading**
> Visit mometrix.com/academy and enter code: 437248

Readers are often required to understand a text that claims and suggests ideas without stating them directly. An **inference** is a piece of information that is implied but not written outright by the author. For instance, consider the following sentence: *After the final out of the inning, the fans were filled with joy and rushed the field*. From this sentence, a reader can infer that the fans were watching a baseball game and their team won the game. Readers should take great care to avoid using information beyond the provided passage before making inferences. As you practice drawing inferences, you will find that they require concentration and attention.

> **Review Video: Inference**
> Visit mometrix.com/academy and enter code: 379203

Test-taking tip: While being tested on your ability to make correct inferences, you must look for contextual clues. An answer can be *true* but not *correct*. The contextual clues will help you find the answer that is the best answer out of the given choices. Be careful in your reading to understand the context in which a phrase is stated. When asked for the implied meaning of a statement made in the passage, you should immediately locate the statement and read the context in which the statement was made. Also, look for an answer choice that has a similar phrase to the statement in question.

In addition to inference and prediction, readers must often **draw conclusions** about the information they have read. When asked for a *conclusion* that may be drawn, look for critical "hedge" phrases, such as *likely, may, can, will often*, among many others. When you are being tested on this knowledge, remember the question that writers insert into these hedge phrases to cover every possibility. Often an answer will be wrong simply because there is no room for exception. Extreme positive or negative answers (such as always or never) are usually not correct. The reader should not use any outside knowledge that is not gathered from the passage to answer the related questions. Correct answers can be derived straight from the passage.

SUMMARIZING A PASSAGE

As an aid to drawing conclusions, **outlining** the information contained in the passage should be a familiar skill to readers. An effective outline will reveal the structure of the passage and will lead to solid conclusions. An effective outline will have a title that refers to the basic subject of the text though the title needs not recapitulate the main idea. In most outlines, the main idea will be the first major section. Each major idea of the passage will be established as the head of a category. For instance, the most common outline format calls for the main ideas of the passage to be indicated with Roman numerals. In an effective outline of this kind, each of the main ideas will be represented by a Roman numeral and none of the Roman numerals will designate minor details or secondary ideas. Moreover, all supporting ideas and details should be placed in the appropriate place on the outline. An outline does not need to include every detail listed in the text, but the outline should feature all of those that are central to the argument or message. Each of these details should be listed under the appropriate main idea.

> **Review Video: Outlining as an Aid to Drawing Conclusions**
> Visit mometrix.com/academy and enter code: 584445

Ideas from a text can also be organized using **graphic organizers**. A graphic organizer is a way to simplify information and take key points from the text. A graphic organizer such as a timeline may have an event listed for a corresponding date on the timeline while an outline may have an event listed under a key point that occurs in the text. Each reader needs to create the type of graphic organizer that works the best for him or her in terms of being able to recall information from a story. Examples include a *spider-map,* which takes a main idea from the story and places it in a bubble with supporting points branching off the main idea. An *outline* is useful for diagramming the main and supporting points of the entire story, and a *Venn diagram* classifies information as separate or overlapping.

> **Review Video: Graphic Organizers**
> Visit mometrix.com/academy and enter code: 665513

A helpful tool is the ability to **summarize** the information that you have read in a paragraph or passage format. This process is similar to creating an effective outline. First, a summary should accurately define the main idea of the passage though the summary does not need to explain this main idea in exhaustive detail. The summary should continue by laying out the most important supporting details or arguments from the passage. All of the significant supporting details should be included, and none of the details included should be irrelevant or insignificant. Also, the summary should accurately report all of these details. Too often, the desire for brevity in a summary leads to the sacrifice of clarity or accuracy. Summaries are often difficult to read because they omit all of the graceful language, digressions, and asides that distinguish great writing. However, an effective summary should contain much the same message as the original text.

> **Review Video: Summarizing Text**
> Visit mometrix.com/academy and enter code: 172903

Paraphrasing is another method that the reader can use to aid in comprehension. When paraphrasing, one puts what they have read into their words by rephrasing what the author has written, or one "translates" all of what the author shared into their words by including as many details as they can.

Vocabulary

Vocabulary is not a discrete section of the exam, but much of the terminology listed here will show up in other sections. Having some familiarity with these terms will give you an advantage when you do encounter them on the exam.

INCREASING VERBAL ABILITY

Nursing, like many professions, requires the ability to **communicate effectively**. Students should prepare for standardized testing and their nursing careers by utilizing some basic techniques for increasing vocabulary. Writing down new words is a good way to increase vocabulary. While reading, watching TV, or talking to others, make a note of any unfamiliar words you encounter. Look up the definition of those words and then attempt to use them in conversation. This will help the word become part of your general store of knowledge. Reading new and different material will also increase vocabulary. For example, if you normally read only for leisure or entertainment, try thumbing through a professional journal of archaeology or mathematics This will introduce new words that you would not encounter in everyday life. Playing games like Scrabble and solving crossword puzzles can also help build verbal ability.

ETYMOLOGY

Etymology is the study of words. It specifically focuses on the **origins** of words: how they have developed over time and between languages. Language is made up of words from different cultures and areas of the world. Some words we use today mean something completely different from what they meant hundreds of years ago. Words are constantly being redefined, changed, and created. New words appear as technology increases. Some words are formed by combining root words with prefixes and suffixes. Students who must improve verbal ability for standardized testing can do so by studying common prefixes and suffixes. By understanding the prefix pre, a student increases their chances of understanding words like predate. The prefix pre means "before", so it can be reasoned that predate means to date something in advance, such as predating a check.

Glossary of Important Terms

A

Abrupt: describes a sudden change that occurs without warning

Abstain: the deliberate effort to refrain from an action, such as drinking alcohol or eating junk food

Access: the freedom to use something as one chooses; the permission or ability to enter or approach a specific entity or area

Accountable: responsible for actions or explanations

Adhere: the process of binding one thing to another using glue, tape, or another agent; refers to the action of maintaining loyalty or support

Adverse: in a contrary fashion; can cause harm; may also refer to something that is in opposition to one's interests

Annual: the duration of a single year; an occurrence that takes place once each year

Apply: to put something to use; having a relevant or valid connection to something else

Audible: capable of being heard

B

Bilateral: having two sides; may refer to something that affects both side of the human body

C

Cardiac: concerning the heart

Cast: the process by which something is given shape through the pouring of a liquid substance into a mold; may also refer to the throwing of an object

Cease: to bring about a gradual end; refers to something that dies out or becomes extinct

Compensatory: an equivalent; the action of making a payment that serves as a counterbalance for another action

Complications: a factor that presents a degree of difficulty; may also refer to a secondary disease or condition

Comply: to carry out the wishes of another person; to perform in the manner prescribed by law

Concave: a surface that is rounded inward like a bowl; surface that is arched or curved

Concise: straightforward and to the point; absent of all excessive detail

Consistency: the agreement of each of the parts that constitute a whole

Constrict: to make something narrow by squeezing or compressing

Contingent: something that may happen; may also refer to something that is dependent upon or conditioned by something else

Contour: the line that represents the shape of a curvy figure

Contract: an agreement between two parties that binds each to perform certain actions

Contraindication: the presence of a symptom or condition that will make a specific treatment unadvisable

D

Defecate: to have feces removed from the bowels

Deficit: a lack in an amount or quality of something, such as money or rainfall

Depress: to press down; the lessening of activity or strength; an action in which something moves to a lower position

Depth: a quality of being complete and thorough

Deteriorating: to make inferior in quality; to diminish in function or condition

Device: something that is devised or thought up; may be a piece of equipment designed for a specific task

Diagnosis: determining the dysfunction/disease

Diameter: the length of a line that passes through the body of an object

Dilate: to enlarge, extend, or widen; to become wide like the pupil of the eye

Dilute: to make a substance thinner or less potent; diminish in flavor or intensity

Discrete: a separate entity; unique and separate from other things

Distended: something that has been enlarged by the force of internal pressure

Dysfunction: a hindered function a body system or organ

E

Elevate: to lift or make something higher; to lift in rank or title

Endogenous: the growth from a deep tissue; refers to conditions that arise from factors that are internal to an organism

Exacerbate: to cause something to become more intense in nature; especially an increase in violence or severity

Excess: surpassing usual limitations; unnecessary indulgence

Exogenous: the growth from superficial or shallow tissue; refers to conditions caused by factors that are external to an organism

Expand: to open or unfold; refers to an increase in number, size, or scope; may refer to the expression of an idea in greater depth

Exposure: being subject to a condition or influence; making a secret fact known publicly

External: being outside the human body; existing outside the confines of a specific space or institution

F

Fatal: something that may cause death; relating to fate or proceeding in a manner that follows a fixed sequence of events

Fatigue: the state of tiredness brought on by labor, exertion, or stress; the tendency of a specified material to break under stress

Flaccid: the state of not being firm; lacking vigor, force, or youthful firmness

Flushed: blushing or an area of the body that becomes reddened

G

Gaping: something that is wide open and exposed

Gastrointestinal: concerning the stomach and intestines

Gender: the behavioral, cultural, or psychological traits that are associated with a specific sex

H

Hematologic: concerning blood

Hygiene: the science of health: inducing practices; the condition or practice of activities that can maintain physical health

I

Impaired: a condition in which one cannot perform or function properly; often refers to a person who is under the influence of drugs or alcohol

Impending: hanging overhead threateningly; bound to occur in the near future

Incidence: the arrival of something at a surface; something that occurs or affects something else

Infection: an area of body tissue that been invaded with pathogenic organisms

Inflamed: to incite an intensely emotional state; also refers to something that has been set on fire

Ingest: to take into one's mouth for digestion

Initiate: to cause something to begin or to set events in motion; as initiation, can also refer to the process through which a person is allowed entry into a club or organization

Insidious: something or someone who is enticing but dangerous; slow: developing dangerousness

Intact: something that remains whole or untouched by destructive forces; having no relevant part removed or altered

Internal: things inside of the body or the mind; something that exists within the limits and confines of something else

Invasive: tending to spread or infringe upon something; may also refer to something that will enter the human body

L

Labile: unstable; constantly undergoing a chemical or physical change or breakdown

Laceration: wound with irregular borders, knife like in appearance

Latent: not presently active but with the potential to become active

Lethargic: sluggish, indifferent, or apathetic

M

Manifestation: the act of becoming outwardly visible; can refer to the occult phenomenon of a supernatural materialization

Musculoskeletal: concerning the connections of the muscle and the skeleton

N

Neurologic: concerning the nervous system

Neurovascular: concerning the blood vessels and the nerves

Nutrient: something that provides nourishment

O

Occluded: closed or blocked off

Ominous: exhibiting an omen; refers to something evil or disastrous that appears likely to occur

Ongoing: in the process of occurring; continuously advancing or moving ahead

Oral: spoken by the mouth; of or relating to the mouth

Overt: something that is openly displayed or obvious

P

Parameter: a limit or boundary; in math, it is an arbitrary value that is used to describe a statistical population

Paroxysmal: characterized by a sudden fit or attack of symptoms; may be a sudden emotion or uncontrollable action

Patent: a clear and easily accessible passage

Pathogenic: disease causing

Pathology: the study of diseases

Posterior: related to the rear/back position

Potent: able to copulate as a male; refers to something that is chemically or medically effective

Potential: having the possibility of becoming a reality

Precaution: the act of taking care in advance; refers to measures taken in advance in order to prevent harm

Precipitous: very steep or difficult to climb or overcome

Predispose: to dispose in advance of or to make susceptible to

Pre-existing: the state of existing before or previous to something else

Primary: first in order; a rank of importance

Priority: the state of being before; coming first in order of date or position; a preferential rating

Prognosis: the possibility of recovery after the diagnosis of an illness or disease

R

Rationale: an explanation regarding the principles, opinions, beliefs, or practices held by a specific party

Recur: something that is revisited for consideration; a thought or idea that enters one's mind for a second time

Renal: concerning the kidneys

Respiration: the act of breathing in and out of air

Restrict: to confine something or someone within specific limitations or boundaries

Retain: to keep in one's possession; to maintain an item or person in security

S

Site: the physical location of a structure; the physical space reserved for a building; the place or scene of an occurrence

Status: the position or rank held in relation to others; a person or object's condition with respect to circumstances

Strict: inflexible; maintained in such a manner that cannot be changed or altered

Sublingual: beneath the tongue

Supplement: an item that completes something else

Suppress: to restrain by authority or force; to omit something from memory; to keep from public knowledge

Symmetric: exhibiting symmetry; capable of being divided by a longitudinal plane into equal sections

Symptom: the evidence of a disease or illness; the presence of a symptom is indicative of something else

Syndrome: a group of symptoms that happen close together and suggest an illness or irregular condition

T

Therapeutic: concerning the treatment of an illness or irregular condition

Transdermal: passing through skin

Transmission: passing something from one place to another

Trauma: an injury done by an outside object

Triage: a system that helps to determine which patients need the most care by evaluating their condition and chances of responding positively to treatment

U

Untoward: difficult to manage; marked by trouble or unpleasantness

Urinate: to expel urine

V

Vascular: concerning the blood vessels

Verbal: relating to or consisting of words; involving words rather than meaning or substance

Virus: a microscopic pathogen that replicates in living cells and can cause disease

Vital: necessary or essential to the existence of life

Void: not occupied or empty; of no legal force or effect

Volume: printed pages bound in a book form; space occupied by a three-dimensional form; degree of loudness

Writing

The Writing section of the exam focuses on the ability to identify errors and make improvements in written passages. There will not only be questions on grammar and punctuation errors, but also on errors related to word usage and misplaced or unnecessary information. You will also be asked to identify the best place to add new information to the passage.

Foundations of Grammar

THE EIGHT PARTS OF SPEECH
NOUNS

When you talk about a person, place, thing, or idea, you are talking about **nouns**. The two main types of nouns are **common** and **proper** nouns. Also, nouns can be abstract (i.e., general) or concrete (i.e., specific).

Common nouns are the class or group of people, places, and things (Note: Do not capitalize common nouns). Examples of common nouns:

People: boy, girl, worker, manager

Places: school, bank, library, home

Things: dog, cat, truck, car

Proper nouns are the names of a specific person, place, or thing (Note: Capitalize all proper nouns). Examples of proper nouns:

People: Abraham Lincoln, George Washington, Martin Luther King, Jr.

Places: Los Angeles, California / New York / Asia

Things: Statue of Liberty, Earth*, Lincoln Memorial

*Note: When you talk about the planet that we live on, you capitalize *Earth*. When you mean the dirt, rocks, or land, you lowercase *earth*.

General nouns are the names of conditions or ideas. **Specific nouns** name people, places, and things that are understood by using your senses.

General nouns:

Condition: beauty, strength

Idea: truth, peace

Specific nouns:

People: baby, friend, father

Places: town, park, city hall

Things: rainbow, cough, apple, silk, gasoline

Collective nouns are the names for a person, place, or thing that may act as a whole. The following are examples of collective nouns: *class, company, dozen, group, herd, team,* and *public*.

PRONOUNS

Pronouns are words that are used to stand in for a noun. A pronoun may be classified as personal, intensive, relative, interrogative, demonstrative, indefinite, and reciprocal.

Personal: *Nominative* is the case for nouns and pronouns that are the subject of a sentence. *Objective* is the case for nouns and pronouns that are an object in a sentence. *Possessive* is the case for nouns and pronouns that show possession or ownership.

SINGULAR

	Nominative	Objective	Possessive
First Person	I	me	my, mine
Second Person	you	you	your, yours
Third Person	he, she, it	him, her, it	his, her, hers, its

PLURAL

	Nominative	Objective	Possessive
First Person	we	us	our, ours
Second Person	you	you	your, yours
Third Person	they	them	their, theirs

Intensive: I myself, you yourself, he himself, she herself, the (thing) itself, we ourselves, you yourselves, they themselves

Relative: which, who, whom, whose

Interrogative: what, which, who, whom, whose

Demonstrative: this, that, these, those

Indefinite: all, any, each, everyone, either/neither, one, some, several

Reciprocal: each other, one another

> **Review Video: Nouns and Pronouns**
> Visit mometrix.com/academy and enter code: 312073

VERBS

If you want to write a sentence, then you need a verb in your sentence. Without a verb, you have no sentence. The verb of a sentence explains action or being. In other words, the verb shows the subject's movement or the movement that has been done to the subject.

TRANSITIVE AND INTRANSITIVE VERBS

A transitive verb is a verb whose action (e.g., drive, run, jump) points to a receiver (e.g., car, dog, kangaroo). Intransitive verbs do not point to a receiver of an action. In other words, the action of the verb does not point to a subject or object.

Transitive: He plays the piano. | The piano was played by him.

Intransitive: He plays. | John writes well.

A dictionary will let you know whether a verb is transitive or intransitive. Some verbs can be transitive and intransitive.

ACTION VERBS AND LINKING VERBS

An action verb is a verb that shows what the subject is doing in a sentence. In other words, an action verb shows action. A sentence can be complete with one word: an action verb. Linking verbs are intransitive verbs that show a condition (i.e., the subject is described but does no action).

Linking verbs link the subject of a sentence to a noun or pronoun, or they link a subject with an adjective. You always need a verb if you want a complete sentence. However, linking verbs are not able to complete a sentence.

Common linking verbs include *appear, be, become, feel, grow, look, seem, smell, sound*, and *taste*. However, any verb that shows a condition and has a noun, pronoun, or adjective that describes the subject of a sentence is a linking verb.

Action: He sings. | Run! | Go! | I talk with him every day. | She reads.

Linking:

Incorrect: I am.

Correct: I am John. | I smell roses. | I feel tired.

Note: Some verbs are followed by words that look like prepositions, but they are a part of the verb and a part of the verb's meaning. These are known as phrasal verbs and examples include *call off, look up,* and *drop off.*

> **Review Video: Action Verbs and Linking Verbs**
> Visit mometrix.com/academy and enter code: 743142

VOICE

Transitive verbs come in active or passive voice. If the subject does an action or receives the action of the verb, then you will know whether a verb is active or passive. When the subject of the sentence is doing the action, the verb is **active voice**. When the subject receives the action, the verb is **passive voice**.

Active: Jon drew the picture. (The subject *Jon* is doing the action of *drawing a picture*.)

Passive: The picture is drawn by Jon. (The subject *picture* is receiving the action from Jon.)

VERB TENSES

A verb tense shows the different form of a verb to point to the time of an action. The present and past tense are shown by changing the verb's form. An action in the present *I talk* can change form for the past: *I talked*. However, for the other tenses, an auxiliary (i.e., helping) verb is needed to show the change in form. These helping verbs include *am, are, is | have, has, had | was, were, will* (or *shall*).

Present: I talk	Present perfect: I have talked
Past: I talked	Past perfect: I had talked
Future: I will talk	Future perfect: I will have talked

Present: The action happens at the current time.

Example: He *walks* to the store every morning.

To show that something is happening right now, use the progressive present tense: I *am walking*.

Past: The action happened in the past.

Example: He *walked* to the store an hour ago.

Future: The action is going to happen later.

Example: I *will walk* to the store tomorrow.

Present perfect: The action started in the past and continues into the present.

Example: I *have walked* to the store three times today.

Past perfect: The second action happened in the past. The first action came before the second.

Example: Before I walked to the store (Action 2), I *had walked* to the library (Action 1).

Future perfect: An action that uses the past and the future. In other words, the action is complete before a future moment.

Example: When she comes for the supplies (future moment), I *will have walked* to the store (action completed in the past).

> **Review Video: Present Perfect, Past Perfect, and Future Perfect Verb Tenses**
> Visit mometrix.com/academy and enter code: 269472

CONJUGATING VERBS

When you need to change the form of a verb, you are **conjugating** a verb. The key parts of a verb are first person singular, present tense (dream); first person singular, past tense (dreamed); and the past participle (dreamed). Note: the past participle needs a helping verb to make a verb tense. For example, I *have dreamed* of this day. | I *am dreaming* of this day.

Present Tense: Active Voice

	Singular	Plural
First Person	I dream	We dream
Second Person	You dream	You dream
Third Person	He, she, it dreams	They dream

Mood

There are three moods in English: the indicative, the imperative, and the subjunctive.

The **indicative mood** is used for facts, opinions, and questions.

> Fact: You can do this.
>
> Opinion: I think that you can do this.
>
> Question: Do you know that you can do this?

The **imperative** is used for orders or requests.

> Order: You are going to do this!
>
> Request: Will you do this for me?

The **subjunctive mood** is for wishes and statements that go against fact.

> Wish: I wish that I were going to do this.
>
> Statement against fact: If I were you, I would do this. (This goes against fact because I am not you. You have the chance to do this, and I do not have the chance.)

The mood that causes trouble for most people is the subjunctive mood. If you have trouble with any of the moods, then be sure to practice.

Adjectives

An adjective is a word that is used to modify a noun or pronoun. An adjective answers a question: *Which one? What kind of?* or *How many?* Usually, adjectives come before the words that they modify, but they may also come after a linking verb.

> Which one? The *third* suit is my favorite.
>
> What kind? This suit is *navy blue*.
>
> How many? Can I look over the *four* neckties for the suit?

Articles

Articles are adjectives that are used to mark nouns. There are only three: the **definite** (i.e., limited or fixed amount) article *the*, and the **indefinite** (i.e., no limit or fixed amount) articles *a* and *an*. Note: *An* comes before words that start with a vowel sound (i.e., vowels include *a, e, i, o, u,* and *y*). For example, "Are you going to get an **u**mbrella?"

> **Definite**: I lost *the* bottle that belongs to me.
>
> **Indefinite**: Does anyone have *a* bottle to share?

Comparison with Adjectives

Some adjectives are relative and other adjectives are absolute. Adjectives that are **relative** can show the comparison between things. Adjectives that are **absolute** can show comparison. However, they show comparison in a different way. Let's say that you are reading two books. You think that one book is perfect, and the other book is not exactly perfect. It is not possible for the book to be more perfect than the other. Either you think that the book is perfect, or you think that the book is not perfect.

The adjectives that are relative will show the different **degrees** of something or someone to something else or someone else. The three degrees of adjectives include positive, comparative, and superlative.

The **positive** degree is the normal form of an adjective.

> Example: This work is *difficult*. | She is *smart*.

The **comparative** degree compares one person or thing to another person or thing.

> Example: This work is *more difficult* than your work. | She is *smarter* than me.

The **superlative** degree compares more than two people or things.

> Example: This is the *most difficult* work of my life. | She is the *smartest* lady in school.

> **Review Video: What is an Adjective?**
> Visit mometrix.com/academy and enter code: 470154

ADVERBS

An adverb is a word that is used to **modify** a verb, adjective, or another adverb. Usually, adverbs answer one of these questions: *When?*, *Where?*, *How?*, and *Why?*. The negatives *not* and *never* are known as adverbs. Adverbs that modify adjectives or other adverbs **strengthen** or **weaken** the words that they modify.

Examples:

> He walks *quickly* through the crowd.
>
> The water flows *smoothly* on the rocks.

Note: While many adverbs end in *-ly*, you need to remember that not all adverbs end in *-ly*. Also, some words that end in *-ly* are adjectives, not adverbs. Some examples include: *early, friendly, holy, lonely, silly,* and *ugly*. To know if a word that ends in *-ly* is an adjective or adverb, you need to check your dictionary.

Examples:

> He is *never* angry.
>
> You talk *too* loudly.

COMPARISON WITH ADVERBS

The rules for comparing adverbs are the same as the rules for adjectives.

The **positive** degree is the standard form of an adverb.

> Example: He arrives *soon*. | She speaks *softly* to her friends.

The **comparative** degree compares one person or thing to another person or thing.

> Example: He arrives sooner than Sarah. | She speaks more softly than him.

The **superlative** degree compares more than two people or things.

> Example: He arrives soonest of the group. | She speaks most softly of any of her friends.

> **Review Video: Adverbs**
> Visit mometrix.com/academy and enter code: 713951

PREPOSITIONS

A preposition is a word placed before a noun or pronoun that shows the relationship between an object and another word in the sentence.

Common prepositions:

about	before	during	on	under
after	beneath	for	over	until
against	between	from	past	up
among	beyond	in	through	with
around	by	of	to	within
at	down	off	toward	without

Examples:

> The napkin is *in* the drawer.
>
> The Earth rotates *around* the Sun.
>
> The needle is *beneath* the haystack.
>
> Can you find me *among* the words?

> **Review Video: Prepositions**
> Visit mometrix.com/academy and enter code: 946763

CONJUNCTIONS

Conjunctions join words, phrases, or clauses, and they show the connection between the joined pieces. **Coordinating** conjunctions connect equal parts of sentences. **Correlative** conjunctions show the connection between pairs. **Subordinating** conjunctions join subordinate (i.e., dependent) clauses with independent clauses.

COORDINATING CONJUNCTIONS

The coordinating conjunctions include: *and, but, yet, or, nor, for,* and *so*

Examples:

> The rock was small, but it was heavy.
>
> She drove in the night, and he drove in the day.

CORRELATIVE CONJUNCTIONS

The correlative conjunctions are: *either...or* | *neither...nor* | *not only...but also*

Examples:

Either you are coming *or* you are staying.

He ran *not only* three miles *but also* swam 200 yards.

> **Review Video: Coordinating and Correlative Conjunctions**
> Visit mometrix.com/academy and enter code: 390329

SUBORDINATING CONJUNCTIONS

Common subordinating conjunctions include:

after	since	whenever
although	so that	where
because	unless	wherever
before	until	whether
in order that	when	while

Examples:

I am hungry *because* I did not eat breakfast.

He went home *when* everyone left.

> **Review Video: Subordinating Conjunctions**
> Visit mometrix.com/academy and enter code: 958913

INTERJECTIONS

An interjection is a word for **exclamation** (i.e., great amount of feeling) that is used alone or as a piece to a sentence. Often, they are used at the beginning of a sentence for an **introduction**. Sometimes, they can be used in the middle of a sentence to show a **change** in thought or attitude.

Common Interjections: Hey! | Oh, | Ouch! | Please! | Wow!

Agreement and Sentence Structure

SUBJECTS AND PREDICATES
SUBJECTS

Every sentence has two things: a subject and a verb. The **subject** of a sentence names who or what the sentence is all about. The subject may be directly stated in a sentence, or the subject may be the implied *you*.

The **complete subject** includes the simple subject and all of its modifiers. To find the complete subject, ask *Who* or *What* and insert the verb to complete the question. The answer is the complete subject. To find the **simple subject**, remove all of the modifiers (adjectives, prepositional phrases, etc.) in the complete subject. Being able to locate the subject of a sentence helps with many problems, such as those involving sentence fragments and subject-verb agreement.

Examples:

The small red car is the one that he wants for Christmas.

(The complete subject is *the small red car*.)

The young artist is coming over for dinner.

(The complete subject is *the young artist*.)

> **Review Video: Subjects in English**
> Visit mometrix.com/academy and enter code: 444771

In **imperative** sentences, the verb's subject is understood (e.g., [You] Run to the store) but not actually present in the sentence. Normally, the subject comes before the verb. However, the subject comes after the verb in sentences that begin with *There are* or *There was*.

Direct:

John knows the way to the park.

(Who knows the way to the park? Answer: John)

The cookies need ten more minutes.

(What needs ten minutes? Answer: The cookies)

By five o' clock, Bill will need to leave.

(Who needs to leave? Answer: Bill)

Remember: The subject can come after the verb.

There are five letters on the table for him.

(What is on the table? Answer: Five letters)

There were coffee and doughnuts in the house.

(What was in the house? Answer: Coffee and doughnuts)

Implied:

>Go to the post office for me.
>
>(Who is going to the post office? Answer: You are.)
>
>Come and sit with me, please?
>
>(Who needs to come and sit? Answer: You do.)

PREDICATES

In a sentence, you always have a predicate and a subject. The subject tells what the sentence is about, and the **predicate** explains or describes the subject.

Think about the sentence: *He sings*. In this sentence, we have a subject (He) and a predicate (sings). This is all that is needed for a sentence to be complete. Would we like more information? Of course, we would like to know more. However, if this is all the information that you are given, you have a complete sentence.

Now, let's look at another sentence:

>*John and Jane sing on Tuesday nights at the dance hall.*

What is the subject of this sentence?

>**Answer**: John and Jane.

What is the predicate of this sentence?

>**Answer**: Everything else in the sentence (sing on Tuesday nights at the dance hall).

SUBJECT-VERB AGREEMENT

Verbs **agree** with their subjects in number. In other words, *singular* subjects need *singular* verbs. *Plural* subjects need *plural* verbs. Singular is for one person, place, or thing. Plural is for more than one person, place, or thing. Subjects and verbs must also agree in person: first, second, or third. The present tense ending -s is used on a verb if its subject is third person singular; otherwise, the verb takes no ending.

> **Review Video: Subject-Verb Agreement**
> Visit mometrix.com/academy and enter code: 479190

NUMBER AGREEMENT EXAMPLES:

>Single Subject and Verb: *Dan calls home.*
>
>(Dan is one person. So, the singular verb *calls* is needed.)
>
>Plural Subject and Verb: *Dan and Bob call home.*
>
>(More than one person needs the plural verb *call*.)

Person Agreement Examples:

First Person: I *am* walking.

Second Person: You *are* walking.

Third Person: He *is* walking.

Complications with Subject-Verb Agreement

Words Between Subject and Verb

Words that come between the simple subject and the verb may serve as an effective distraction, but they have no bearing on subject-verb agreement.

Examples:

The joy of my life returns home tonight.

(**Singular Subject**: joy. **Singular Verb**: returns)

The phrase *of my life* does not influence the verb *returns*.

The question that still remains unanswered is "Who are you?"

(**Singular Subject**: question. **Singular Verb**: is)

Don't let the phrase *"that still remains…"* trouble you. The subject *question* goes with *is*.

Compound Subjects

A compound subject is formed when two or more nouns joined by *and*, *or*, or *nor* jointly act as the subject of the sentence.

Joined by And

When a compound subject is joined by *and*, it is treated as a plural subject and requires a plural verb.

Examples:

You and Jon are invited to come to my house.

(**Plural Subject**: You and Jon. **Plural Verb**: are)

The pencil and paper belong to me.

(**Plural Subject**: pencil and paper. **Plural Verb**: belong)

Joined by Or/Nor

For a compound subject joined by *or* or *nor*, the verb must agree in number with the part of the subject that is closest to the verb (italicized in the examples below).

Examples:

Today or *tomorrow is* the day.

(**Subject**: Today / tomorrow. **Verb**: is)

Stan or *Phil wants* to read the book.

(**Subject**: Stan / Phil. **Verb**: wants)

Neither the books nor the *pen is* on the desk.

(**Subject**: Books / Pen. **Verb**: is)

Either the blanket or *pillows arrive* this afternoon.

(**Subject**: Blanket / Pillows. **Verb**: arrive)

INDEFINITE PRONOUNS AS SUBJECT

An indefinite pronoun is a pronoun that does not refer to a specific noun. Indefinite pronouns may be only singular, be only plural, or change depending on how they are used.

ALWAYS SINGULAR

Pronouns such as *each*, *either*, *everybody*, *anybody*, *somebody*, and *nobody* are always singular.

Examples:

Each of the runners *has* a different bib number.

(**Singular Subject**: Each. **Singular Verb**: has)

Is either of you ready for the game?

(**Singular Subject**: Either. **Singular Verb**: is)

Note: The words *each* and *either* can also be used as adjectives (e.g., *each* person is unique). When one of these adjectives modifies the subject of a sentence, it is always a singular subject.

Everybody grows a day older every day.

(**Singular Subject**: Everybody. **Singular Verb**: grows)

Anybody is welcome to bring a tent.

(**Singular Subject**: Anybody. **Singular Verb**: is)

ALWAYS PLURAL

Pronouns such as *both*, *several*, and *many* are always plural.

Examples:

Both of the siblings *were* too tired to argue.

(**Plural Subject**: Both. **Plural Verb**: were)

Many have tried, but none have succeeded.

(**Plural Subject**: Many. **Plural Verb**: have tried)

DEPEND ON CONTEXT

Pronouns such as *some*, *any*, *all*, *none*, *more*, and *most* can be either singular or plural depending on what they are representing in the context of the sentence.

Examples:

All of my dog's food *was* still there in his bowl

(**Singular Subject**: All. **Singular Verb**: was)

By the end of the night, *all* of my guests *were* already excited about coming to my next party.

(**Plural Subject**: All. **Plural Verb**: were)

OTHER CASES INVOLVING PLURAL OR IRREGULAR FORM

Some nouns are **singular in meaning but plural in form**: news, mathematics, physics, and economics.

The *news is* coming on now.

Mathematics is my favorite class.

Some nouns are plural in form and meaning, and have **no singular equivalent**: scissors and pants.

Do these *pants come* with a shirt?

The *scissors are* for my project.

Mathematical operations are **irregular** in their construction, but are normally considered to be **singular in meaning**.

One plus one is two.

Three times three is nine.

Note: Look to your **dictionary** for help when you aren't sure whether a noun with a plural form has a singular or plural meaning.

COMPLEMENTS

A complement is a noun, pronoun, or adjective that is used to give more information about the subject or verb in the sentence.

DIRECT OBJECTS

A direct object is a noun or pronoun that takes or receives the **action** of a verb. (Remember: a complete sentence does not need a direct object, so not all sentences will have them. A sentence needs only a subject and a verb.) When you are looking for a direct object, find the verb and ask *who* or *what*.

Examples:

>I took the blanket. (Who or what did I take? *The blanket*)

>Jane read books. (Who or what does Jane read? *Books*)

INDIRECT OBJECTS

An indirect object is a word or group of words that show how an action had an **influence** on someone or something. If there is an indirect object in a sentence, then you always have a direct object in the sentence. When you are looking for the indirect object, find the verb and ask *to/for whom or what*.

Examples:

>We taught the old dog a new trick.

>(To/For Whom or What was taught? *The old dog*)

>I gave them a math lesson.

>(To/For Whom or What was given? *Them*)

>**Review Video: Direct and Indirect Objects**
>Visit mometrix.com/academy and enter code: 817385

PREDICATE NOMINATIVES AND PREDICATE ADJECTIVES

As we looked at previously, verbs may be classified as either action verbs or linking verbs. A linking verb is so named because it links the subject to words in the predicate that describe or define the subject. These words are called predicate nominatives (if nouns or pronouns) or predicate adjectives (if adjectives).

Examples:

>My father is a *lawyer*.

>(Father is the **subject**. Lawyer is the **predicate nominative**.)

>Your mother is *patient*.

>(Mother is the **subject**. Patient is the **predicate adjective**.)

PRONOUN USAGE

The **antecedent** is the noun that has been replaced by a pronoun. A pronoun and its antecedent **agree** when they have the same number (singular or plural) and gender (male, female, or neuter).

Examples:

>**Singular agreement**: *John* came into town, and *he* played for us.

>(The word *he* replaces *John*.)

>**Plural agreement**: *John and Rick* came into town, and *they* played for us.

>(The word *they* replaces *John and Rick*.)

To determine which is the correct pronoun to use in a compound subject or object, try each pronoun **alone** in place of the compound in the sentence. Your knowledge of pronouns will tell you which one is correct.

Example:

Bob and (I, me) will be going.

Test: (1) *I will be going* or (2) *Me will be going*. The second choice cannot be correct because *me* cannot be used as the subject of a sentence. Instead, *me* is used as an object.

Answer: Bob and I will be going.

When a pronoun is used with a noun immediately following (as in "we boys"), try the sentence **without the added noun**.

Example:

(We/Us) boys played football last year.

Test: (1) *We played football last year* or (2) *Us played football last year*. Again, the second choice cannot be correct because *us* cannot be used as a subject of a sentence. Instead, *us* is used as an object.

Answer: We boys played football last year.

> **Review Video: Pronoun Usage**
> Visit mometrix.com/academy and enter code: 666500
>
> **Review Video: What is Pronoun-Antecedent Agreement?**
> Visit mometrix.com/academy and enter code: 919704

A pronoun should point clearly to the **antecedent**. Here is how a pronoun reference can be unhelpful if it is not directly stated or puzzling.

Unhelpful: Ron and Jim went to the store, and *he* bought soda.

(Who bought soda? Ron or Jim?)

Helpful: Jim went to the store, and *he* bought soda.

(The sentence is clear. Jim bought the soda.)

Some pronouns change their form by their placement in a sentence. A pronoun that is a subject in a sentence comes in the **subjective case**. Pronouns that serve as objects appear in the **objective case**. Finally, the pronouns that are used as possessives appear in the **possessive case**.

Examples:

Subjective case: *He* is coming to the show.

(The pronoun *He* is the subject of the sentence.)

Objective case: Josh drove *him* to the airport.

(The pronoun *him* is the object of the sentence.)

Possessive case: The flowers are *mine*.

(The pronoun *mine* shows ownership of the flowers.)

The word *who* is a subjective-case pronoun that can be used as a **subject**. The word *whom* is an objective-case pronoun that can be used as an **object**. The words *who* and *whom* are common in subordinate clauses or in questions.

Examples:

Subject: He knows who wants to come.

(*Who* is the subject of the verb *wants*.)

Object: He knows the man whom we want at the party.

(*Whom* is the object of *we want*.)

CLAUSES

A clause is a group of words that contains both a subject and a predicate (verb). There are two types of clauses: independent and dependent. An **independent clause** contains a complete thought, while a **dependent (or subordinate) clause** does not. A dependent clause includes a subject and a verb, and may also contain objects or complements, but it cannot stand as a complete thought without being joined to an independent clause. Dependent clauses function within sentences as adjectives, adverbs, or nouns.

Example:

Independent Clause: I am running

Dependent Clause: because I want to stay in shape

The clause *I am running* is an independent clause: it has a subject and a verb, and it gives a complete thought. The clause *because I want to stay in shape* is a dependent clause: it has a subject and a verb, but it does not express a complete thought. It adds detail to the independent clause to which it is attached.

Combined: I am running because I want to stay in shape.

> **Review Video: What is a Clause?**
> Visit mometrix.com/academy and enter code: 940170
>
> **Review Video: Independent and Dependent Clause Examples**
> Visit mometrix.com/academy and enter code: 556903

Types of Dependent Clauses
Adjective Clauses

An **adjective clause** is a dependent clause that modifies a noun or a pronoun. Adjective clauses begin with a relative pronoun (*who, whose, whom, which,* and *that*) or a relative adverb (*where, when,* and *why*).

Also, adjective clauses come after the noun that the clause needs to explain or rename. This is done to have a clear connection to the independent clause.

Examples:

I learned the reason *why I won the award*.

This is the place *where I started my first job*.

An adjective clause can be an essential or nonessential clause. An essential clause is very important to the sentence. **Essential clauses** explain or define a person or thing. **Nonessential clauses** give more information about a person or thing but are not necessary to define them. Nonessential clauses are set off with commas while essential clauses are not.

Examples:

Essential: A person *who works hard at first* can often rest later in life.

Nonessential: Neil Armstrong, *who walked on the moon*, is my hero.

Adverb Clauses

An **adverb clause** is a dependent clause that modifies a verb, adjective, or adverb. In sentences with multiple dependent clauses, adverb clauses are usually placed immediately before or after the independent clause. An adverb clause is introduced with words such as *after, although, as, before, because, if, since, so, unless, when, where,* and *while*.

Examples:

When you walked outside, I called the manager.

I will go with you *unless you want to stay*.

Noun Clauses

A **noun clause** is a dependent clause that can be used as a subject, object, or complement. Noun clauses begin with words such as *how, that, what, whether, which, who,* and *why*. These words can also come with an adjective clause. Unless the noun clause is being used as the subject of the sentence, it should come after the verb of the independent clause.

Examples:

The real mystery is *how you avoided serious injury*.

What you learn from each other depends on your honesty with others.

SUBORDINATION

When two related ideas are not of equal importance, the ideal way to combine them is to make the more important idea an independent clause, and the less important idea a dependent or subordinate clause. This is called **subordination**.

Example:

Separate ideas: The team had a perfect regular season. The team lost the championship.

Subordinated: Despite having a perfect regular season, *the team lost the championship.*

PHRASES

A phrase is a group of words that functions as a single part of speech, usually a noun, adjective, or adverb. A phrase is not a complete thought, but it adds **detail** or **explanation** to a sentence, or **renames** something within the sentence.

PREPOSITIONAL PHRASES

One of the most common types of phrases is the prepositional phrase. A **prepositional phrase** begins with a preposition and ends with a noun or pronoun that is the object of the preposition. Normally, the prepositional phrase functions as an **adjective** or an **adverb** within the sentence.

Examples:

The picnic is *on the blanket.*

I am sick *with a fever* today.

Among the many flowers, John found a four-leaf clover.

VERBAL PHRASES

A verbal is a word or phrase that is formed from a verb but does not function as a verb. Depending on its particular form, it may be used as a noun, adjective, or adverb. A verbal does **not** replace a verb in a sentence.

Examples:

Correct: *Walk* a mile daily.

(*Walk* is the verb of this sentence. The subject is the implied *you.*)

Incorrect: *To walk* a mile.

(*To walk* is a type of verbal. This is not a sentence since there is no functional verb)

There are three types of verbals: **participles**, **gerunds**, and **infinitives**. Each type of verbal has a corresponding **phrase** that consists of the verbal itself along with any complements or modifiers.

PARTICIPLES

A **participle** is a type of verbal that always functions as an adjective. The present participle always ends with *-ing*. Past participles end with *-d, -ed, -n,* or *-t*.

Examples: Verb: *dance* | Present Participle: *dancing* | Past Participle: *danced*

Participial phrases most often come right before or right after the noun or pronoun that they modify.

Examples:

Shipwrecked on an island, the boys started to fish for food.

Having been seated for five hours, we got out of the car to stretch our legs.

Praised for their work, the group accepted the first-place trophy.

GERUNDS

A **gerund** is a type of verbal that always functions as a noun. Like present participles, gerunds always end with *-ing*, but they can be easily distinguished from one another by the part of speech they represent (participles always function as adjectives). Since a gerund or gerund phrase always functions as a noun, it can be used as the subject of a sentence, the predicate nominative, or the object of a verb or preposition.

Examples:

We want to be known for *teaching the poor*. (Object of preposition)

Coaching this team is the best job of my life. (Subject)

We like *practicing our songs* in the basement. (Object of verb)

INFINITIVES

An **infinitive** is a type of verbal that can function as a noun, an adjective, or an adverb. An infinitive is made of the word *to* + the basic form of the verb. As with all other types of verbal phrases, an infinitive phrase includes the verbal itself and all of its complements or modifiers.

Examples:

To join the team is my goal in life. (Noun)

The animals have enough food *to eat for the night*. (Adjective)

People lift weights *to exercise their muscles*. (Adverb)

> **Review Video: Gerunds, Participles, and Infinitives**
> Visit mometrix.com/academy and enter code: 634263

APPOSITIVE PHRASES

An **appositive** is a word or phrase that is used to explain or rename nouns or pronouns. Noun phrases, gerund phrases, and infinitive phrases can all be used as appositives.

Examples:

> Terriers, *hunters at heart*, have been dressed up to look like lap dogs.
>
> (The noun phrase *hunters at heart* renames the noun *terriers*.)
>
> His plan, *to save and invest his money*, was proven as a safe approach.
>
> (The infinitive phrase explains what the plan is.)

Appositive phrases can be **essential** or **nonessential**. An appositive phrase is essential if the person, place, or thing being described or renamed is too general for its meaning to be understood without the appositive.

Examples:

> **Essential**: Two Founding Fathers George Washington and Thomas Jefferson served as presidents.
>
> **Nonessential**: George Washington and Thomas Jefferson, two Founding Fathers, served as presidents.

ABSOLUTE PHRASES

An absolute phrase is a phrase that consists of **a noun followed by a participle**. An absolute phrase provides **context** to what is being described in the sentence, but it does not modify or explain any particular word; it is essentially independent.

Examples:

> *The alarm ringing*, he pushed the snooze button.
>
> *The music paused*, she continued to dance through the crowd.

Note: Absolute phrases can be confusing, so don't be discouraged if you have a difficult time with them.

PARALLELISM

When multiple items or ideas are presented in a sentence in series, such as in a list, the items or ideas must be stated in grammatically equivalent ways. In other words, if one idea is stated in gerund form, the second cannot be stated in infinitive form. For example, to write, *I enjoy reading and to study* would be incorrect. An infinitive and a gerund are not equivalent. Instead, you should write *I enjoy reading and studying*. In lists of more than two, it can be harder to keep everything straight, but all items in a list must be parallel.

Example:

> **Incorrect**: He stopped at the office, grocery store, and the pharmacy before heading home.
>
> The first and third items in the list of places include the article *the*, so the second item needs it as well.
>
> **Correct**: He stopped at the office, *the* grocery store, and the pharmacy before heading home.

Example:

> **Incorrect**: While vacationing in Europe, she went biking, skiing, and climbed mountains.
>
> The first and second items in the list are gerunds, so the third item must be as well.
>
> **Correct**: While vacationing in Europe, she went biking, skiing, and *mountain climbing*.

SENTENCE PURPOSE

There are four types of sentences: declarative, imperative, interrogative, and exclamatory.

A **declarative** sentence states a fact and ends with a period.

> Example: *The football game starts at seven o'clock.*

An **imperative** sentence tells someone to do something and generally ends with a period. (An urgent command might end with an exclamation point instead.)

> Example: *Don't forget to buy your ticket.*

An **interrogative** sentence asks a question and ends with a question mark.

> Example: *Are you going to the game on Friday?*

An **exclamatory** sentence shows strong emotion and ends with an exclamation point.

> Example: *I can't believe we won the game!*

SENTENCE STRUCTURE

Sentences are classified by structure based on the type and number of clauses present. The four classifications of sentence structure are the following:

Simple: A simple sentence has one independent clause with no dependent clauses. A simple sentence may have **compound elements** (i.e., compound subject or verb).

Examples:

> <u>Judy</u> *watered* the lawn. (single <u>subject</u>, single *verb*)
>
> <u>Judy and Alan</u> *watered* the lawn. (compound <u>subject</u>, single *verb*)
>
> <u>Judy</u> *watered* the lawn and *pulled* weeds. (single <u>subject</u>, compound *verb*)
>
> <u>Judy and Alan</u> *watered* the lawn and *pulled* weeds. (compound <u>subject</u>, compound *verb*)

Compound: A compound sentence has two or more <u>independent clauses</u> with no dependent clauses. Usually, the independent clauses are joined with a comma and a coordinating conjunction or with a semicolon.

Examples:

> <u>The time has come</u>, and <u>we are ready</u>.
>
> <u>I woke up at dawn</u>; <u>the sun was just coming up</u>.

Complex: A complex sentence has one independent clause and at least one *dependent clause*.

Examples:

Although he had the flu, Harry went to work.

Marcia got married *after she finished college*.

Compound-Complex: A compound-complex sentence has at least two independent clauses and at least one *dependent clause*.

Examples:

John is my friend *who went to India*, and he brought back souvenirs.

You may not realize this, but we heard the music *that you played last night*.

> **Review Video: Sentence Structure**
> Visit mometrix.com/academy and enter code: 700478

SENTENCE FRAGMENTS

Usually when the term *sentence fragment* comes up, it is because you have to decide whether or not a group of words is a complete sentence, and if it's not a complete sentence, you're about to have to fix it. Recall that a group of words must contain at least one **independent clause** in order to be considered a sentence. If it doesn't contain even one independent clause, it would be called a **sentence fragment**. (If it contains two or more independent clauses that are not joined correctly, it would be called a run-on sentence.)

The process to use for **repairing** a sentence fragment depends on what type of fragment it is. If the fragment is a dependent clause, it can sometimes be as simple as removing a subordinating word (e.g., when, because, if) from the beginning of the fragment. Alternatively, a dependent clause can be incorporated into a closely related neighboring sentence. If the fragment is missing some required part, like a subject or a verb, the fix might be as simple as adding it in.

Examples:

Fragment: Because he wanted to sail the Mediterranean.

Removed subordinating word: He wanted to sail the Mediterranean.

Combined with another sentence: Because he wanted to sail the Mediterranean, he booked a Greek island cruise.

RUN-ON SENTENCES

Run-on sentences consist of multiple independent clauses that have not been joined together properly. Run-on sentences can be corrected in several different ways:

Join clauses properly: This can be done with a comma and coordinating conjunction, with a semicolon, or with a colon or dash if the second clause is explaining something in the first.

Example:

> **Incorrect**: I went on the trip, we visited lots of castles.
>
> **Corrected**: I went on the trip, and we visited lots of castles.

Split into separate sentences: This correction is most effective when the independent clauses are very long or when they are not closely related.

Example:

> **Incorrect**: The drive to New York takes ten hours, my uncle lives in Boston.
>
> **Corrected**: The drive to New York takes ten hours. My uncle lives in Boston.

Make one clause dependent: This is the easiest way to make the sentence correct and more interesting at the same time. It's often as simple as adding a subordinating word between the two clauses

Example:

> **Incorrect**: I finally made it to the store and I bought some eggs.
>
> **Corrected**: When I finally made it to the store, I bought some eggs.

Reduce to one clause with a compound verb: If both clauses have the same subject, remove the subject from the second clause, and you now have just one clause with a compound verb.

Example:

> **Incorrect**: The drive to New York takes ten hours, it makes me very tired.
>
> **Corrected**: The drive to New York takes ten hours and makes me very tired.

Note: While these are the simplest ways to correct a run-on sentence, often the best way is to completely reorganize the thoughts in the sentence and rewrite it.

> **Review Video: Fragments and Run-on Sentences**
> Visit mometrix.com/academy and enter code: 541989

DANGLING AND MISPLACED MODIFIERS
DANGLING MODIFIERS

A dangling modifier is a dependent clause or verbal phrase that does not have a **clear logical connection** to a word in the sentence.

Example:

> **Dangling**: *Reading each magazine article*, the stories caught my attention.
>
> The word *stories* cannot be modified by *Reading each magazine article*. People can read, but stories cannot read. Therefore, the subject of the sentence must be a person.
>
> **Corrected**: Reading each magazine article, *I* was entertained by the stories.

Example:

Dangling: Ever since childhood, my grandparents have visited me for Christmas.

The speaker in this sentence can't have been visited by her grandparents when *they* were children, since she wouldn't have been born yet. Either the modifier should be **clarified** or the sentence should be **rearranged** to specify whose childhood is being referenced.

Clarified: Ever since I was a child, my grandparents have visited for Christmas.

Rearranged: Ever since childhood, I have enjoyed my grandparents visiting for Christmas.

MISPLACED MODIFIERS

Because modifiers are grammatically versatile, they can be put in many different places within the structure of a sentence. The danger of this versatility is that a modifier can accidentally be placed where it is modifying the wrong word or where it is not clear which word it is modifying.

Example:

Misplaced: She read the book to a crowd *that was filled with beautiful pictures*.

The book was filled with beautiful pictures, not the crowd.

Corrected: She read the book *that was filled with beautiful pictures* to a crowd.

Example:

Ambiguous: Derek saw a bus nearly hit a man *on his way to work*.

Was Derek on his way to work? Or was the other man?

Derek: *On his way to work*, Derek saw a bus nearly hit a man.

The other man: Derek saw a bus nearly hit a man *who was on his way to work*.

SPLIT INFINITIVES

A split infinitive occurs when a modifying word comes between the word *to* and the verb that pairs with *to*.

Example: To *clearly* explain vs. To explain *clearly* | To *softly* sing vs. To sing *softly*

Though considered improper by some, split infinitives may provide better clarity and simplicity in some cases than the alternatives. As such, avoiding them should not be considered a universal rule.

DOUBLE NEGATIVES

Standard English allows **two negatives** only when a **positive** meaning is intended. For example, *The team was not displeased with their performance.* Double negatives to emphasize negation are not used in standard English.

Negative modifiers (e.g., never, no, and not) should not be paired with other negative modifiers or negative words (e.g., none, nobody, nothing, or neither). The modifiers *hardly, barely,* and *scarcely* are considered negatives in standard English, so they should not be used with other negatives.

Punctuation

END PUNCTUATION

PERIODS
Use a period to end all sentences except direct questions, exclamations.

DECLARATIVE SENTENCE
A declarative sentence gives information or makes a statement.

> Examples: I can fly a kite. | The plane left two hours ago.

IMPERATIVE SENTENCE
An imperative sentence gives an order or command.

> Examples: You are coming with me. | Bring me that note.

PERIODS FOR ABBREVIATIONS
> Examples: 3 P.M. | 2 A.M. | Mr. Jones | Mrs. Stevens | Dr. Smith | Bill Jr. | Pennsylvania Ave.

Note: an abbreviation is a shortened form of a word or phrase.

QUESTION MARKS
Question marks should be used following a direct question. A polite request can be followed by a period instead of a question mark.

> **Direct Question**: What is for lunch today? | How are you? | Why is that the answer?

> **Polite Requests**: Can you please send me the item tomorrow. | Will you please walk with me on the track.

> **Review Video: When to Use a Question Mark**
> Visit mometrix.com/academy and enter code: 118471

EXCLAMATION MARKS
Exclamation marks are used after a word group or sentence that shows much feeling or has special importance. Exclamation marks should not be overused. They are saved for proper **exclamatory interjections**.

> Example: We're going to the finals! | You have a beautiful car! | That's crazy!

> **Review Video: What Does an Exclamation Point Mean?**
> Visit mometrix.com/academy and enter code: 199367

COMMAS
The comma is a punctuation mark that can help you understand connections in a sentence. Not every sentence needs a comma. However, if a sentence needs a comma, you need to put it in the right place. A comma in the wrong place (or an absent comma) will make a sentence's meaning unclear. These are some of the rules for commas:

1. Use a comma **before a coordinating conjunction** joining independent clauses
   Example: Bob caught three fish, and I caught two fish.

2. Use a comma after an introductory phrase or an adverbial clause
   Examples:
   After the final out, we went to a restaurant to celebrate.
   Studying the stars, I was surprised at the beauty of the sky.

3. Use a comma between items in a series.
   Example: I will bring the turkey, the pie, and the coffee.

4. Use a comma **between coordinate adjectives** not joined with *and*
   Incorrect: The kind, brown dog followed me home.
   Correct: The *kind, loyal* dog followed me home.
   Not all adjectives are **coordinate** (i.e., equal or parallel). There are two simple ways to know if your adjectives are coordinate. One, you can join the adjectives with *and*: *The kind and loyal dog.* Two, you can change the order of the adjectives: *The loyal, kind dog.*

5. Use commas for **interjections** and **after *yes* and *no*** responses
   Examples:
   Interjection: *Oh,* I had no idea. | *Wow,* you know how to play this game.
   Yes and No: *Yes,* I heard you. | *No,* I cannot come tomorrow.

6. Use commas to separate nonessential modifiers and nonessential appositives
   Examples:
   Nonessential Modifier: John Frank, who is coaching the team, was promoted today.
   Nonessential Appositive: Thomas Edison, an American inventor, was born in Ohio.

7. Use commas to set off nouns of direct address, interrogative tags, and contrast
   Examples:
   Direct Address: You, *John,* are my only hope in this moment.
   Interrogative Tag: This is the last time, *correct*?
   Contrast: You are my friend, *not my enemy.*

8. Use commas with dates, addresses, geographical names, and titles
   Examples:
   Date: *July 4, 1776,* is an important date to remember.
   Address: He is meeting me at *456 Delaware Avenue, Washington, D.C.,* tomorrow morning.
   Geographical Name: *Paris, France,* is my favorite city.
   Title: John Smith, *Ph. D.,* will be visiting your class today.

9. Use commas to **separate expressions like *he said*** and ***she said*** if they come between a sentence of a quote
   Examples:
   "I want you to know," he began, "that I always wanted the best for you."
   "You can start," Jane said, "with an apology."

Review Video: When To Use a Comma
Visit mometrix.com/academy and enter code: 786797

SEMICOLONS

The semicolon is used to connect major sentence pieces of equal value. Some rules for semicolons include:

1. Use a semicolon **between closely connected independent clauses** that are not connected with a coordinating conjunction.

    Examples:

    > She is outside; we are inside.
    > You are right; we should go with your plan.

2. Use a semicolon **between independent clauses linked with a transitional word.**

    Examples:

    > I think that we can agree on this; *however,* I am not sure about my friends.
    > You are looking in the wrong places; *therefore,* you will not find what you need.

3. Use a semicolon **between items in a series that has internal punctuation.**

    Example: I have visited New York, New York; Augusta, Maine; and Baltimore, Maryland.

    > **Review Video: How to Use Semicolons**
    > Visit mometrix.com/academy and enter code: 370605

COLONS

The colon is used to call attention to the words that follow it. A colon must come after a **complete independent clause**. The rules for colons are as follows:

1. Use a colon after an independent clause to **make a list**

    Example: I want to learn many languages: Spanish, German, and Italian.

2. Use a colon for **explanations** or to **give a quote**

    Examples:

    > **Quote**: He started with an idea: "We are able to do more than we imagine."
    > **Explanation**: There is one thing that stands out on your resume: responsibility.

3. Use a colon **after the greeting in a formal letter**, to **show hours and minutes**, and to **separate a title and subtitle**

    Examples:

    > **Greeting in a formal letter**: Dear Sir: | To Whom It May Concern:
    > **Time**: It is 3:14 P.M.
    > **Title**: The essay is titled "America: A Short Introduction to a Modern Country"

    > **Review Video: What is a Colon?**
    > Visit mometrix.com/academy and enter code: 868673

PARENTHESES

Parentheses are used for additional information. Also, they can be used to put labels for letters or numbers in a series. Parentheses should be not be used very often. If they are overused, parentheses can be a distraction instead of a help.

Examples:

Extra Information: The rattlesnake (see Image 2) is a dangerous snake of North and South America.

Series: Include in the email (1) your name, (2) your address, and (3) your question for the author.

> **Review Video: When to Use Parentheses**
> Visit mometrix.com/academy and enter code: 947743

QUOTATION MARKS

Use quotation marks to close off **direct quotations** of a person's spoken or written words. Do not use quotation marks around indirect quotations. An indirect quotation gives someone's message without using the person's exact words. Use **single quotation marks** to close off a quotation inside a quotation.

Direct Quote: Nancy said, "I am waiting for Henry to arrive."

Indirect Quote: Henry said that he is going to be late to the meeting.

Quote inside a Quote: The teacher asked, "Has everyone read 'The Gift of the Magi'?"

Quotation marks should be used around the titles of **short works**: newspaper and magazine articles, poems, short stories, songs, television episodes, radio programs, and subdivisions of books or web sites.

Examples:

"Rip van Winkle" (short story by Washington Irving)

"O Captain! My Captain!" (poem by Walt Whitman)

Although it is not standard usage, quotation marks are sometimes used to highlight **irony**, or the use of words to mean something other than their dictionary definition. This type of usage should be employed sparingly, if at all.

Examples:

The boss warned Frank that he was walking on "thin ice."

(Frank is not walking on real ice. Instead, Frank is being warned to avoid mistakes.)

The teacher thanked the young man for his "honesty."

(In this example, the quotation marks around *honesty* show that the teacher does not believe the young man's explanation.)

> **Review Video: Quotation Marks**
> Visit mometrix.com/academy and enter code: 884918

Periods and commas are put **inside** quotation marks. Colons and semicolons are put **outside** the quotation marks. Question marks and exclamation points are placed inside quotation marks when they are part of a quote. When the question or exclamation mark goes with the whole sentence, the mark is left outside of the quotation marks.

Examples:

Period and comma: We read "The Gift of the Magi," "The Skylight Room," and "The Cactus."

Semicolon: They watched "The Nutcracker"; then, they went home.

Exclamation mark that is a part of a quote: The crowd cheered, "Victory!"

Question mark that goes with the whole sentence: Is your favorite short story "The Tell-Tale Heart"?

APOSTROPHES

An apostrophe is used to show **possession** or the **deletion of letters in contractions**. An apostrophe is not needed with the possessive pronouns *his, hers, its, ours, theirs, whose*, and *yours*.

Singular Nouns: David's car | a book's theme | my brother's board game

Plural Nouns with -s: the scissors' handle | boys' basketball

Plural Nouns without -s: Men's department | the people's adventure

> **Review Video: When to Use an Apostrophe**
> Visit mometrix.com/academy and enter code: 213068
>
> **Review Video: Punctuation Errors in Possessive Pronouns**
> Visit mometrix.com/academy and enter code: 221438

HYPHENS

Hyphens are used to **separate compound words**. Use hyphens in the following cases:

1. **Compound numbers** between 21 and 99 when written out in words
   Example: This team needs *twenty-five* points to win the game.

2. **Written-out fractions** that are used as **adjectives**
   Correct: The recipe says that we need a *three-fourths* cup of butter.
   Incorrect: *One-fourth* of the road is under construction.

3. Compound words used as **adjectives that come before a noun**
   Correct: The *well-fed* dog took a nap.
   Incorrect: The dog was *well-fed* for his nap.

4. Compound words that would be **hard to read** or **easily confused with other words**
   Examples: Semi-irresponsible | Anti-itch | Re-sort

Note: This is not a complete set of the rules for hyphens. A dictionary is the best tool for knowing if a compound word needs a hyphen.

DASHES

Dashes are used to show a **break** or a **change in thought** in a sentence or to act as parentheses in a sentence. When typing, use two hyphens to make a dash. Do not put a space before or after the dash. The following are the rules for dashes:

1. To set off **parenthetical statements** or an **appositive with internal punctuation**

    Example: The three trees—oak, pine, and magnolia—are coming on a truck tomorrow.

2. To show a **break or change in tone or thought**

    Example: The first question—how silly of me—does not have a correct answer.

ELLIPSIS MARKS

The ellipsis mark has three periods (...) to show when **words have been removed** from a quotation. If a full sentence or more is removed from a quoted passage, you need to use four periods to show the removed text and the end punctuation mark. The ellipsis mark should not be used at the beginning of a quotation. The ellipsis mark should also not be used at the end of a quotation unless some words have been deleted from the end of the final sentence.

Example:

"Then he picked up the groceries...paid for them...later he went home."

BRACKETS

There are two main reasons to use brackets:

1. When **placing parentheses inside of parentheses**

    Example: The hero of this story, Paul Revere (a silversmith and industrialist [see Ch. 4]), rode through towns of Massachusetts to warn of advancing British troops.

2. When adding **clarification or detail** to a quotation that is **not part of the quotation**

    Example:

    The father explained, "My children are planning to attend my alma mater [State University]."

> **Review Video: Using Brackets in Sentences**
> Visit mometrix.com/academy and enter code: 727546

Common Errors

WORD CONFUSION
WHICH, THAT, AND WHO

The words *which*, *that*, and *who* can act as **relative pronouns** to help clarify or describe a noun.

Which is used for things only.

> Example: Andrew's car, *which is old and rusty*, broke down last week.

That is used for people or things. *That* is usually informal when used to describe people.

> Example: Is this the only book *that Louis L'Amour wrote?*

> Example: Is Louis L'Amour the author *that wrote Western novels?*

Who is used for people or for animals that have a name.

> Example: Mozart was the composer *who wrote those operas.*

> Example: John's dog, *who is called Max,* is large and fierce.

HOMOPHONES

Homophones are words that sound alike (or similar), but they have different **spellings** and **definitions**.

TO, TOO, AND TWO

To can be an adverb or a preposition for showing direction, purpose, and relationship. See your dictionary for the many other ways use *to* in a sentence.

> Examples: I went to the store. | I want to go with you.

Too is an adverb that means *also, as well, very, or more than enough*.

> Examples: I can walk a mile too. | You have eaten too much.

Two is the second number in the series of numbers (e.g., one (1), two, (2), three (3)...)

> Example: You have two minutes left.

THERE, THEIR, AND THEY'RE

There can be an adjective, adverb, or pronoun. Often, *there* is used to show a place or to start a sentence.

> Examples: I went there yesterday. | There is something in his pocket.

Their is a pronoun that is used to show ownership.

> Examples: He is their father. | This is their fourth apology this week.

They're is a contraction of *they are*.

> Example: Did you know that they're in town?

KNEW AND NEW

Knew is the past tense of *know*.

>Example: I knew the answer.

New is an adjective that means something is current, has not been used, or modern.

>Example: This is my new phone.

THEN AND THAN

Then is an adverb that indicates sequence or order:

>Example: I'm going to run to the library and then come home.

Than is special-purpose word used only for comparisons:

>Example: Susie likes chips better than candy.

ITS AND IT'S

Its is a pronoun that shows ownership.

>Example: The guitar is in its case.

It's is a contraction of *it is*.

>Example: It's an honor and a privilege to meet you.

Note: The *h* in honor is silent, so the sound of the vowel *o* must have the article *an*.

YOUR AND YOU'RE

Your is a pronoun that shows ownership.

>Example: This is your moment to shine.

You're is a contraction of *you are*.

>Example: Yes, you're correct.

AFFECT AND EFFECT

There are two main reasons that **affect** and **effect** are so often confused: 1) both words can be used as either a noun or a verb, and 2) unlike most homophones, their usage and meanings are closely related to each other. Here is a quick rundown of the four usage options:

Affect (n): feeling, emotion, or mood that is displayed

>Example: The patient had a flat *affect*. (i.e., his face showed little or no emotion)

Affect (v): to alter, to change, to influence

>Example: The sunshine *affects* the plant's growth.

Effect (n): a result, a consequence

>Example: What *effect* will this weather have on our schedule?

Effect (v): to bring about, to cause to be

Example: These new rules will *effect* order in the office.

The noun form of *affect* is rarely used outside of technical medical descriptions, so if a noun form is needed on the test, you can safely select *effect*. The verb form of *effect* is not as rare as the noun form of *affect*, but it's still not all that likely to show up on your test. If you need a verb and you can't decide which to use based on the definitions, choosing *affect* is your best bet.

Homographs

Homographs are words that share the same spelling, and they have multiple meanings. To figure out which meaning is being used, you should be looking for context clues. The context clues give hints to the meaning of the word. For example, the word *spot* has many meanings. It can mean "a place" or "a stain or blot." In the sentence "After my lunch, I saw a spot on my shirt," the word *spot* means "a stain or blot." The context clues of "After my lunch..." and "on my shirt" guide you to this decision.

Bank

(noun): an establishment where money is held for savings or lending

(verb): to collect or pile up

Content

(noun): the topics that will be addressed within a book

(adjective): pleased or satisfied

Fine

(noun): an amount of money that acts a penalty for an offense

(adjective): very small or thin

Incense

(noun): a material that is burned in religious settings and makes a pleasant aroma

(verb): to frustrate or anger

Lead

(noun): the first or highest position

(verb): to direct a person or group of followers

Object

(noun): a lifeless item that can be held and observed

(verb): to disagree

Produce

(noun): fruits and vegetables

(verb): to make or create something

REFUSE

    (noun): garbage or debris that has been thrown away

    (verb): to not allow

SUBJECT

    (noun): an area of study

    (verb): to force or subdue

TEAR

    (noun): a fluid secreted by the eyes

    (verb): to separate or pull apart

Mathematics

Numbers

CLASSIFICATIONS OF NUMBERS

Numbers are the basic building blocks of mathematics. Specific features of numbers are identified by the following terms:

Integer – any positive or negative whole number, including zero. Integers do not include fractions $\left(\frac{1}{3}\right)$, decimals (0.56), or mixed numbers $\left(7\frac{3}{4}\right)$.

Prime number – any whole number greater than 1 that has only two factors, itself and 1; that is, a number that can be divided evenly only by 1 and itself.

Composite number – any whole number greater than 1 that has more than two different factors; in other words, any whole number that is not a prime number. For example: The composite number 8 has the factors of 1, 2, 4, and 8.

Even number – any integer that can be divided by 2 without leaving a remainder. For example: 2, 4, 6, 8, and so on.

Odd number – any integer that cannot be divided evenly by 2. For example: 3, 5, 7, 9, and so on.

Decimal number – any number that uses a decimal point to show the part of the number that is less than one. Example: 1.234.

Decimal point – a symbol used to separate the ones place from the tenths place in decimals or dollars from cents in currency.

Decimal place – the position of a number to the right of the decimal point. In the decimal 0.123, the 1 is in the first place to the right of the decimal point, indicating tenths; the 2 is in the second place, indicating hundredths; and the 3 is in the third place, indicating thousandths.

The **decimal**, or base 10, system is a number system that uses ten different digits (0, 1, 2, 3, 4, 5, 6, 7, 8, 9). An example of a number system that uses something other than ten digits is the **binary**, or base 2, number system, used by computers, which uses only the numbers 0 and 1. It is thought that the decimal system originated because people had only their 10 fingers for counting.

Rational numbers include all integers, decimals, and fractions. Any terminating or repeating decimal number is a rational number.

Irrational numbers cannot be written as fractions or decimals because the number of decimal places is infinite and there is no recurring pattern of digits within the number. For example, pi (π) begins with 3.141592 and continues without terminating or repeating, so pi is an irrational number.

Real numbers are the set of all rational and irrational numbers.

> **Review Video and Practice: Numbers and Their Classifications**
> Visit mometrix.com/academy and enter code: 461071
>
> **Review Video and Practice: Rational and Irrational Numbers**
> Visit mometrix.com/academy and enter code: 280645
>
> **Review Video and Practice: Prime and Composite Numbers**
> Visit mometrix.com/academy and enter code: 565581

THE NUMBER LINE

A number line is a graph to see the distance between numbers. Basically, this graph shows the relationship between numbers. So a number line may have a point for zero and may show negative numbers on the left side of the line. Any positive numbers are placed on the right side of the line. For example, consider the points labeled on the following number line:

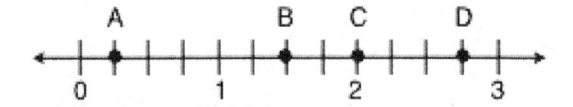

We can use the dashed lines on the number line to identify each point. Each dashed line between two whole numbers is $\frac{1}{4}$. The line halfway between two numbers is $\frac{1}{2}$.

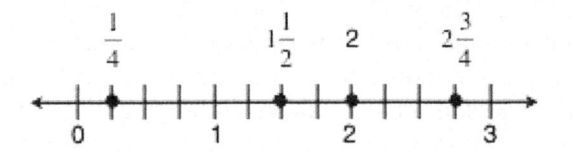

> **Review Video: The Number Line**
> Visit mometrix.com/academy and enter code: 816439

NUMBERS IN WORD FORM AND PLACE VALUE

When writing numbers out in word form or translating word form to numbers, it is essential to understand how a place value system works. In the decimal or base-10 system, each digit of a number represents how many of the corresponding place value – a specific factor of 10 – are contained in the number being represented. To make reading numbers easier, every three digits to the left of the decimal place is preceded by a comma. The following table demonstrates some of the place values:

Power of 10	10^3	10^2	10^1	10^0	10^{-1}	10^{-2}	10^{-3}
Value	1,000	100	10	1	0.1	0.01	0.001
Place	thousands	hundreds	tens	ones	tenths	hundredths	thousandths

For example, consider the number 4,546.09, which can be separated into each place value like this:

4: thousands
5: hundreds
4: tens
6: ones
0: tenths
9: hundredths

This number in word form would be *four thousand five hundred forty-six and nine hundredths*.

> **Review Video: Number Place Value**
> Visit mometrix.com/academy and enter code: 205433

ABSOLUTE VALUE

A precursor to working with negative numbers is understanding what **absolute values** are. A number's absolute value is simply the distance away from zero a number is on the number line. The absolute value of a number is always positive and is written $|x|$. For example, the absolute value of 3, written as $|3|$, is 3 because the distance between 0 and 3 on a number line is three units. Likewise, the absolute value of −3, written as $|-3|$, is 3 because the distance between 0 and −3 on a number line is three units. So $|3| = |-3|$.

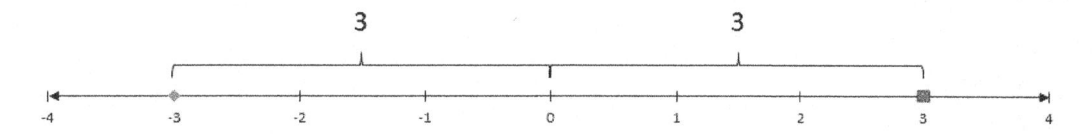

> **Review Video: Absolute Value**
> Visit mometrix.com/academy and enter code: 314669

PRACTICE

P1. Write the place value of each digit in 14,059.826

P2. Write out each of the following in words:

  (a) 29
  (b) 478
  (c) 98,542
  (d) 0.06
  (e) 13.113

P3. Write each of the following in numbers:

  (a) nine thousand four hundred thirty-five   9,435
  (b) three hundred two thousand eight hundred seventy-six   302,876
  (c) nine hundred one thousandths   .901
  (d) nineteen thousandths   .019
  (e) seven thousand one hundred forty-two and eighty-five hundredths   7,142.85

67

Practice Solutions

P1. The place value for each digit would be as follows:

Digit	Place Value
1	ten-thousands
4	thousands
0	hundreds
5	tens
9	ones
8	tenths
2	hundredths
6	thousandths

P2. Each written out in words would be:

(a) twenty-nine
(b) four hundred seventy-eight
(c) ninety-eight thousand five hundred forty-two
(d) six hundredths
(e) thirteen and one hundred thirteen thousandths

P3. Each in numeric form would be:

(a) 9,435
(b) 302, 876
(c) 0.901
(d) 0.019
(e) 7,142.85

Operations

OPERATIONS

An **operation** is simply a mathematical process that takes some value(s) as input(s) and produces an output. Elementary operations are often written in the following form: *value operation value*. For instance, in the expression $1 + 2$ the values are 1 and 2 and the operation is addition. Performing the operation gives the output of 3. In this way we can say that $1 + 2$ and 3 are equal, or $1 + 2 = 3$.

ADDITION

Addition increases the value of one quantity by the value of another quantity (both called **addends**). For example, $2 + 4 = 6; 8 + 9 = 17$. The result is called the **sum**. With addition, the order does not matter, $4 + 2 = 2 + 4$.

When adding signed numbers, if the signs are the same simply add the absolute values of the addends and apply the original sign to the sum. For example, $(+4) + (+8) = +12$ and $(-4) + (-8) = -12$. When the original signs are different, take the absolute values of the addends and subtract the smaller value from the larger value, then apply the original sign of the larger value to the difference. For instance, $(+4) + (-8) = -4$ and $(-4) + (+8) = +4$.

SUBTRACTION

Subtraction is the opposite operation to addition; it decreases the value of one quantity (the **minuend**) by the value of another quantity (the **subtrahend**). For example, $6 - 4 = 2; 17 - 8 = 9$. The result is called the **difference**. Note that with subtraction, the order does matter, $6 - 4 \neq 4 - 6$.

For subtracting signed numbers, change the sign of the subtrahend and then follow the same rules used for addition. For example, $(+4) - (+8) = (+4) + (-8) = -4$.

MULTIPLICATION

Multiplication can be thought of as repeated addition. One number (the **multiplier**) indicates how many times to add the other number (the **multiplicand**) to itself. For example, 3×2 (three times two) $= 2 + 2 + 2 = 6$. With multiplication, the order does not matter: $2 \times 3 = 3 \times 2$ or $3 + 3 = 2 + 2 + 2$, either way the result (the **product**) is the same.

If the signs are the same the product is positive when multiplying signed numbers. For example, $(+4) \times (+8) = +32$ and $(-4) \times (-8) = +32$. If the signs are opposite, the product is negative. For example, $(+4) \times (-8) = -32$ and $(-4) \times (+8) = -32$. When more than two factors are multiplied together, the sign of the product is determined by how many negative factors are present. If there are an odd number of negative factors then the product is negative, whereas an even number of negative factors indicates a positive product. For instance, $(+4) \times (-8) \times (-2) = +64$ and $(-4) \times (-8) \times (-2) = -64$.

DIVISION

Division is the opposite operation to multiplication; one number (the **divisor**) tells us how many parts to divide the other number (the **dividend**) into. The result of division is called the **quotient**. For example, $20 \div 4 = 5$; if 20 is split into 4 equal parts, each part is 5. With division, the order of the numbers does matter, $20 \div 4 \neq 4 \div 20$.

The rules for dividing signed numbers are similar to multiplying signed numbers. If the dividend and divisor have the same sign, the quotient is positive. If the dividend and divisor have opposite signs, the quotient is negative. For example, $(-4) \div (+8) = -0.5$.

> **Review Video: Mathematical Operations**
> Visit mometrix.com/academy and enter code: 208095

PARENTHESES

Parentheses are used to designate which operations should be done first when there are multiple operations. Example: $4 - (2 + 1) = 1$; the parentheses tell us that we must add 2 and 1, and then subtract the sum from 4, rather than subtracting 2 from 4 and then adding 1 (this would give us an answer of 3).

> **Review Video: Mathematical Parentheses**
> Visit mometrix.com/academy and enter code: 978600

EXPONENTS

An **exponent** is a superscript number placed next to another number at the top right. It indicates how many times the base number is to be multiplied by itself. Exponents provide a shorthand way to write what would be a longer mathematical expression, for example: $2^4 = 2 \times 2 \times 2 \times 2$. A number with an exponent of 2 is said to be "squared," while a number with an exponent of 3 is said to be "cubed." The value of a number raised to an exponent is called its power. So 8^4 is read as "8 to the 4th power," or "8 raised to the power of 4."

The properties of exponents are as follows:

Property	Description
$a^1 = a$	Any number to the power of 1 is equal to itself
$1^n = 1$	The number 1 raised to any power is equal to 1
$a^0 = 1$	Any number raised to the power of 0 is equal to 1
$a^n \times a^m = a^{n+m}$	Add exponents to multiply powers of the same base number
$a^n \div a^m = a^{n-m}$	Subtract exponents to divide powers of the same base number
$(a^n)^m = a^{n \times m}$	When a power is raised to a power, the exponents are multiplied
$(a \times b)^n = a^n \times b^n$	Multiplication and division operations inside parentheses can be raised to
$(a \div b)^n = a^n \div b^n$	a power. This is the same as each term being raised to that power.
$a^{-n} = \dfrac{1}{a^n}$	A negative exponent is the same as the reciprocal of a positive exponent

Note that exponents do not have to be integers. Fractional or decimal exponents follow all the rules above as well. Example: $5^{\frac{1}{4}} \times 5^{\frac{3}{4}} = 5^{\frac{1}{4} + \frac{3}{4}} = 5^1 = 5$.

> **Review Video: What is an Exponent?**
> Visit mometrix.com/academy and enter code: 600998
>
> **Review Video: Properties of Exponents**
> Visit mometrix.com/academy and enter code: 532558

ROOTS

A **root**, such as a square root, is another way of writing a fractional exponent. Instead of using a superscript, roots use the radical symbol ($\sqrt{}$) to indicate the operation. A radical will have a

perfect roots
1, 4, 9, 16, 25, 36, 49, 64, 81, 100, 121, 144, 169, 196, 225

number underneath the bar, and may sometimes have a number in the upper left: $\sqrt[n]{a}$, read as "the nth root of a." The relationship between radical notation and exponent notation can be described by this equation: $\sqrt[n]{a} = a^{\frac{1}{n}}$. The two special cases of $n = 2$ and $n = 3$ are called square roots and cube roots. If there is no number to the upper left, it is understood to be a square root ($n = 2$). Nearly all of the roots you encounter will be square roots. A square root is the same as a number raised to the one-half power. When we say that a is the square root of b ($a = \sqrt{b}$), we mean that a multiplied by itself equals b: ($a \times a = b$).

A **perfect square** is a number that has an integer for its square root. There are 10 perfect squares from 1 to 100: 1, 4, 9, 16, 25, 36, 49, 64, 81, 100 (the squares of integers 1 through 10).

> **Review Video: Roots**
> Visit mometrix.com/academy and enter code: 795655
>
> **Review Video: Square Root and Perfect Squares**
> Visit mometrix.com/academy and enter code: 648063

ORDER OF OPERATIONS

The **order of operations** is a set of rules that dictates the order in which we must perform each operation in an expression so that we will evaluate it accurately. If we have an expression that includes multiple different operations, the order of operations tells us which operations to do first. The most common mnemonic for the order of operations is **PEMDAS**, or "Please Excuse My Dear Aunt Sally." PEMDAS stands for parentheses, exponents, multiplication, division, addition, and subtraction. It is important to understand that multiplication and division have equal precedence, as do addition and subtraction, so those pairs of operations are simply worked from left to right in order.

For example, evaluating the expression $5 + 20 \div 4 \times (2 + 3) - 6$ using the correct order of operations would be done like this:

- **P:** Perform the operations inside the parentheses: $(2 + 3) = 5$
- **E:** Simplify the exponents.
  - The equation now looks like this: $5 + 20 \div 4 \times 5 - 6$
- **MD:** Perform multiplication and division from left to right: $20 \div 4 = 5$; then $5 \times 5 = 25$
  - The equation now looks like this: $5 + 25 - 6$
- **AS:** Perform addition and subtraction from left to right: $5 + 25 = 30$; then $30 - 6 = 24$

> **Review Video: Order of Operations**
> Visit mometrix.com/academy and enter code: 259675

SUBTRACTION WITH REGROUPING

A great way to make use of some of the features built into the decimal system would be regrouping when attempting longform subtraction operations. When subtracting within a place value, sometimes the minuend is smaller than the subtrahend, **regrouping** enables you to 'borrow' a unit from a place value to the left in order to get a positive difference. For example, consider subtracting 189 from 525 with regrouping.

First, set up the subtraction problem in vertical form:

```
   525
-  189
```

Notice that the numbers in the ones and tens columns of 525 are smaller than the numbers in the ones and tens columns of 189. This means you will need to use regrouping to perform subtraction:

```
   5  2  5
-  1  8  9
```

To subtract 9 from 5 in the ones column you will need to borrow from the 2 in the tens columns:

```
   5  1  15
-  1  8   9
            6
```

Next, to subtract 8 from 1 in the tens column you will need to borrow from the 5 in the hundreds column:

```
   4  11  15
-  1   8   9
       3   6
```

Last, subtract the 1 from the 4 in the hundreds column:

```
   4  11  15
-  1   8   9
   3   3   6
```

PRACTICE

P1. Demonstrate how to subtract 477 from 620 using regrouping.

P2. Simplify the following expressions with exponents:

  (a) 37^0
  (b) 1^{30}
  (c) $2^3 \times 2^4 \times 2^x$
  (d) $(3^x)^3$
  (e) $(12 \div 3)^2$

PRACTICE SOLUTIONS

P1. First, set up the subtraction problem in vertical form:

```
    6   2   0
-   4   7   7
_____
```

To subtract 7 from 0 in the ones column you will need to borrow from the 2 in the tens column:

```
    6   1   10
-   4   7   7
_____
            3
```

Next, to subtract 7 from the 1 that's still in the tens column you will need to borrow from the 6 in the hundreds column:

```
    5   11  10
-   4   7   7
_____
        4   3
```

Lastly, subtract 4 from the 5 remaining in the hundreds column:

```
    5   11  10
-   4   7   7
_____
    1   4   3
```

P2. Using the properties of exponents and the proper order of operations:

    (a) Any number raised to the power of 0 is equal to 1: $37^0 = 1$
    (b) The number 1 raised to any power is equal to 1: $1^{30} = 1$
    (c) Add exponents to multiply powers of the same base: $2^3 \times 2^4 \times 2^x = 2^{(3+4+x)} = 2^{(7+x)}$
    (d) When a power is raised to a power, the exponents are multiplied: $(3^x)^3 = 3^{3x}$
    (e) Perform the operation inside the parentheses first: $(12 \div 3)^2 = 4^2 = 16$

Factoring

FACTORS AND GREATEST COMMON FACTOR

Factors are numbers that are multiplied together to obtain a **product**. For example, in the equation $2 \times 3 = 6$, the numbers 2 and 3 are factors. A **prime number** has only two factors (1 and itself), but other numbers can have many factors.

A **common factor** is a number that divides exactly into two or more other numbers. For example, the factors of 12 are 1, 2, 3, 4, 6, and 12, while the factors of 15 are 1, 3, 5, and 15. The common factors of 12 and 15 are 1 and 3.

A **prime factor** is also a prime number. Therefore, the prime factors of 12 are 2 and 3. For 15, the prime factors are 3 and 5.

The **greatest common factor (GCF)** is the largest number that is a factor of two or more numbers. For example, the factors of 15 are 1, 3, 5, and 15; the factors of 35 are 1, 5, 7, and 35. Therefore, the greatest common factor of 15 and 35 is 5.

> **Review Video: Factors**
> Visit mometrix.com/academy and enter code: 920086
>
> **Review Video: GCF and LCM**
> Visit mometrix.com/academy and enter code: 838699

MULTIPLES AND LEAST COMMON MULTIPLE

Often listed out in multiplication tables, **multiples** are integer increments of a given factor. In other words, dividing a multiple by the factor number will result in an integer. For example, the multiples of 7 include: $1 \times 7 = 7$, $2 \times 7 = 14$, $3 \times 7 = 21$, $4 \times 7 = 28$, $5 \times 7 = 35$. Dividing 7, 14, 21, 28, or 35 by 7 will result in the integers 1, 2, 3, 4, and 5, respectively.

The least common multiple **(LCM)** is the smallest number that is a multiple of two or more numbers. For example, the multiples of 3 include 3, 6, 9, 12, 15, etc.; the multiples of 5 include 5, 10, 15, 20, etc. Therefore, the least common multiple of 3 and 5 is 15.

> **Review Video: Multiples**
> Visit mometrix.com/academy and enter code: 626738

Rational Numbers

FRACTIONS

A **fraction** is a number that is expressed as one integer written above another integer, with a dividing line between them $\left(\frac{x}{y}\right)$. It represents the **quotient** of the two numbers "x divided by y." It can also be thought of as x out of y equal parts.

The top number of a fraction is called the **numerator**, and it represents the number of parts under consideration. The 1 in $\frac{1}{4}$ means that 1 part out of the whole is being considered in the calculation. The bottom number of a fraction is called the **denominator**, and it represents the total number of equal parts. The 4 in $\frac{1}{4}$ means that the whole consists of 4 equal parts. A fraction cannot have a denominator of zero; this is referred to as "*undefined.*"

Fractions can be manipulated, without changing the value of the fraction, by multiplying or dividing (but not adding or subtracting) both the numerator and denominator by the same number. If you divide both numbers by a common factor, you are **reducing** or simplifying the fraction. Two fractions that have the same value but are expressed differently are known as **equivalent fractions**. For example, $\frac{2}{10}, \frac{3}{15}, \frac{4}{20}$, and $\frac{5}{25}$ are all equivalent fractions. They can also all be reduced or simplified to $\frac{1}{5}$.

When two fractions are manipulated so that they have the same denominator, this is known as finding a **common denominator**. The number chosen to be that common denominator should be the least common multiple of the two original denominators. Example: $\frac{3}{4}$ and $\frac{5}{6}$; the least common multiple of 4 and 6 is 12. Manipulating to achieve the common denominator: $\frac{3}{4} = \frac{9}{12}; \frac{5}{6} = \frac{10}{12}$.

PROPER FRACTIONS AND MIXED NUMBERS

A fraction whose denominator is greater than its numerator is known as a **proper fraction**, while a fraction whose numerator is greater than its denominator is known as an **improper fraction**. Proper fractions have values *less than one* and improper fractions have values *greater than one*.

A **mixed number** is a number that contains both an integer and a fraction. Any improper fraction can be rewritten as a mixed number. Example: $\frac{8}{3} = \frac{6}{3} + \frac{2}{3} = 2 + \frac{2}{3} = 2\frac{2}{3}$. Similarly, any mixed number can be rewritten as an improper fraction. Example: $1\frac{3}{5} = 1 + \frac{3}{5} = \frac{5}{5} + \frac{3}{5} = \frac{8}{5}$.

> **Review Video: Fractions and Mixed Numbers**
> Visit mometrix.com/academy and enter code: 211077
>
> **Review Video: Overview of Fractions**
> Visit mometrix.com/academy and enter code: 262335

ADDING AND SUBTRACTING FRACTIONS

If two fractions have a common denominator, they can be added or subtracted simply by adding or subtracting the two numerators and retaining the same denominator. If the two fractions do not already have the same denominator, one or both of them must be manipulated to achieve a common denominator before they can be added or subtracted. Example: $\frac{1}{2}+\frac{1}{4}=\frac{2}{4}+\frac{1}{4}=\frac{3}{4}$.

> **Review Video: Adding and Subtracting Fractions**
> Visit mometrix.com/academy and enter code: 378080

MULTIPLYING FRACTIONS

Two fractions can be multiplied by multiplying the two numerators to find the new numerator and the two denominators to find the new denominator. Example: $\frac{1}{3}\times\frac{2}{3}=\frac{1\times 2}{3\times 3}=\frac{2}{9}$.

DIVIDING FRACTIONS

Two fractions can be divided by flipping the numerator and denominator of the second fraction and then proceeding as though it were a multiplication. Example: $\frac{2}{3}\div\frac{3}{4}=\frac{2}{3}\times\frac{4}{3}=\frac{8}{9}$.

> **Review Video: Multiplying and Dividing Fractions**
> Visit mometrix.com/academy and enter code: 473632

MULTIPLYING A MIXED NUMBER BY A WHOLE NUMBER OR A DECIMAL

When multiplying a mixed number by something, it is usually best to convert it to an improper fraction first. Additionally, if the multiplicand is a decimal, it is most often simplest to convert it to a fraction. For instance, to multiply $4\frac{3}{8}$ by 3.5, begin by rewriting each quantity as a whole number plus a proper fraction. Remember, a mixed number is a fraction added to a whole number and a decimal is a representation of the sum of fractions, specifically tenths, hundredths, thousandths, and so on:

$$4\frac{3}{8}\times 3.5 = \left(4+\frac{3}{8}\right)\times\left(3+\frac{1}{2}\right)$$

Next, the quantities being added need to be expressed with the same denominator. This is achieved by multiplying and dividing the whole number by the denominator of the fraction. Recall that a whole number is equivalent to that number divided by 1:

$$=\left(\frac{4}{1}\times\frac{8}{8}+\frac{3}{8}\right)\times\left(\frac{3}{1}\times\frac{2}{2}+\frac{1}{2}\right)$$

When multiplying fractions, remember to multiply the numerators and denominators separately:

$$=\left(\frac{4\times 8}{1\times 8}+\frac{3}{8}\right)\times\left(\frac{3\times 2}{1\times 2}+\frac{1}{2}\right)$$
$$=\left(\frac{32}{8}+\frac{3}{8}\right)\times\left(\frac{6}{2}+\frac{1}{2}\right)$$

Now that the fractions have the same denominators, they can be added:

$$=\frac{35}{8}\times\frac{7}{2}$$

Finally, perform the last multiplication and then simplify:

$$= \frac{35 \times 7}{8 \times 2} = \frac{245}{16} = \frac{240}{16} + \frac{5}{16} = 15\frac{5}{16}$$

DECIMALS

Decimals are one way to represent parts of a whole. Using the place value system, each digit to the right of a decimal point denotes the number of units of a corresponding *negative* power of ten. For example, consider the decimal 0.24. We can use a model to represent the decimal. Since a dime is worth one-tenth of a dollar and a penny is worth one-hundredth of a dollar, one possible model to represent this fraction is to have 2 dimes representing the 2 in the tenths place and 4 pennies representing the 4 in the hundredths place:

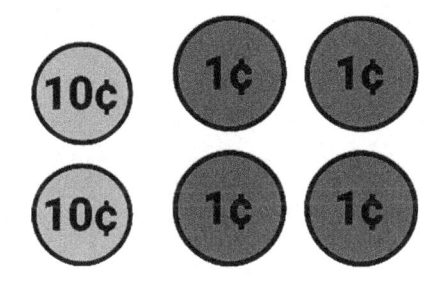

To write the decimal as a fraction, put the decimal in the numerator with 1 in the denominator. Multiply the numerator and denominator by tens until there are no more decimal places. Then simplify the fraction to lowest terms. For example, converting 0.24 to a fraction:

$$0.24 = \frac{0.24}{1} = \frac{0.24 \times 100}{1 \times 100} = \frac{24}{100} = \frac{6}{25}$$

> **Review Video: Decimals**
> Visit mometrix.com/academy and enter code: 837268

OPERATIONS WITH DECIMALS
ADDING AND SUBTRACTING DECIMALS

When adding and subtracting decimals, the decimal points must always be aligned. Adding decimals is just like adding regular whole numbers. Example: $4.5 + 2 = 6.5$.

If the problem-solver does not properly align the decimal points, an incorrect answer of 4.7 may result. An easy way to add decimals is to align all of the decimal points in a vertical column visually. This will allow you to see exactly where the decimal should be placed in the final answer. Begin adding from right to left. Add each column in turn, making sure to carry the number to the left if a column adds up to more than 9. The same rules apply to the subtraction of decimals.

> **Review Video: Adding and Subtracting Decimals**
> Visit mometrix.com/academy and enter code: 381101

MULTIPLYING DECIMALS

A simple multiplication problem has two components: a **multiplicand** and a **multiplier**. When multiplying decimals, work as though the numbers were whole rather than decimals. Once the final product is calculated, count the number of places to the right of the decimal in both the multiplicand and the multiplier. Then, count that number of places from the right of the product and place the decimal in that position.

For example, 12.3 × 2.56 has a total of three places to the right of the respective decimals. Multiply 123 × 256 to get 31488. Now, beginning on the right, count three places to the left and insert the decimal. The final product will be 31.488.

> **Review Video: How to Multiply Decimals**
> Visit mometrix.com/academy and enter code: 731574

DIVIDING DECIMALS

Every division problem has a **divisor** and a **dividend**. The dividend is the number that is being divided. In the problem 14 ÷ 7, 14 is the dividend and 7 is the divisor. In a division problem with decimals, the divisor must be converted into a whole number. Begin by moving the decimal in the divisor to the right until a whole number is created. Next, move the decimal in the dividend the same number of spaces to the right. For example, 4.9 into 24.5 would become 49 into 245. The decimal was moved one space to the right to create a whole number in the divisor, and then the same was done for the dividend. Once the whole numbers are created, the problem is carried out normally: 245 ÷ 49 = 5.

> **Review Video: How to Divide Decimals**
> Visit mometrix.com/academy and enter code: 560690

PERCENTAGES

Percentages can be thought of as fractions that are based on a whole of 100; that is, one whole is equal to 100%. The word **percent** means "per hundred." Percentage problems are often presented in three main ways:

- Find what percentage of some number another number is.
  o Example: What percentage of 40 is 8?
- Find what number is some percentage of a given number.
  o Example: What number is 20% of 40?
- Find what number another number is a given percentage of.
  o Example: What number is 8 20% of?

There are three components in each of these cases: a **whole** (W), a **part** (P), and a **percentage** (%). These are related by the equation: $P = W \times \%$. This can easily be rearranged into other forms that may suit different questions better: $\% = \frac{P}{W}$ and $W = \frac{P}{\%}$. Percentage problems are often also word problems. As such, a large part of solving them is figuring out which quantities are what. For example, consider the following word problem:

In a school cafeteria, 7 students choose pizza, 9 choose hamburgers, and 4 choose tacos. What percentage of student choose tacos?

To find the whole, you must first add all of the parts: $7 + 9 + 4 = 20$. The percentage can then be found by dividing the part by the whole ($\% = \frac{P}{W}$): $\frac{4}{20} = \frac{20}{100} = 20\%$.

CONVERTING BETWEEN PERCENTAGES, FRACTIONS, AND DECIMALS

Converting decimals to percentages and percentages to decimals is as simple as moving the decimal point. To *convert from a decimal to a percentage*, move the decimal point **two places to the right**. To *convert from a percentage to a decimal*, move it **two places to the left**. It may be helpful to remember that the percentage number will always be larger than the equivalent decimal number. For example:

$$0.23 = 23\% \quad 5.34 = 534\% \quad 0.007 = 0.7\%$$
$$700\% = 7.00 \quad 86\% = 0.86 \quad 0.15\% = 0.0015$$

To convert a fraction to a decimal, simply divide the numerator by the denominator in the fraction. To convert a decimal to a fraction, put the decimal in the numerator with 1 in the denominator. Multiply the numerator and denominator by tens until there are no more decimal places. Then simplify the fraction to lowest terms. For example, converting 0.24 to a fraction:

$$0.24 = \frac{0.24}{1} = \frac{0.24 \times 100}{1 \times 100} = \frac{24}{100} = \frac{6}{25}$$

Fractions can be converted to a percentage by finding equivalent fractions with a denominator of 100. Example:

$$\frac{7}{10} = \frac{70}{100} = 70\% \quad \frac{1}{4} = \frac{25}{100} = 25\%$$

To convert a percentage to a fraction, divide the percentage number by 100 and reduce the fraction to its simplest possible terms. Example:

$$60\% = \frac{60}{100} = \frac{3}{5} \quad 96\% = \frac{96}{100} = \frac{24}{25}$$

> **Review Video: Converting Fractions to Percentages and Decimals**
> Visit mometrix.com/academy and enter code: 306233
>
> **Review Video: Converting Percentages to Decimals and Fractions**
> Visit mometrix.com/academy and enter code: 287297
>
> **Review Video: Converting Decimals to Fractions and Percentages**
> Visit mometrix.com/academy and enter code: 986765
>
> **Review Video: Converting Decimals, Improper Fractions, and Mixed Numbers**
> Visit mometrix.com/academy and enter code: 696924

RATIONAL NUMBERS

The term **rational** means that the number can be expressed as a ratio or fraction. That is, a number, r, is rational if and only if it can be represented by a fraction $\frac{a}{b}$ where a and b are integers and b does not equal 0. The set of rational numbers includes integers and decimals. If there is no finite way to represent a value with a fraction of integers, then the number is **irrational**. Common examples of irrational numbers include: $\sqrt{5}, (1 + \sqrt{2})$, and π.

Practice

P1. What is 30% of 120?

P2. What is 150% of 20?

P3. What is 14.5% of 96?

P4. Simplify the following expressions:

(a) $\left(\frac{2}{5}\right)/\left(\frac{4}{7}\right)$
(b) $\frac{7}{8} - \frac{8}{16}$
(c) $\frac{1}{2} + \left(3\left(\frac{3}{4}\right) - 2\right) + 4$
(d) $0.22 + 0.5 - (5.5 + 3.3 \div 3)$
(e) $\frac{3}{2} + (4(0.5) - 0.75) + 2$

P5. Convert the following to a fraction and to a decimal: (a) 15%; (b) 24.36%

P6. Convert the following to a decimal and to a percentage. (a) $\frac{4}{5}$; (b) $3\frac{2}{5}$

P7. A woman's age is thirteen more than half of 60. How old is the woman?

P8. A patient was given pain medicine at a dosage of 0.22 grams. The patient's dosage was then increased to 0.80 grams. By how much was the patient's dosage increased?

P9. At a hotel, $\frac{3}{4}$ of the 100 rooms are occupied today. Yesterday, $\frac{4}{5}$ of the 100 rooms were occupied. On which day were more of the rooms occupied and by how much more?

P10. At a school, 40% of the teachers teach English. If 20 teachers teach English, how many teachers work at the school?

P11. A patient was given blood pressure medicine at a dosage of 2 grams. The patient's dosage was then decreased to 0.45 grams. By how much was the patient's dosage decreased?

P12. Two weeks ago, $\frac{2}{3}$ of the 60 customers at a skate shop were male. Last week, $\frac{3}{6}$ of the 80 customers were male. During which week were there more male customers?

P13. Jane ate lunch at a local restaurant. She ordered a $4.99 appetizer, a $12.50 entrée, and a $1.25 soda. If she wants to tip her server 20%, how much money will she spend in all?

P14. According to a survey, about 82% of engineers were highly satisfied with their job. If 145 engineers were surveyed, how many reported that they were highly satisfied?

P15. A patient was given 40 mg of a certain medicine. Later, the patient's dosage was increased to 45 mg. What was the percent increase in his medication?

P16. Order the following rational numbers from least to greatest: 0.55, 17%, $\sqrt{25}$, $\frac{64}{4}$, $\frac{25}{50}$, 3.

P17. Order the following rational numbers from greatest to least: 0.3, 27%, $\sqrt{100}$, $\frac{72}{9}$, $\frac{1}{9}$, 4.5

P18. Perform the following multiplication. Write each answer as a mixed number.

(a) $\left(1\frac{11}{16}\right) \times 4$

(b) $\left(12\frac{1}{3}\right) \times 1.1$

(c) $3.71 \times \left(6\frac{1}{5}\right)$

P19. Suppose you are making doughnuts and you want to triple the recipe you have. If the following list is the original amounts for the ingredients, what would be the amounts for the tripled recipe?

$1\frac{3}{4}$	cup	Flour
$1\frac{1}{4}$	tsp	Baking powder
$\frac{3}{4}$	tsp	Salt
$\frac{3}{8}$	cup	Sugar
$1\frac{1}{2}$	Tbsp	Butter
2	large	Eggs
$\frac{3}{4}$	tsp	Vanilla extract
$\frac{3}{8}$	cup	Sour cream

PRACTICE SOLUTIONS

P1. The word *of* indicates multiplication, so 30% of 120 is found by multiplying 120 by 30%. Change 30% to a decimal, then multiply: $120 \times 0.3 = 36$

P2. The word *of* indicates multiplication, so 150% of 20 is found by multiplying 20 by 150%. Change 150% to a decimal, then multiply: $20 \times 1.5 = 30$

P3. Change 14.5% to a decimal before multiplying. $0.145 \times 96 = 13.92$.

P4. Follow the order of operations and utilize properties of fractions to solve each:

(a) Rewrite the problem as a multiplication problem: $\frac{2}{5} \times \frac{7}{4} = \frac{2 \times 7}{5 \times 4} = \frac{14}{20}$. Make sure the fraction is reduced to lowest terms. Both 14 and 20 can be divided by 2.

$$\frac{14}{20} = \frac{14 \div 2}{20 \div 2} = \frac{7}{10}$$

(b) The denominators of $\frac{7}{8}$ and $\frac{8}{16}$ are 8 and 16, respectively. The lowest common denominator of 8 and 16 is 16 because 16 is the least common multiple of 8 and 16. Convert the first fraction to its equivalent with the newly found common denominator of 16: $\frac{7 \times 2}{8 \times 2} = \frac{14}{16}$. Now that the fractions have the same denominator, you can subtract them.

$$\frac{14}{16} - \frac{8}{16} = \frac{6}{16} = \frac{3}{8}$$

(c) When simplifying expressions, first perform operations within groups. Within the set of parentheses are multiplication and subtraction operations. Perform the multiplication first to get $\frac{1}{2} + \left(\frac{9}{4} - 2\right) + 4$. Then, subtract two to obtain $\frac{1}{2} + \frac{1}{4} + 4$. Finally, perform addition from left to right:

$$\frac{1}{2} + \frac{1}{4} + 4 = \frac{2}{4} + \frac{1}{4} + \frac{16}{4} = \frac{19}{4} = 4\frac{3}{4}$$

(d) First, evaluate the terms in the parentheses $(5.5 + 3.3 \div 3)$ using order of operations. $3.3 \div 3 = 1.1$, and $5.5 + 1.1 = 6.6$. Next, rewrite the problem: $0.22 + 0.5 - 6.6$. Finally, add and subtract from left to right: $0.22 + 0.5 = 0.72$; $0.72 - 6.6 = -5.88$. The answer is -5.88.

(e) First, simplify within the parentheses, then change the fraction to a decimal and perform addition from left to right:

$$\frac{3}{2} + (2 - 0.75) + 2 =$$
$$\frac{3}{2} + 1.25 + 2 =$$
$$1.5 + 1.25 + 2 = 4.75$$

P5. (a) 15% can be written as $\frac{15}{100}$. Both 15 and 100 can be divided by 5: $\frac{15 \div 5}{100 \div 5} = \frac{3}{20}$

When converting from a percentage to a decimal, drop the percent sign and move the decimal point two places to the left: $15\% = 0.15$

(b) 24.36% written as a fraction is $\frac{24.36}{100}$, or $\frac{2436}{10,000}$, which reduces to $\frac{609}{2500}$. 24.36% written as a decimal is 0.2436. Recall that dividing by 100 moves the decimal two places to the left.

P6. (a) Recall that in the decimal system the first decimal place is one tenth: $\frac{4 \times 2}{5 \times 2} = \frac{8}{10} = 0.8$

Percent means "per hundred." $\frac{4 \times 20}{5 \times 20} = \frac{80}{100} = 80\%$

(b) The mixed number $3\frac{2}{5}$ has a whole number and a fractional part. The fractional part $\frac{2}{5}$ can be written as a decimal by dividing 5 into 2, which gives 0.4. Adding the whole to the part gives 3.4.

To find the equivalent percentage, multiply the decimal by 100. $3.4(100) = 340\%$. Notice that this percentage is greater than 100%. This makes sense because the original mixed number $3\frac{2}{5}$ is greater than 1.

P7. "More than" indicates addition, and "of" indicates multiplication. The expression can be written as $\frac{1}{2}(60) + 13$. So the woman's age is equal to $\frac{1}{2}(60) + 13 = 30 + 13 = 43$. The woman is 43 years old.

P8. The first step is to determine what operation (addition, subtraction, multiplication, or division) the problem requires. Notice the keywords and phrases "by how much" and "increased." "Increased" means that you go from a smaller amount to a larger amount. This change can be found by subtracting the smaller amount from the larger amount: 0.80 grams – 0.22 grams = 0.58 grams.

Remember to line up the decimal when subtracting:

$$\begin{array}{r} 0.80 \\ -0.22 \\ \hline 0.58 \end{array}$$

P9. First, find the number of rooms occupied each day. To do so, multiply the fraction of rooms occupied by the number of rooms available:

$$\text{Number occupied} = \text{Fraction occupied} \times \text{Total number}$$
$$\text{Number of rooms occupied today} = \frac{3}{4} \times 100 = 75$$
$$\text{Number of rooms occupied} = \frac{4}{5} \times 100 = 80$$

The difference in the number of rooms occupied is: $80 - 75 = 5$ rooms

P10. To answer this problem, first think about the number of teachers that work at the school. Will it be more or less than the number of teachers who work in a specific department such as English? More teachers work at the school, so the number you find to answer this question will be greater than 20.

40% of the teachers are English teachers. "Of" indicates multiplication, and words like "is" and "are" indicate equivalence. Translating the problem into a mathematical sentence gives $40\% \times t = 20$, where t represents the total number of teachers. Solving for t gives $t = \frac{20}{40\%} = \frac{20}{0.40} = 50$. Fifty teachers work at the school.

P11. The decrease is represented by the difference between the two amounts:

$$2 \text{ grams} - 0.45 \text{ grams} = 1.55 \text{ grams}.$$

Remember to line up the decimal point before subtracting.

$$\begin{array}{r} 2.00 \\ -0.45 \\ \hline 1.55 \end{array}$$

P12. First, you need to find the number of male customers that were in the skate shop each week. You are given this amount in terms of fractions. To find the actual number of male customers, multiply the fraction of male customers by the number of customers in the store.

$$\text{Actual number of male customers} = \text{fraction of male customers} \times \text{total customers}$$
$$\text{Number of male customers two weeks ago} = \frac{2}{3} \times 60 = \frac{120}{3} = 40$$
$$\text{Number of male customers last week} = \frac{3}{6} \times 80 = \frac{1}{2} \times 80 = \frac{80}{2} = 40$$

The number of male customers was the same both weeks.

P13. To find total amount, first find the sum of the items she ordered from the menu and then add 20% of this sum to the total.

$$\$4.99 + \$12.50 + \$1.25 = \$18.74$$

$$\$18.74 \times 20\% = (0.20)(\$18.74) = \$3.748 \approx \$3.75$$

$$\text{Total} = \$18.74 + \$3.75 = \$22.49$$

P14. 82% of 145 is $0.82 \times 145 = 118.9$. Because you can't have 0.9 of a person, we must round up to say that 119 engineers reported that they were highly satisfied with their jobs.

P15. To find the percent increase, first compare the original and increased amounts. The original amount was 40 mg, and the increased amount is 45 mg, so the dosage of medication was increased by 5 mg ($45 - 40 = 5$). Note, however, that the question asks not by how much the dosage increased but by what percentage it increased.

$$\text{Percent increase} = \frac{\text{new amount} - \text{original amount}}{\text{original amount}} \times 100\%$$
$$= \frac{45 \text{ mg} - 40 \text{ mg}}{40 \text{ mg}} \times 100\% = \frac{5}{40} \times 100\% = 0.125 \times 100\% = 12.5\%$$

P16. Recall that the term rational simply means that the number can be expressed as a ratio or fraction. Notice that each of the numbers in the problem can be written as a decimal or integer:

$$17\% = 0.1717$$
$$\sqrt{25} = 5$$
$$\frac{64}{4} = 16$$
$$\frac{25}{50} = \frac{1}{2} = 0.5$$

So, the answer is $17\%, \frac{25}{50}, 0.55, 3, \sqrt{25}, \frac{64}{4}$.

P17. Converting all the numbers to integers and decimals makes it easier to compare the values:

$$27\% = 0.27$$
$$\sqrt{100} = 10$$
$$\frac{72}{9} = 8$$
$$\frac{1}{9} \approx 0.11$$

So, the answer is $\sqrt{100}, \frac{72}{9}, 4.5, 0.3, 27\%, \frac{1}{9}$.

> **Review Video: Ordering Rational Numbers**
> Visit mometrix.com/academy and enter code: 419578

P18. For each, convert improper fractions, adjust to a common denominator, perform the operations, and then simplify:

(a) Sometimes, you can skip converting the denominator and just distribute the multiplication.

$$\left(1\frac{11}{16}\right) \times 4 = \left(1 + \frac{11}{16}\right) \times 4$$
$$= 1 \times 4 + \frac{11}{16} \times 4$$
$$= 4 + \frac{11}{16} \times \frac{4}{1}$$
$$= 4 + \frac{44}{16} = 4 + \frac{11}{4} = 4 + 2\frac{3}{4} = 6\frac{3}{4}$$

(b)

$$\left(12\frac{1}{3}\right) \times 1.1 = \left(12 + \frac{1}{3}\right) \times \left(1 + \frac{1}{10}\right)$$
$$= \left(\frac{12}{1} \times \frac{3}{3} + \frac{1}{3}\right) \times \left(\frac{10}{10} + \frac{1}{10}\right)$$
$$= \left(\frac{36}{3} + \frac{1}{3}\right) \times \frac{11}{10}$$
$$= \frac{37}{3} \times \frac{11}{10}$$
$$= \frac{407}{30} = \frac{390}{30} + \frac{17}{30} = 13\frac{17}{30}$$

(c)

$$3.71 \times \left(6\frac{1}{5}\right) = \left(3 + \frac{71}{100}\right) \times \left(6 + \frac{1}{5}\right)$$
$$= \left(\frac{300}{100} + \frac{71}{100}\right) \times \left(\frac{6}{1} \times \frac{5}{5} + \frac{1}{5}\right)$$
$$= \frac{371}{100} \times \left(\frac{30}{5} + \frac{1}{5}\right)$$
$$= \frac{371}{100} \times \frac{31}{5}$$
$$= \frac{11501}{500} = \frac{11500}{500} + \frac{1}{500} = 23\frac{1}{500}$$

P19. Fortunately, some of the amounts are duplicated, so we do not need to figure out every amount.

$$1\frac{3}{4} \times 3 = (1 \times 3) + \left(\frac{3}{4} \times 3\right) \qquad 1\frac{1}{4} \times 3 = (1 \times 3) + \left(\frac{1}{4} \times 3\right) \qquad \frac{3}{4} \times 3 = \frac{3}{4} \times 3$$
$$= 3 + \frac{9}{4} \qquad\qquad\qquad = 3 + \frac{3}{4} \qquad\qquad\qquad = \frac{9}{4}$$
$$= 3 + 2\frac{1}{4} \qquad\qquad\qquad = 3\frac{3}{4} \qquad\qquad\qquad = 2\frac{1}{4}$$
$$= 5\frac{1}{4}$$

$$\frac{3}{8} \times 3 = \frac{3}{8} \times 3 \qquad\qquad 1\frac{1}{2} \times 3 = 1 \times 3 + \frac{1}{2} \times 3 \qquad 2 \times 3 = 6$$
$$= \frac{9}{8} \qquad\qquad\qquad\qquad = 3 + \frac{3}{2}$$
$$= 1\frac{1}{8} \qquad\qquad\qquad\qquad = 3 + 1\frac{1}{2}$$
$$\qquad\qquad\qquad\qquad\qquad\quad = 4\frac{1}{2}$$

So, the result for the triple recipe is:

$5\frac{1}{4}$	cup	Flour
$3\frac{3}{4}$	tsp	Baking powder
$2\frac{1}{4}$	tsp	Salt
$1\frac{1}{8}$	cup	Sugar
$4\frac{1}{2}$	Tbsp	Butter
6	large	Eggs
$2\frac{1}{4}$	tsp	Vanilla extract
$1\frac{1}{8}$	cup	Sour cream

Proportions and Ratios

PROPORTIONS

A proportion is a relationship between two quantities that dictates how one changes when the other changes. A **direct proportion** describes a relationship in which a quantity increases by a set amount for every increase in the other quantity, or decreases by that same amount for every decrease in the other quantity. Example: Assuming a constant driving speed, the time required for a car trip increases as the distance of the trip increases. The distance to be traveled and the time required to travel are directly proportional.

An **inverse proportion** is a relationship in which an increase in one quantity is accompanied by a decrease in the other, or vice versa. Example: the time required for a car trip decreases as the speed increases, and increases as the speed decreases, so the time required is inversely proportional to the speed of the car.

> **Review Video: Proportions**
> Visit mometrix.com/academy and enter code: 505355

RATIOS

A **ratio** is a comparison of two quantities in a particular order. Example: If there are 14 computers in a lab, and the class has 20 students, there is a student to computer ratio of 20 to 14, commonly written as 20:14. Ratios are normally reduced to their smallest whole number representation, so 20:14 would be reduced to 10:7 by dividing both sides by 2.

> **Review Video: Ratios**
> Visit mometrix.com/academy and enter code: 996914

CONSTANT OF PROPORTIONALITY

When two quantities have a proportional relationship, there exists a **constant of proportionality** between the quantities. The product of this constant and one of the quantities is equal to the other quantity. For example, if one lemon costs $0.25, two lemons cost $0.50, and three lemons cost $0.75, there is a proportional relationship between the total cost of lemons and the number of lemons purchased. The constant of proportionality is the **unit price**, namely $0.25/lemon. Notice that the total price of lemons, t, can be found by multiplying the unit price of lemons, p, and the number of lemons, n: $t = pn$.

WORK/UNIT RATE

Unit rate expresses a quantity of one thing in terms of one unit of another. For example, if you travel 30 miles every two hours, a unit rate expresses this comparison in terms of one hour: in one hour you travel 15 miles, so your unit rate is 15 miles per hour. Other examples are how much one ounce of food costs (price per ounce) or figuring out how much one egg costs out of the dozen (price per 1 egg, instead of price per 12 eggs). The denominator of a unit rate is always 1. Unit rates are used to compare different situations to solve problems. For example, to make sure you get the best deal when deciding which kind of soda to buy, you can find the unit rate of each. If soda #1 costs $1.50 for a 1-liter bottle, and soda #2 costs $2.75 for a 2-liter bottle, it would be a better deal to buy soda #2, because its unit rate is only $1.375 per 1-liter, which is cheaper than soda #1. Unit rates can also help determine the length of time a given event will take. For example, if you can paint 2 rooms in 4.5 hours, you can determine how long it will take you to paint 5 rooms by solving for the unit rate per room and then multiplying that by 5.

> **Review Video: Rates and Unit Rates**
> Visit mometrix.com/academy and enter code: 185363

SLOPE

On a graph with two points, (x_1, y_1) and (x_2, y_2), the **slope** is found with the formula $m = \frac{y_2 - y_1}{x_2 - x_1}$; where $x_1 \neq x_2$ and m stands for slope. If the value of the slope is **positive**, the line has an *upward direction* from left to right. If the value of the slope is **negative**, the line has a *downward direction* from left to right. Consider the following example:

A new book goes on sale in bookstores and online stores. In the first month, 5,000 copies of the book are sold. Over time, the book continues to grow in popularity. The data for the number of copies sold is in the table below.

# of Months on Sale	1	2	3	4	5
# of Copies Sold (In Thousands)	5	10	15	20	25

So, the number of copies that are sold and the time that the book is on sale is a proportional relationship. In this example, an equation can be used to show the data: $y = 5x$, where x is the number of months that the book is on sale, and y is the number of copies sold. So, the slope of the corresponding line is $\frac{\text{rise}}{\text{run}} = \frac{5}{1} = 5$.

> **Review Video: Finding the Slope of a Line**
> Visit mometrix.com/academy and enter code: 766664

FINDING AN UNKNOWN IN EQUIVALENT EXPRESSIONS

It is often necessary to apply information given about a rate or proportion to a new scenario. For example, if you know that Jedha can run a marathon (26 miles) in 3 hours, how long would it take her to run 10 miles at the same pace? Start by setting up equivalent expressions:

$$\frac{26 \text{ mi}}{3 \text{ hr}} = \frac{10 \text{ mi}}{x \text{ hr}}$$

Now, cross multiply and, solve for x:

$$26x = 30$$
$$x = \frac{30}{26} = \frac{15}{13}$$
$$x \cong 1.15 \text{ hrs } or \text{ 1 hr 9 min}$$

So, at this pace, Jedha could run 10 miles in about 1.15 hours or about 1 hour and 9 minutes.

Practice

P1. Solve the following for x.

(a) $\frac{45}{12} = \frac{15}{x}$

(b) $\frac{0.50}{2} = \frac{1.50}{x}$

(c) $\frac{40}{8} = \frac{x}{24}$

P2. At a school, for every 20 female students there are 15 male students. This same student ratio happens to exist at another school. If there are 100 female students at the second school, how many male students are there?

P3. In a hospital emergency room, there are 4 nurses for every 12 patients. What is the ratio of nurses to patients? If the nurse-to-patient ratio remains constant, how many nurses must be present to care for 24 patients?

P4. In a bank, the banker-to-customer ratio is 1:2. If seven bankers are on duty, how many customers are currently in the bank?

P5. Janice made $40 during the first 5 hours she spent babysitting. She will continue to earn money at this rate until she finishes babysitting in 3 more hours. Find how much money Janice earns per hour and the total she earned babysitting.

P6. The McDonalds are taking a family road trip, driving 300 miles to their cabin. It took them 2 hours to drive the first 120 miles. They will drive at the same speed all the way to their cabin. Find the speed at which the McDonalds are driving and how much longer it will take them to get to their cabin.

P7. It takes Andy 10 minutes to read 6 pages of his book. He has already read 150 pages in his book that is 210 pages long. Find how long it takes Andy to read 1 page and also find how long it will take him to finish his book if he continues to read at the same speed.

PRACTICE SOLUTIONS

P1. First, cross multiply; then, solve for x:

(a) $45x = 12 \times 15$
$45x = 180$
$x = \frac{180}{45} = 4$

(b) $0.5x = 1.5 \times 2$
$0.5x = 3$
$x = \frac{3}{0.5} = 6$

(c) $8x = 40 \times 24$
$8x = 960$
$x = \frac{960}{8} = 120$

P2. One way to find the number of male students is to set up and solve a proportion.

$$\frac{\text{number of female students}}{\text{number of male students}} = \frac{20}{15} = \frac{100}{\text{number of male students}}$$

Represent the unknown number of male students as the variable x: $\frac{20}{15} = \frac{100}{x}$

Cross multiply and then solve for x:

$$20x = 15 \times 100$$
$$x = \frac{1500}{20}$$
$$x = 75$$

P3. The ratio of nurses to patients can be written as 4 to 12, 4:12, or $\frac{4}{12}$. Because four and twelve have a common factor of four, the ratio should be reduced to 1:3, which means that there is one nurse present for every three patients. If this ratio remains constant, there must be eight nurses present to care for 24 patients.

P4. Use proportional reasoning or set up a proportion to solve. Because there are twice as many customers as bankers, there must be fourteen customers when seven bankers are on duty. Setting up and solving a proportion gives the same result:

$$\frac{\text{number of bankers}}{\text{number of customers}} = \frac{1}{2} = \frac{7}{\text{number of customers}}$$

Represent the unknown number of customers as the variable x: $\frac{1}{2} = \frac{7}{x}$.

To solve for x, cross multiply: $1 \times x = 7 \times 2$, so $x = 14$.

P5. Janice earns $8 per hour. This can be found by taking her initial amount earned, $40, and dividing it by the number of hours worked, 5. Since $\frac{40}{5} = 8$, Janice makes $8 in one hour. This can also be found by finding the unit rate, money earned per hour: $\frac{40}{5} = \frac{x}{1}$. Since cross multiplying yields $5x = 40$, and division by 5 shows that $x = 8$, Janice earns $8 per hour.

Janice will earn $64 babysitting in her 8 total hours (adding the first 5 hours to the remaining 3 gives the 8-hour total). Since Janice earns $8 per hour and she worked 8 hours, $\frac{\$8}{hr} \times 8$ hrs = $64. This can also be found by setting up a proportion comparing money earned to babysitting hours. Since she earns $40 for 5 hours and since the rate is constant, she will earn a proportional amount in 8 hours: $\frac{40}{5} = \frac{x}{8}$. Cross multiplying will yield $5x = 320$, and division by 5 shows that $x = 64$.

P6. The McDonalds are driving 60 miles per hour. This can be found by setting up a proportion to find the unit rate, the number of miles they drive per one hour: $\frac{120}{2} = \frac{x}{1}$. Cross multiplying yields $2x = 120$ and division by 2 shows that $x = 60$.

Since the McDonalds will drive this same speed for the remaining miles, it will take them another 3 hours to get to their cabin. This can be found by first finding how many miles the McDonalds have left to drive, which is $300 - 120 = 180$. The McDonalds are driving at 60 miles per hour, so a proportion can be set up to determine how many hours it will take them to drive 180 miles: $\frac{180}{x} = \frac{60}{1}$. Cross multiplying yields $60x = 180$, and division by 60 shows that $x = 3$. This can also be found by using the formula $D = r \times t$ (or distance = rate × time), where $180 = 60 \times t$, and division by 60 shows that $t = 3$.

P7. It takes Andy 10 minutes to read 6 pages, $\frac{10}{6} = 1\frac{2}{3}$ minutes, which is 1 minute and 40 seconds.

Next, determine how many pages Andy has left to read, $210 - 150 = 60$. Since it is now known that it takes him $1\frac{2}{3}$ minutes to read each page, then that rate must be multiplied by however many pages he has left to read (60) to find the time he'll need: $60 \times 1\frac{2}{3} = 100$, so it will take him 100 minutes, or 1 hour and 40 minutes, to read the rest of his book.

Expressions and Equations

TERMS AND COEFFICIENTS

Mathematical expressions consist of a combination of one or more values arranged in terms that are added together. As such, an expression could be just a single number, including zero. A **variable term** is the product of a real number, also called a **coefficient**, and one or more variables, each of which may be raised to an exponent. Expressions may also include numbers without a variable, called **constants** or **constant terms**. The expression $6s^2$, for example, is a single term where the coefficient is the real number 6 and the variable is s^2. Note that if a term is written as simply a variable to some exponent, like t^2, then the coefficient is 1, because $t^2 = 1t^2$.

LINEAR EXPRESSIONS

A **single variable linear expression** is the sum of a single variable term, where the variable has no exponent, and a constant, which may be zero. For instance, the expression $2w + 7$ has $2w$ as the variable term and 7 as the constant term. It is important to realize that terms are separated by addition or subtraction. Since an expression is a sum of terms, expressions such as $5x - 3$ can be written as $5x + (-3)$ to emphasize that the constant term is negative. A real-world example of a single variable linear expression is the perimeter of a square, four times the side length, often expressed: $4s$.

In general, a **linear expression** is the sum of any number of variable terms so long as none of the variables have an exponent. For example, $3m + 8n - \frac{1}{4}p + 5.5q - 1$ is a linear expression, but $3y^3$ is not. In the same way, the expression for the perimeter of a general triangle, the sum of the side lengths $(a + b + c)$ is considered to be linear, but the expression for the area of a square, the side length squared (s^2) is not.

LINEAR EQUATIONS

Equations that can be written as $ax + b = 0$, where $a \neq 0$, are referred to as **one variable linear equations**. A solution to such an equation is called a **root**. In the case where we have the equation $5x + 10 = 0$, if we solve for x we get a solution of $x = -2$. In other words, the root of the equation is -2. This is found by first subtracting 10 from both sides, which gives $5x = -10$. Next, simply divide both sides by the coefficient of the variable, in this case 5, to get $x = -2$. This can be checked by plugging -2 back into the original equation $(5)(-2) + 10 = -10 + 10 = 0$.

The **solution set** is the set of all solutions of an equation. In our example, the solution set would simply be -2. If there were more solutions (there usually are in multivariable equations) then they would also be included in the solution set. When an equation has no true solutions, this is referred to as an **empty set**. Equations with identical solution sets are **equivalent equations**. An **identity** is a term whose value or determinant is equal to 1.

Linear equations can be written many ways. Below is a list of some forms linear equations can take:

- **Standard Form**: $Ax + By = C$; the slope is $\frac{-A}{B}$ and the y-intercept is $\frac{C}{B}$
- **Slope Intercept Form**: $y = mx + b$, where m is the slope and b is the y-intercept
- **Point-Slope Form**: $y - y_1 = m(x - x_1)$, where m is the slope and (x_1, y_1) is a point on the line
- **Two-Point Form**: $\frac{y - y_1}{x - x_1} = \frac{y_2 - y_1}{x_2 - x_1}$, where (x_1, y_1) and (x_2, y_2) are two points on the given line

- **Intercept Form**: $\frac{x}{x_1} + \frac{y}{y_1} = 1$, where $(x_1, 0)$ is the point at which a line intersects the x-axis, and $(0, y_1)$ is the point at which the same line intersects the y-axis

> **Review Video: Slope-Intercept and Point-Slope Forms**
> Visit mometrix.com/academy and enter code: 113216

SOLVING ONE-VARIABLE LINEAR EQUATIONS

Multiply all terms by the lowest common denominator to eliminate any fractions. Look for addition or subtraction to undo so you can isolate the variable on one side of the equal sign. Divide both sides by the coefficient of the variable. When you have a value for the variable, substitute this value into the original equation to make sure you have a true equation. Consider the following example:

Kim's savings are represented by the table below. Represent her savings using an equation.

X (Months)	Y (Total Savings)
2	$1300
5	$2050
9	$3050
11	$3550
16	$4800

The table shows a function with a constant rate of change, or slope, of 250. Given the points on the table, the slopes can be calculated as $(2050 - 1300)/(5 - 2)$, $(3050 - 2050)/(9 - 5)$, $(3550 - 3050)/(11 - 9)$, and $(4800 - 3550)/(16 - 11)$, each of which equals 250. Thus, the table shows a constant rate of change, indicating a linear function. The slope-intercept form of a linear equation is written as $y = mx + b$, where m represents the slope and b represents the y-intercept. Substituting the slope into this form gives $y = 250x + b$. Substituting corresponding x- and y-values from any point into this equation will give the y-intercept, or b. Using the point, (2, 1300), gives $1300 = 250(2) + b$, which simplifies as b = 800. Thus, her savings may be represented by the equation $y = 250x + 800$.

RULES FOR MANIPULATING EQUATIONS
LIKE TERMS

Like terms are terms in an equation that have the same variable, regardless of whether or not they also have the same coefficient. This includes terms that *lack* a variable; all constants (i.e. numbers without variables) are considered like terms. If the equation involves terms with a variable raised to different powers, the like terms are those that have the variable raised to the same power.

For example, consider the equation $x^2 + 3x + 2 = 2x^2 + x - 7 + 2x$. In this equation, 2 and –7 are like terms; they are both constants. $3x$, x, and $2x$ are like terms: they all include the variable x raised to the first power. x^2 and $2x^2$ are like terms; they both include the variable x, raised to the second power. $2x$ and $2x^2$ are not like terms; although they both involve the variable x, the variable is not raised to the same power in both terms. The fact that they have the same coefficient, 2, is not relevant.

CARRYING OUT THE SAME OPERATION ON BOTH SIDES OF AN EQUATION

When solving an equation, the general procedure is to carry out a series of operations on both sides of an equation, choosing operations that will tend to simplify the equation when doing so. The reason why the same operation must be carried out on both sides of the equation is because that leaves the meaning of the equation unchanged, and yields a result that is equivalent to the original equation. This would not be the case if we carried out an operation on one side of an equation and not the other. Consider what an equation means: it is a statement that two values or expressions are equal. If we carry out the same operation on both sides of the equation—add 3 to both sides, for example—then the two sides of the equation are changed in the same way, and so remain equal. If we do that to only one side of the equation—add 3 to one side but not the other—then that wouldn't be true; if we change one side of the equation but not the other then the two sides are no longer equal.

Advantage of Combining Like Terms

Combining like terms refers to adding or subtracting like terms—terms with the same variable—and therefore reducing sets of like terms to a single term. The main advantage of doing this is that it simplifies the equation. Often combining like terms can be done as the first step in solving an equation, though it can also be done later, such as after distributing terms in a product.

For example, consider the equation $2(x + 3) + 3(2 + x + 3) = -4$. The 2 and the 3 in the second set of parentheses are like terms, and we can combine them, yielding $2(x + 3) + 3(x + 5) = -4$. Now we can carry out the multiplications implied by the parentheses, distributing outer 2 and 3 accordingly: $2x + 6 + 3x + 15 = -4$. The $2x$ and the $3x$ are like terms, and we can add them together: $5x + 6 + 15 = -4$. Now, the constants 6, 15, and –4 are also like terms, and we can combine them as well: subtracting 6 and 15 from both sides of the equation, we get $5x = -4 - 6 - 15$, or $5x = -25$, which simplifies further to $x = -5$.

Canceling Terms on Opposite Sides of an Equation

Two terms on opposite sides of an equation can be canceled if and only if they *exactly* match each other. They must have the same variable raised to the same power and the same coefficient. For example, in the equation $3x + 2x^2 + 6 = 2x^2 - 6$, $2x^2$ appears on both sides of the equation, and can be canceled, leaving $3x + 6 = -6$. The 6 on each side of the equation can*not* be canceled, because it is added on one side of the equation and subtracted on the other. While they cannot be canceled, however, the 6 and –6 are like terms and can be combined, yielding $3x = -12$, which simplifies further to $x = -4$.

It's also important to note that the terms to be canceled must be independent terms and cannot be part of a larger term. For example, consider the equation $2(x + 6) = 3(x + 4) + 1$. We cannot cancel the xs, because even though they match each other they are part of the larger terms $2(x + 6)$ and $3(x + 4)$. We must first distribute the 2 and 3, yielding $2x + 12 = 3x + 12 + 1$. Now we see that the terms with the x's do not match, but the 12s do, and can be canceled, leaving $2x = 3x + 1$, which simplifies to $x = -1$.

Process for Manipulating Equations
Isolating Variables

To **isolate a variable** means to manipulate the equation so that the variable appears by itself on one side of the equation, and does not appear at all on the other side. Generally, an equation or inequality is considered to be solved once the variable is isolated and the other side of the equation or inequality is simplified as much as possible. In the case of a two-variable equation or inequality, only one variable needs to be isolated; it will not usually be possible to simultaneously isolate both variables.

For a linear equation—an equation in which the variable only appears raised to the first power—isolating a variable can be done by first moving all the terms with the variable to one side of the equation and all other terms to the other side. (*Moving* a term really means adding the inverse of the term to both sides; when a term is *moved* to the other side of the equation its sign is flipped.) Then combine like terms on each side. Finally, divide both sides by the coefficient of the variable, if applicable. The steps need not necessarily be done in this order, but this order will always work.

EQUATIONS WITH MORE THAN ONE SOLUTION

Some types of non-linear equations, such as equations involving squares of variables, may have more than one solution. For example, the equation $x^2 = 4$ has two solutions: 2 and –2. Equations with absolute values can also have multiple solutions: $|x| = 1$ has the solutions $x = 1$ and $x = -1$.

It is also possible for a linear equation to have more than one solution, but only if the equation is true regardless of the value of the variable. In this case, the equation is considered to have infinitely many solutions, because any possible value of the variable is a solution. We know a linear equation has infinitely many solutions if when we combine like terms the variables cancel, leaving a true statement. For example, consider the equation $2(3x + 5) = x + 5(x + 2)$. Distributing, we get $6x + 10 = x + 5x + 10$; combining like terms gives $6x + 10 = 6x + 10$, and the $6x$ terms cancel to leave $10 = 10$. This is clearly true, so the original equation is true for any value of x. We could also have canceled the 10s leaving $0 = 0$, but again this is clearly true—in general if both sides of the equation match exactly, it has infinitely many solutions.

EQUATIONS WITH NO SOLUTION

Some types of non-linear equations, such as equations involving squares of variables, may have no solution. For example, the equation $x^2 = -2$ has no solutions in the real numbers, because the square of any real number must be positive. Similarly, $|x| = -1$ has no solution, because the absolute value of a number is always positive.

It is also possible for an equation to have no solution even if does not involve any powers greater than one or absolute values or other special functions. For example, the equation $2(x + 3) + x = 3x$ has no solution. We can see that if we try to solve it. First, we distribute, leaving $2x + 6 + x = 3x$. But now if we try to combine all the terms with the variable, we find that they cancel: we have $3x$ on the left and $3x$ on the right, canceling to leave us with $6 = 0$. This is clearly false. In general, whenever the variable terms in an equation cancel leaving different constants on both sides, it means that the equation has no solution. (If we are left with the *same* constant on both sides, the equation has infinitely many solutions instead.)

FEATURES OF EQUATIONS THAT REQUIRE SPECIAL TREATMENT

LINEAR EQUATIONS

A linear equation is an equation in which variables only appear by themselves; they are not multiplied together, not with exponents other than one, and not inside absolute value signs or any other functions. For example, the equation $x + 1 - 3x = 5 - x$ is a linear equation; while x appears multiple times, it never appears with an exponent other than one, or inside any function. The two-variable equation $2x - 3y = 5 + 2x$ is also a linear equation. In contrast, the equation $x^2 - 5 = 3x$ is *not* a linear equation, because it involves the term x^2. $\sqrt{x} = 5$ is not a linear equation, because it involves a square root. $(x - 1)^2 = 4$ is not a linear equation because even though there's no exponent on the x directly, it appears as part of an expression that is squared. The two-variable equation $x + xy - y = 5$ is not a linear equation because it includes the term xy, where two variables are multiplied together.

Linear equations can always be solved (or shown to have no solution) by combining like terms and performing simple operations on both sides of the equation. Some non-linear equations can be solved by similar methods, but others may require more advanced methods of solution, if they can be solved analytically at all.

Solving Equations Involving Roots

In an equation involving roots, the first step is to isolate the term with the root, if possible, and then raise both sides of the equation to the appropriate power to eliminate it. Consider an example equation, $2\sqrt{x+1} - 1 = 3$. In this case, begin by adding 1 to both sides, yielding $2\sqrt{x+1} = 4$, and then dividing both sides by 2, yielding $\sqrt{x+1} = 2$. Now square both sides, yielding $x + 1 = 4$. Finally, subtracting 1 from both sides yields $x = 3$.

Squaring both sides of an equation may, however, yield a spurious solution—a solution to the squared equation that is *not* a solution of the original equation. It's therefore necessary to plug the solution back into the original equation to make sure it works. In this case, it does: $2\sqrt{3+1} - 1 = 2\sqrt{4} - 1 = 2(2) - 1 = 4 - 1 = 3$.

The same procedure applies for other roots as well. For example, given the equation $3 + \sqrt[3]{2x} = 5$, we can first subtract 3 from both sides, yielding $\sqrt[3]{2x} = 2$ and isolating the root. Raising both sides to the third power yields $2x = 2^3$, i.e. $2x = 8$. We can now divide both sides by 2 to get $x = 4$.

Solving Equations with Exponents

To solve an equation involving an exponent, the first step is to isolate the variable with the exponent. We can then take the appropriate root of both sides to eliminate the exponent. For instance, for the equation $2x^3 + 17 = 5x^3 - 7$, we can subtract $5x^3$ from both sides to get $-3x^3 + 17 = -7$, and then subtract 17 from both sides to get $-3x^3 = -24$. Finally, we can divide both sides by -3 to get $x^3 = 8$. Finally, we can take the cube root of both sides to get $x = \sqrt[3]{8} = 2$.

One important but often overlooked point is that equations with an exponent greater than 1 may have more than one answer. The solution to $x^2 = 9$ isn't simply $x = 3$; it's $x = \pm 3$: that is, $x = 3$ or $x = -3$. For a slightly more complicated example, consider the equation $(x - 1)^2 - 1 = 3$. Adding one to both sides yields $(x - 1)^2 = 4$; taking the square root of both sides yields $x - 1 = 2$. We can then add 1 to both sides to get $x = 3$. However, there's a second solution: we also have the possibility that $x - 1 = -2$, in which case $x = -1$. Both $x = 3$ and $x = -1$ are valid solutions, as can be verified by substituting them both into the original equation.

Solving Equations with Absolute Values

When solving an equation with an absolute value, the first step is to isolate the absolute value term. We then consider two possibilities: when the expression inside the absolute value is positive or when it is negative. In the former case, the expression in the absolute value equals the expression on the other side of the equation; in the latter, it equals the additive inverse of that expression—the expression times negative one. We consider each case separately and finally check for spurious solutions.

For instance, consider solving $|2x - 1| + x = 5$ for x. We can first isolate the absolute value by moving the x to the other side: $|2x - 1| = -x + 5$. Now, we have two possibilities. First, that $2x - 1$ is positive, and hence $2x - 1 = -x + 5$. Rearranging and combining like terms yields $3x = 6$, and hence $x = 2$. The other possibility is that $2x - 1$ is negative, and hence $2x - 1 = -(-x + 5) = x - 5$. In this case, rearranging and combining like terms yields $x = -4$. Substituting $x = 2$ and $x = -4$ back into the original equation, we see that they are both valid solutions.

Note that the absolute value of a sum or difference applies to the sum or difference as a whole, not to the individual terms; in general, $|2x - 1|$ is not equal to $|2x + 1|$ or to $|2x| - 1$.

SPURIOUS SOLUTIONS

A **spurious solution** may arise when we square both sides of an equation as a step in solving it, or under certain other operations on the equation. It is a solution to the squared or otherwise modified equation that is *not* a solution of the original equation. To identify a spurious solution, it's useful when you solve an equation involving roots or absolute values to plug the solution back into the original equation to make sure it's valid.

CHOOSING WHICH VARIABLE TO ISOLATE IN TWO-VARIABLE EQUATIONS

Similar to methods for a one-variable equation, solving a two-variable equation involves isolating a variable: manipulating the equation so that a variable appears by itself on one side of the equation, and not at all on the other side. However, in a two-variable equation, you will usually only be able to isolate one of the variables; the other variable may appear on the other side along with constant terms, or with exponents or other functions.

Often one variable will be much more easily isolated than the other, and therefore that's the variable you should choose. If one variable appears with various exponents, and the other only raised it to the first power, the latter variable is the one to isolate. Given the equation $a^2 + 2b = a^3 + b + 3$, the b only appears to the first power, whereas a appears squared and cubed, so b is the variable that can be solved for: combining like terms and isolating the b on the left side of the equation, we get $b = a^3 - a^2 + 3$. If both variables are equally easy to isolate, then it's best to isolate the independent variable, if one is defined. If the two variables are x and y, the convention is that y is the independent variable.

PRACTICE

P1. Seeing the equation $2x + 4 = 4x + 7$, a student divides the first terms on each side by 2, yielding $x + 4 = 2x + 7$, and then combines like terms to get $x = -3$. However, this is incorrect, as can be seen by substituting –3 into the original equation. Explain what is wrong with the student's reasoning.

P2. Describe the steps necessary to solve the equation $2x + 1 - x = 4 + 3x + 7$.

P3. Describe the steps necessary to solve the equation $2(x + 5) = 7(4 - x)$.

P4. Find all real solutions to the equation $1 - \sqrt{x} = 2$.

P5. Find all real solutions to the equation $|x + 1| = 2x + 5$.

P6. Solve for x: $-x + 2\sqrt{x + 5} + 1 = 3$.

P7. Ray earns $10 an hour at his job. Write an equation for his earnings as a function of time spent working. Determine how long Ray has to work in order to earn $360.

P8. Simplify the following: $3x + 2 + 2y = 5y - 7 + |2x - 1|$

PRACTICE SOLUTIONS

P1. As stated, it's easy to verify that the student's solution is incorrect: $2(-3) + 4 = -2$ and $4(-3) + 7 = -5$; clearly $-2 \neq -5$. The mistake was in the first step, which illustrates a common type of error in solving equations. The student tried to simplify the two variable terms by dividing them by 2. However, it's not valid to multiply or divide only one term on each side of an equation by a number; when multiplying or dividing, the operation must be applied to *every* term in the equation. So, dividing by 2 would yield not $x + 4 = 2x + 7$, but $x + 2 = 2x + \frac{7}{2}$. While this is now valid, that fraction is inconvenient to work with, so this may not be the best first step in solving the equation. Rather, it may have been better to first combine like terms: subtracting $4x$ from both sides yields $-2x + 4 = 7$; subtracting 4 from both sides yields $-2x = 3$; and *now* we can divide both sides by -2 to get $x = -\frac{3}{2}$.

P2. Our ultimate goal is to isolate the variable, x. To that end we first move all the terms containing x to the left side of the equation, and all the constant terms to the right side. Note that when we move a term to the other side of the equation its sign changes. We are therefore now left with $2x - x - 3x = 4 + 7 - 1$.

Next, we combine the like terms on each side of the equation, adding and subtracting the terms as appropriate. This leaves us with $-2x = 10$.

At this point, we're almost done; all that remains is to divide both sides by -2 to leave the x by itself. We now have our solution, $x = -5$. We can verify that this is a correct solution by substituting it back into the original equation.

P3. Generally, in equations that have a sum or difference of terms multiplied by another value or expression, the first step is to multiply those terms, distributing as necessary: $2(x + 5) = 2(x) + 2(5) = 2x + 10$, and $7(4 - x) = 7(4) - 7(x) = 28 - 7x$. So, the equation becomes $2x + 10 = 28 - 7x$. We can now add $7x$ to both sides to eliminate the variable from the right-hand side: $9x + 10 = 28$. Similarly, we can subtract 10 from both sides to move all the constants to the right: $9x = 18$. Finally, we can divide both sides by 9, yielding the final answer, $x = 2$.

P4. It's not hard to isolate the root: subtract one from both sides, yielding $-\sqrt{x} = 1$. Finally, multiply both sides by -1, yielding $\sqrt{x} = -1$. Squaring both sides of the equation yields $x = 1$. However, if we plug this back into the original equation, we get $1 - \sqrt{1} = 2$, which is false. Therefore $x = 1$ is a spurious solution, and the equation has no real solutions.

P5. This equation has two possibilities: $x + 1 = 2x + 5$, which simplifies to $x = -4$; or $x + 1 = -(2x + 5) = -2x - 5$, which simplifies to $x = -2$. However, if we try substituting both values back into the original equation, we see that only $x = -2$ yields a true statement. $x = -4$ is a spurious solution; $x = -2$ is the only valid solution to the equation.

P6. Start by isolating the term with the root. We can do that by moving the $-x$ and the 1 to the other side, yielding $2\sqrt{x + 5} = 3 + x - 1$, or $2\sqrt{x + 5} = x + 2$. Dividing both sides of the equation by 2 would give us a fractional term that could be messy to deal with, so we won't do that for now. Instead, we square both sides of the equation; note that on the left-hand side the 2 is outside the square root sign, so we have to square it. As a result, we get $4(x + 5) = (x + 2)^2$. Expanding both sides gives us $4x + 20 = x^2 + 4x + 4$. In this case, we see that we have $4x$ on both sides, so we can cancel the $4x$ (which is what allows us to solve this equation despite the different powers of x). We now have $20 = x^2 + 4$, or $x^2 = 16$. Since the variable is raised to an even power, we need to take the positive and negative roots, so $x = \pm 4$: that is, $x = 4$ or $x = -4$. Substituting both values into the original equation, we see that $x = 4$ satisfies the equation but $x = -4$ does not; hence $x = -4$ is a spurious solution, and the only solution to the equation is $x = 4$.

P7. The number of dollars that Ray earns is dependent on the number of hours he works, so earnings will be represented by the dependent variable y and hours worked will be represented by the independent variable x. He earns 10 dollars per hour worked, so his earnings can be calculated as $y = 10x$. To calculate the number of hours Ray must work in order to earn $360, plug in 360 for y and solve for x:

$$360 = 10x$$
$$x = \frac{360}{10} = 36$$

P8. To simplify this equation, we must isolate one of its variables on one side of the equation. In this case, the x appears under an absolute value sign, which makes it difficult to isolate. The y, on the other hand, only appears without an exponent—the equation is linear in y. We will therefore choose to isolate the y. The first step, then, is to move all the terms with y to the left side of the equation, which we can do by subtracting $5y$ from both sides:

$$3x + 2 - 3y = -7 + |2x - 1|$$

We can then move all the terms that do *not* include y to the right side of the equation, by subtracting $3x$ and 2 from both sides of the equation:

$$-3y = -3x - 9 + |2x - 1|$$

Finally, we can isolate the y by dividing both sides by -3.

$$y = x + 3 - \frac{1}{3}|2x - 1|$$

This is as far as we can simplify the equation; we cannot combine the terms inside and outside the absolute value sign. We can therefore consider the equation to be solved.

Units of Measurement

METRIC MEASUREMENT PREFIXES

Giga-: one billion (1 *giga*watt is one billion watts)
Mega-: one million (1 *mega*hertz is one million hertz)
Kilo-: one thousand (1 *kilo*gram is one thousand grams)
Deci-: one tenth (1 *deci*meter is one tenth of a meter)
Centi-: one hundredth (1 *centi*meter is one hundredth of a meter)
Milli-: one thousandth (1 *milli*liter is one thousandth of a liter)
Micro-: one millionth (1 *micro*gram is one millionth of a gram)

MEASUREMENT CONVERSION

When converting between units, the goal is to maintain the same meaning but change the way it is displayed. In order to go from a larger unit to a smaller unit, multiply the number of the known amount by the equivalent amount. When going from a smaller unit to a larger unit, divide the number of the known amount by the equivalent amount.

For complicated conversions, it may be helpful to set up conversion fractions. In these fractions, one fraction is the **conversion factor**. The other fraction has the unknown amount in the numerator. So, the known value is placed in the denominator. Sometimes the second fraction has the known value from the problem in the numerator, and the unknown in the denominator. Multiply the two fractions to get the converted measurement. Note that since the numerator and the denominator of the factor are equivalent, the value of the fraction is 1. That is why we can say that the result in the new units is equal to the result in the old units even though they have different numbers.

It can often be necessary to chain known conversion factors together. As an example, consider converting 512 square inches to square meters. We know that there are 2.54 centimeters in an inch and 100 centimeters in a meter, and that we will need to square each of these factors to achieve the conversion we are looking for.

$$\frac{512 \text{ in}^2}{1} \times \left(\frac{2.54 \text{ cm}}{1 \text{ in}}\right)^2 \times \left(\frac{1 \text{ m}}{100 \text{ cm}}\right)^2 = \frac{512 \text{ in}^2}{1} \times \left(\frac{6.4516 \text{ cm}^2}{1 \text{ in}^2}\right) \times \left(\frac{1 \text{ m}^2}{10000 \text{ cm}^2}\right) = 0.330 \text{ m}^2$$

COMMON UNITS AND EQUIVALENTS

METRIC EQUIVALENTS

1000 µg (microgram)	1 mg
1000 mg (milligram)	1 g
1000 g (gram)	1 kg
1000 kg (kilogram)	1 metric ton
1000 mL (milliliter)	1 L
1000 µm (micrometer)	1 mm
1000 mm (millimeter)	1 m
100 cm (centimeter)	1 m
1000 m (meter)	1 km

Distance and Area Measurement

Unit	Abbreviation	U.S. equivalent	Metric equivalent
Inch	in	1 inch	2.54 centimeters
Foot	ft	12 inches	0.305 meters
Yard	yd	3 feet	0.914 meters
Mile	mi	5280 feet	1.609 kilometers
Acre	ac	4840 square yards	0.405 hectares
Square Mile	mi^2	640 acres	2.590 square kilometers

Capacity Measurements

Unit	Abbreviation	U.S. equivalent	Metric equivalent
Fluid Ounce	fl oz	8 fluid drams	29.573 milliliters
Cup	cp	8 fluid ounces	0.237 liter
Pint	pt	16 fluid ounces	0.473 liter
Quart	qt	2 pints	0.946 liter
Gallon	gal	4 quarts	3.785 liters
Teaspoon	t or tsp	1 fluid dram	5 milliliters
Tablespoon	T or tbsp	4 fluid drams	15 or 16 milliliters
Cubic Centimeter	cc or cm^3	0.271 drams	1 milliliter

Weight Measurements

Unit	Abbreviation	U.S. equivalent	Metric equivalent
Ounce	oz	16 drams	28.35 grams
Pound	lb	16 ounces	453.6 grams
Ton	t	2,000 pounds	907.2 kilograms

Volume and Weight Measurement Clarifications

Always be careful when using ounces and fluid ounces. They are not equivalent.

1 pint = 16 fluid ounces	1 fluid ounce ≠ 1 ounce
1 pound = 16 ounces	1 pint ≠ 1 pound

Having one pint of something does not mean you have one pound of it. In the same way, just because something weighs one pound does not mean that its volume is one pint.

In the United States, the word "ton" by itself refers to a short ton or a net ton. Do not confuse this with a long ton (also called a gross ton) or a metric ton (also spelled *tonne*), which have different measurement equivalents.

$$1 \text{ U.S. ton} = 2000 \text{ pounds} \quad \neq \quad 1 \text{ metric ton} = 1000 \text{ kilograms}$$

Military Time

The **24-hour clock** is a time system used by the military and on some digital clocks. On the 24-hour clock, minutes and seconds are the same as the standard 12-hour clock. However, time is expressed in 4 figures, and the hours run from 0000 hour (12 a.m.) to 2359 hours (11:59 p.m.).

To convert from 12-hour to 24-hour time, remove the colon and:

- for a.m. times, if the time has 3 digits, add a 0 to the beginning (e.g., 8:12 a.m. becomes 0812 hours). For times between 12 a.m. and 1 a. m., replace the 12 with a pair of zeros (e.g., 12:41 a.m. becomes 0041 hours).
- for p.m. times, add 12 to the hour number (e.g., 3:40 p.m. = 1540 hours), except for times between 12 p.m. and 1 p.m., which do not require any further change.

To convert from 24-hour to 12-hour time, add a colon between the second and third digits. If the first two digits are less than 12, the time is a.m.; otherwise it is p.m. If the first two digits are zeros, the hour becomes 12 a.m. (e.g., 0020 becomes 12:20 a.m.) If only the first digit is zero, remove it (e.g., 0730 becomes 7:30 a.m.). If the first two digits are greater than 12, subtract 12 (e.g., 2325 becomes 11:25 p.m.).

ROMAN NUMERALS

Roman numerals are used today only in limited circumstances, but for the test you will still need to know what numbers they represent. Each numeral has a specific value:

Roman Numeral	Value
I	1
V	5
X	10
L	50
C	100
D	500
M	1000

When multiple numerals are placed together, their values are generally added:

$$XVI = 10 + 5 + 1 = 16$$

The exception to this rule is when a smaller number is placed in front of a larger number. In those cases, the smaller number must be subtracted from the larger number that immediately follows it:

$$IX = 10 - 1 = 9$$

$$XL = 50 - 10 = 40$$

Further complicating things, these combinations can be used as part of a larger number as well:

$$MCMXCIX = 1000 + (1000 - 100) + (100 - 10) + (10 - 1)$$

$$MCMXCIX = 1000 + 900 + 90 + 9 = 1999$$

Though it's not likely to show up on your test, a line over a Roman numeral means that its value is 1000 times its normal value:

$$\overline{V} = 5{,}000; \ \overline{X} = 10{,}000; \ \overline{C} = 100{,}000$$

PRACTICE

P1. Perform the following conversions:

(a) 1.4 meters to centimeters

(b) 218 centimeters to meters

(c) 42 inches to feet

(d) 15 kilograms to pounds

(e) 80 ounces to pounds

(f) 2 miles to kilometers

(g) 5 feet to centimeters

(h) 15.14 liters to gallons

(i) 8 quarts to liters

(j) 13.2 pounds to grams

PRACTICE SOLUTIONS

P1. (a) $\frac{100 \text{ cm}}{1 \text{ m}} = \frac{x \text{ cm}}{1.4 \text{ m}}$ Cross multiply to get $x = 140$

(b) $\frac{100 \text{ cm}}{1 \text{ m}} = \frac{218 \text{ cm}}{x \text{ m}}$ Cross multiply to get $100x = 218$, or $x = 2.18$

(c) $\frac{12 \text{ in}}{1 \text{ ft}} = \frac{42 \text{ in}}{x \text{ ft}}$ Cross multiply to get $12x = 42$, or $x = 3.5$

(d) 15 kilograms $\times \frac{2.2 \text{ pounds}}{1 \text{ kilogram}} = 33$ pounds

(e) 80 ounces $\times \frac{1 \text{ pound}}{16 \text{ ounces}} = 5$ pounds

(f) 2 miles $\times \frac{1.609 \text{ kilometers}}{1 \text{ mile}} = 3.218$ kilometers

(g) 5 feet $\times \frac{12 \text{ inches}}{1 \text{ foot}} \times \frac{2.54 \text{ centimeters}}{1 \text{ inch}} = 152.4$ centimeters

(h) 15.14 liters $\times \frac{1 \text{ gallon}}{3.785 \text{ liters}} = 4$ gallons

(i) 8 quarts $\times \frac{1 \text{ gallon}}{4 \text{ quarts}} \times \frac{3.785 \text{ liters}}{1 \text{ gallon}} = 7.57$ liters

(j) 13.2 pounds $\times \frac{1 \text{ kilogram}}{2.2 \text{ pounds}} \times \frac{1000 \text{ grams}}{1 \text{ kilogram}} = 6000$ grams

Science

Macromolecules

Macromolecules are large and complex, and play an important role in cell structure and function. The four basic organic macromolecules produced by anabolic reactions are **carbohydrates** (polysaccharides), **nucleic acids**, **proteins**, and **lipids**. The four basic building blocks involved in catabolic reactions are **monosaccharides** (glucose), **amino acids**, **fatty acids** (glycerol), and **nucleotides**.

An **anabolic reaction** is one that builds larger and more complex molecules (macromolecules) from smaller ones. **Catabolic reactions** are the opposite. Larger molecules are broken down into smaller, simpler molecules. Catabolic reactions *release energy*, while anabolic ones *require energy*.

Endothermic reactions are chemical reactions that *absorb* heat and **exothermic reactions** are chemical reactions that *release* heat.

> **Review Video: Macromolecules**
> Visit mometrix.com/academy and enter code: 220156

CARBOHYDRATE

Carbohydrates are the primary source of energy and are responsible for providing energy as they can be easily converted to **glucose**. It is the oxidation of carbohydrates that provides the cells with most of their energy. Glucose can be further broken down by respiration or fermentation by **glycolysis**. They are involved in the metabolic energy cycles of photosynthesis and respiration.

Structurally, carbohydrates usually take the form of some variation of CH_2O as they are made of carbon, hydrogen, and oxygen. Carbohydrates (**polysaccharides**) are broken down into sugars or glucose.

The simple sugars can be grouped into monosaccharides (glucose, fructose, and galactose) and disaccharides. These are both types of carbohydrates. Monosaccharides have one monomer of sugar and disaccharides have two. Monosaccharides (CH_2O) have one carbon for every water molecule.

A **monomer** is a small molecule. It is a single compound that forms chemical bonds with other monomers to make a polymer. A **polymer** is a compound of large molecules formed by repeating monomers. Carbohydrates, proteins, and nucleic acids are groups of macromolecules that are polymers.

> **Review Video: What are Carbohydrates?**
> Visit mometrix.com/academy and enter code: 601714

LIPIDS

Lipids are molecules that are soluble in nonpolar solvents, but are hydrophobic, meaning they do not bond well with water or mix well with water solutions. Lipids have numerous **C–H bonds**. In this way, they are similar to **hydrocarbons** (substances consisting only of carbon and hydrogen). The major roles of lipids include *energy storage and structural functions*. Examples of lipids include fats, phospholipids, steroids, and waxes. **Fats** (which are triglycerides) are made of long chains of fatty acids (three fatty acids bound to a glycerol). **Fatty acids** are chains with reduced carbon at one end and a carboxylic acid group at the other. An example is soap, which contains the sodium salts of free fatty acids. **Phospholipids** are lipids that have a phosphate group rather than a fatty acid. **Glycerides** are another type of lipid. Examples of glycerides are fat and oil. Glycerides are formed from fatty acids and glycerol (a type of alcohol).

> **Review Video: Lipids**
> Visit mometrix.com/academy and enter code: 269746

PROTEINS

Proteins are macromolecules formed from amino acids. They are **polypeptides**, which consist of many (10 to 100) peptides linked together. The peptide connections are the result of condensation reactions. A **condensation reaction** results in a loss of water when two molecules are joined together. A **hydrolysis reaction** is the opposite of a condensation reaction. During hydrolysis, water is added. –H is added to one of the smaller molecules and OH is added to another molecule being formed. A **peptide** is a compound of two or more amino acids. **Amino acids** are formed by the partial hydrolysis of protein, which forms an **amide bond**. This partial hydrolysis involves an amine group and a carboxylic acid. In the carbon chain of amino acids, there is a **carboxylic acid group** (–COOH), an **amine group** (–NH$_2$), a **central carbon atom** between them with an attached hydrogen, and an attached **"R" group** (side chain), which is different for different amino acids. It is the "R" group that determines the properties of the protein.

> **Review Video: Proteins**
> Visit mometrix.com/academy and enter code: 903713

ENZYMES

Enzymes are proteins with strong **catalytic** power. They greatly accelerate the speed at which specific reactions approach equilibrium. Although enzymes do not start chemical reactions that would not eventually occur by themselves, they do make these reactions happen *faster and more often*. This acceleration can be substantial, sometimes making reactions happen a million times faster. Each type of enzyme deals with **reactants**, also called **substrates**. Each enzyme is highly selective, only interacting with substrates that are a match for it at an active site on the enzyme. This is the "key in the lock" analogy: a certain enzyme only fits with certain substrates. Even with a matching substrate, sometimes an enzyme must reshape itself to fit well with the substrate, forming a strong bond that aids in catalyzing a reaction before it returns to its original shape. An unusual quality of enzymes is that they are not permanently consumed in the reactions they speed up. They can be used again and again, providing a constant source of energy accelerants for cells. This allows for a tremendous increase in the number and rate of reactions in cells.

NUCLEIC ACIDS

Nucleic acids are macromolecules that are composed of **nucleotides**. **Hydrolysis** is a reaction in which water is broken down into **hydrogen cations** (H or H$^+$) and **hydroxide anions** (OH or OH-). This is part of the process by which nucleic acids are broken down by enzymes to produce shorter strings of RNA and DNA (oligonucleotides). **Oligonucleotides** are broken down into smaller sugar nitrogenous units called **nucleosides**. These can be digested by cells since the sugar is divided from the nitrogenous base. This, in turn, leads to the formation of the five types of nitrogenous bases, sugars, and the preliminary substances involved in the synthesis of new RNA and DNA. DNA and RNA have a double helix shape.

Macromolecular nucleic acid polymers, such as RNA and DNA, are formed from nucleotides, which are monomeric units joined by **phosphodiester bonds**. Cells require energy in the form of ATP to synthesize proteins from amino acids and replicate DNA. **Nitrogen fixation** is used to synthesize nucleotides for DNA and amino acids for proteins. Nitrogen fixation uses the enzyme nitrogenase in the reduction of dinitrogen gas (N_2) to ammonia (NH_3).

Nucleic acids store information and energy and are also important catalysts. It is the **RNA** that catalyzes the transfer of **DNA genetic information** into protein coded information. ATP is an RNA nucleotide. **Nucleotides** are used to form the nucleic acids. Nucleotides are made of a five-carbon sugar, such as ribose or deoxyribose, a nitrogenous base, and one or more phosphates. Nucleotides consisting of more than one phosphate can also store energy in their bonds.

> **Review Video: Nucleic Acids**
> Visit mometrix.com/academy and enter code: 503931

DNA

Chromosomes consist of **genes**, which are single units of genetic information. Genes are made up of deoxyribonucleic acid (DNA). DNA is a nucleic acid located in the cell nucleus. There is also DNA in the **mitochondria**. DNA replicates to pass on genetic information. The DNA in almost all cells is the same. It is also involved in the biosynthesis of proteins.

> **Review Video: Chromosomes**
> Visit mometrix.com/academy and enter code: 132083

The model or structure of DNA is described as a **double helix**. A helix is a curve, and a double helix is two congruent curves connected by horizontal members. The model can be likened to a spiral staircase. It is right-handed. The British scientist Rosalind Elsie Franklin is credited with taking the x-ray diffraction image in 1952 that was used by Francis Crick and James Watson to formulate the double-helix model of DNA and speculate about its important role in carrying and transferring genetic information.

> **Review Video: DNA**
> Visit mometrix.com/academy and enter code: 639552

DNA STRUCTURE

DNA has a double helix shape, resembles a twisted ladder, and is compact. It consists of **nucleotides**. Nucleotides consist of a **five-carbon sugar** (pentose), a **phosphate group**, and a **nitrogenous base**. Two bases pair up to form the rungs of the ladder. The "side rails" or backbone consists of the covalently bonded sugar and phosphate. The bases are attached to each other with hydrogen bonds, which are easily dismantled so replication can occur. Each base is attached to a phosphate and to a sugar. There are four types of nitrogenous bases: **adenine** (A), **guanine** (G), **cytosine** (C), and **thymine** (T). There are about 3 billion bases in human DNA. The bases are mostly the same in everybody, but their order is different. It is the order of these bases that creates diversity in people. *Adenine (A) pairs with thymine (T)*, and *cytosine (C) pairs with guanine (G)*.

PURINES AND PYRIMIDINES

The five bases in DNA and RNA can be categorized as either pyrimidine or purine according to their structure. The **pyrimidine bases** include *cytosine, thymine, and uracil*. They are six-sided and have a single ring shape. The **purine bases** are *adenine and guanine*, which consist of two attached rings.

One ring has five sides and the other has six. When combined with a sugar, any of the five bases become **nucleosides**. Nucleosides formed from purine bases end in "osine" and those formed from pyrimidine bases end in "idine." **Adenosine** and **thymidine** are examples of nucleosides. Bases are the most basic components, followed by nucleosides, nucleotides, and then DNA or RNA.

CODONS

Codons are groups of three nucleotides on the messenger RNA, and can be visualized as three rungs of a ladder. A **codon** has the code for a single amino acid. There are 64 codons but 20 amino acids. More than one combination, or triplet, can be used to synthesize the necessary amino acids. For example, AAA (adenine-adenine-adenine) or AAG (adenine-adenine-guanine) can serve as codons for lysine. These groups of three occur in strings, and might be thought of as frames. For example, AAAUCUUCGU, if read in groups of three from the beginning, would be AAA, UCU, UCG, which are codons for lysine, serine, and serine, respectively. If the same sequence was read in groups of three starting from the second position, the groups would be AAU (asparagine), CUU (proline), and so on. The resulting amino acids would be completely different. For this reason, there are **start and stop codons** that indicate the beginning and ending of a sequence (or frame). **AUG** (methionine) is the start codon. **UAA**, **UGA**, and **UAG**, also known as ocher, opal, and amber, respectively, are stop codons.

> **Review Video: Codons**
> Visit mometrix.com/academy and enter code: 978172

DNA REPLICATION

Pairs of chromosomes are composed of DNA, which is tightly wound to conserve space. When replication starts, it unwinds. The steps in **DNA replication** are controlled by enzymes. The enzyme **helicase** instigates the deforming of hydrogen bonds between the bases to split the two strands. The splitting starts at the A-T bases (adenine and thymine) as there are only two hydrogen bonds. The cytosine-guanine base pair has three bonds. The term "**origin of replication**" is used to refer to where the splitting starts. The portion of the DNA that is unwound to be replicated is called the **replication fork**. Each strand of DNA is transcribed by an mRNA. It copies the DNA onto itself, base by base, in a complementary manner. The exception is that uracil replaces thymine.

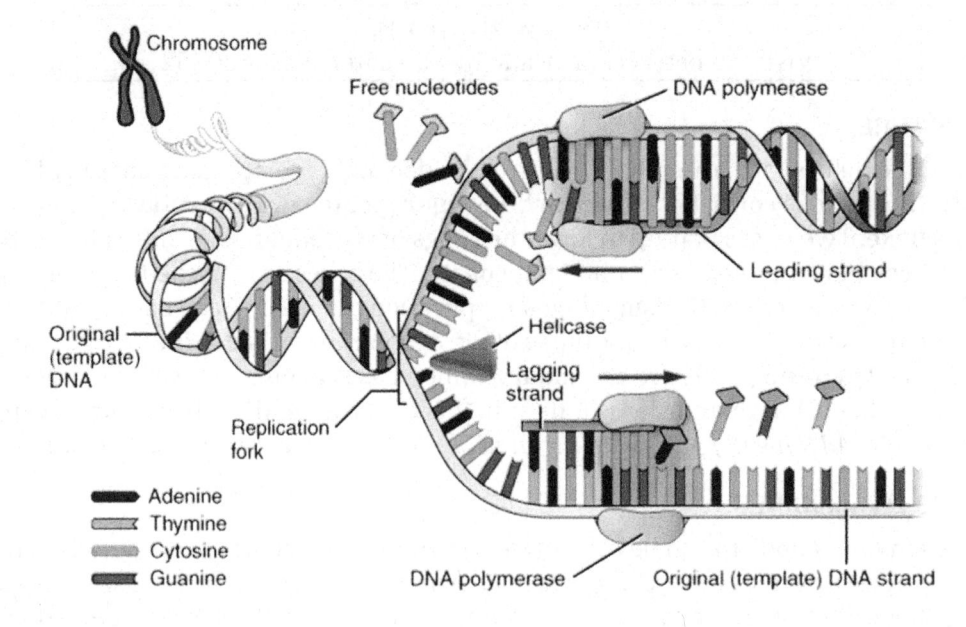

RNA

TYPES OF RNA

RNA acts as a *helper* to DNA and carries out a number of other functions. Types of RNA include ribosomal RNA (rRNA), transfer RNA (tRNA), and messenger RNA (mRNA). Viruses can use RNA to carry their genetic material to DNA. **Ribosomal RNA** is not believed to have changed much over time. For this reason, it can be used to study relationships in organisms. **Messenger RNA** carries a copy of a strand of DNA and transports it from the nucleus to the cytoplasm. **Transcription** is the process in which RNA polymerase copies DNA into RNA. DNA unwinds itself and serves as a template while RNA is being assembled. The DNA molecules are copied to RNA. **Translation** is the process whereby ribosomes use transcribed RNA to put together the needed protein. **Transfer RNA** is a molecule that helps in the translation process, and is found in the cytoplasm.

DIFFERENCES BETWEEN RNA AND DNA

RNA and DNA differ in terms of structure and function. RNA has a different sugar than DNA. It has **ribose** rather than **deoxyribose** sugar. The RNA nitrogenous bases are adenine (A), guanine (G), cytosine (C), and uracil (U). **Uracil** is found only in RNA and **thymine** in found only in DNA. RNA consists of a single strand and DNA has two strands. If straightened out, DNA has two side rails. RNA only has one "backbone," or strand of sugar and phosphate group components. RNA uses the fully hydroxylated sugar **pentose**, which includes an extra oxygen compared to deoxyribose, which is the sugar used by DNA. RNA supports the functions carried out by DNA. It aids in gene expression, replication, and transportation.

> **Review Video: DNA vs. RNA**
> Visit mometrix.com/academy and enter code: 184871

Mendel's Laws

Mendel's laws are the law of segregation (the first law), the law of independent assortment (the second law), and the law of dominance (the third law). The **law of segregation** states that there are two **alleles** and that half of the total number of alleles are contributed by each parent organism. The **law of independent assortment** states that traits are passed on randomly and are not influenced by other traits. The exception to this is linked traits. A **Punnett square** can illustrate how alleles combine from the contributing genes to form various **phenotypes**. One set of a parent's genes are put in columns, while the genes from the other parent are placed in rows. The allele combinations are shown in each cell. The **law of dominance** states that when two different alleles are present in a pair, the **dominant** one is expressed. A Punnett square can be used to predict the outcome of crosses.

GENE, GENOTYPE, PHENOTYPE, AND ALLELE

A gene is a portion of DNA that identifies how traits are expressed and passed on in an organism. A gene is part of the **genetic code**. Collectively, all genes form the **genotype** of an individual. The genotype includes genes that may not be expressed, such as **recessive genes**. The **phenotype** is the physical, visual manifestation of genes. It is determined by the basic genetic information and how genes have been affected by their environment.

An **allele** is a variation of a gene. Also known as a trait, it determines the manifestation of a gene. This manifestation results in a specific physical appearance of some facet of an organism, such as eye color or height. For example, the genetic information for eye color is a gene. The gene variations responsible for blue, green, brown, or black eyes are called alleles. **Locus** (pl. loci) refers to the location of a gene or alleles.

> **Review Video: Genotype vs Phenotype**
> Visit mometrix.com/academy and enter code: 922853

DOMINANT AND RECESSIVE

Gene traits are represented in pairs with an uppercase letter for the dominant trait (A) and a lowercase letter for the recessive trait (a). Genes occur in pairs (AA, Aa, or aa). There is one gene on each chromosome half supplied by each parent organism. Since half the genetic material is from each parent, the offspring's traits are represented as a combination of these. A **dominant trait** only requires one gene of a gene pair for it to be expressed in a **phenotype**, whereas a **recessive** requires both genes in order to be manifested. For example, if the mother's genotype is Dd and the father's is dd, the possible combinations are Dd and dd. The dominant trait will be manifested if the genotype is DD or Dd. The recessive trait will be manifested if the genotype is dd. Both DD and dd are **homozygous** pairs. Dd is **heterozygous**.

MONOHYBRID AND HYBRID CROSSES

Genetic crosses are the possible combinations of alleles, and can be represented using Punnett squares. A **monohybrid cross** refers to a cross involving only one trait. Typically, the ratio is 3:1 (DD, Dd, Dd, dd), which is the ratio of dominant gene manifestation to recessive gene manifestation. This ratio occurs when both parents have a pair of dominant and recessive genes. If one parent has a pair of dominant genes (DD) and the other has a pair of recessive (dd) genes, the recessive trait cannot be expressed in the next generation because the resulting crosses all have the Dd genotype.

A **dihybrid cross** refers to one involving more than one trait, which means more combinations are possible. The ratio of genotypes for a dihybrid cross is 9:3:3:1 when the traits are not linked. The ratio for incomplete dominance is 1:2:1, which corresponds to dominant, mixed, and recessive phenotypes.

MONOHYBRID CROSS EXAMPLE

A monohybrid cross is a genetic cross for a single trait that has two alleles. A monohybrid cross can be used to show which allele is **dominant** for a single trait. The first monohybrid cross typically occurs between two **homozygous** parents. Each parent is homozygous for a separate allele for a particular trait. For example, in pea plants, green pods (G) are dominant over yellow pods (g). In a genetic cross of two pea plants that are homozygous for pod color, the F_1 generation will be 100% heterozygous green pods.

	g	g
G	Gg	Gg
G	Gg	Gg

If the plants with the heterozygous green pods are crossed, the F_2 generation should be 50% heterozygous green, 25% homozygous green, and 25% homozygous yellow.

	G	g
G	GG	Gg
g	Gg	gg

DIHYBRID CROSS EXAMPLE

A dihybrid cross is a genetic cross for **two traits** that each have two alleles. For example, in pea plants, green pods (G) are dominant over yellow pods (g), and yellow seeds (Y) are dominant over green seeds (y). In a genetic cross of two pea plants that are homozygous for pod color and seed color, the F_1 generation will be 100% heterozygous green pods and yellow seeds (GgYy). If these F_1 plants are crossed, the resulting F_2 generation is shown below. There are nine genotypes for green-pod, yellow-seed plants: one GGYY, two GGYy, two GgYY, and four GgYy. There are three genotypes for green-pod, green-seed plants: one GGyy and two Ggyy. There are three genotypes for yellow-pod, yellow-seed plants: one ggYY and two ggYy. There is only one genotype for yellow-pod, green-seed plants: ggyy. This cross has a 9:3:3:1 ratio.

	GY	Gy	gY	gy
GY	GGYY	GGYy	GgYY	GgYy
Gy	GGYy	GGyy	GgYy	Ggyy
gY	GgYY	GgYy	ggYY	ggYy
gy	GgYy	Ggyy	ggYy	ggyy

Non-Mendelian Concepts

CO-DOMINANCE

Co-dominance refers to the expression of *both alleles* so that both traits are shown. Cows, for example, can have hair colors of red, white, or red and white (not pink). In the latter color, both traits are fully expressed. The ABO human blood typing system is also co-dominant.

INCOMPLETE DOMINANCE

Incomplete dominance is when both the **dominant** and **recessive** genes are expressed, resulting in a phenotype that is a mixture of the two. The fact that snapdragons can be red, white, or pink is a good example. The dominant red gene (RR) results in a red flower because of large amounts of red pigment. White (rr) occurs because both genes call for no pigment. Pink (Rr) occurs because one gene is for red and one is for no pigment. The colors blend to produce pink flowers. A cross of pink flowers (Rr) can result in red (RR), white (rr), or pink (Rr) flowers.

> **Review Video: Mendelian and Non-Mendelian Genetics**
> Visit mometrix.com/academy and enter code: 113159

POLYGENIC INHERITANCE

Polygenic inheritance goes beyond the simplistic Mendelian concept that one gene influences one trait. It refers to traits that are influenced by *more than one gene*, and takes into account environmental influences on development.

MULTIPLE ALLELES

Each gene is made up of only two alleles, but in some cases, there are more than two possibilities for what those two alleles might be. For example, in blood typing, there are three alleles (A, B, O), but each person has only two of them. A gene with more than two possible alleles is known as a multiple allele. A gene that can result in two or more possible forms or expressions is known as a polymorphic gene.

General Anatomy and Physiology

CELL

The cell is the basic *organizational unit* of all living things. Each piece within a cell has a function that helps organisms grow and survive. There are many different types of cells, but cells are unique to each type of organism. The one thing that all cells have in common is a **membrane**, which is comparable to a semi-permeable plastic bag. The membrane is composed of **phospholipids**. There are also some **transport holes**, which are proteins that help certain molecules and ions move in and out of the cell. The cell is filled with a fluid called **cytoplasm** or cytosol.

Within the cell are a variety of **organelles**, groups of complex molecules that help a cell survive, each with its own unique membrane that has a different chemical makeup from the cell membrane. The larger the cell, the more organelles it will need to live.

All organisms, whether plants, animals, fungi, protists, or bacteria, exhibit structural organization on the cellular and organism level. All cells contain **DNA** and **RNA** and can synthesize proteins. All organisms have a highly organized cellular structure. Each cell consists of **nucleic acids**, **cytoplasm**, and a **cell membrane**. Specialized organelles such as **mitochondria** and **chloroplasts** have specific functions within the cell. In single-celled organisms, that single cell contains all of the components necessary for life. In multicellular organisms, cells can become specialized. Different types of cells can have different functions. Life begins as a single cell whether by **asexual** or **sexual reproduction**. Cells are grouped together in **tissues**. Tissues are grouped together in **organs**. Organs are grouped together in **systems**. An **organism** is a complete individual.

> **Review Video: Cell Structure**
> Visit mometrix.com/academy and enter code: 591293

CELL STRUCTURE

Ribosomes: Ribosomes are involved in *synthesizing proteins from amino acids*. They are numerous, making up about one quarter of the cell. Some cells contain thousands of ribosomes. Some are mobile and some are embedded in the rough **endoplasmic reticulum**.

Golgi complex (Golgi apparatus): This is involved in *synthesizing materials* such as proteins that are transported out of the cell. It is located near the nucleus and consists of layers of **membranes**.

Vacuoles: These are sacs used for *storage, digestion, and waste removal*. There is one large vacuole in plant cells. Animal cells have small, sometimes numerous vacuoles.

Vesicle: This is a small organelle within a cell. It has a membrane and performs varying functions, including *moving materials within a cell*.

Cytoskeleton: This consists of **microtubules** that help *shape and support the cell*.

Microtubules: These are part of the **cytoskeleton** and help *support the cell*. They are made of protein.

Cytosol: This is the *liquid material in the cell*. It is mostly water, but also contains some floating molecules.

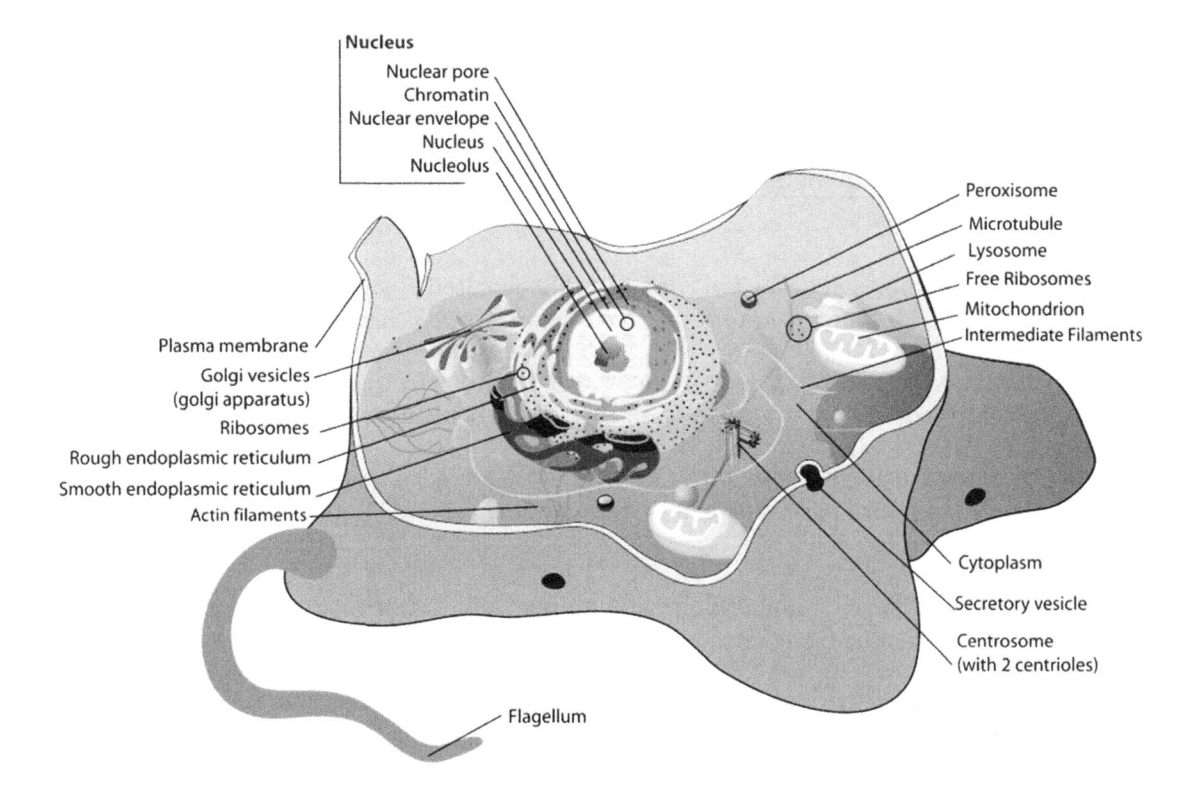

Cytoplasm: This is a general term that refers to cytosol and the substructures (organelles) found *within the plasma membrane*, but not within the nucleus.

Cell membrane (plasma membrane): This defines the cell by acting as a *barrier*. It helps keeps cytoplasm in and substances located outside the cell out. It also determines what is allowed to enter and exit the cell.

Endoplasmic reticulum: The two types of endoplasmic reticulum are **rough** (has ribosomes on the surface) and **smooth** (does not have ribosomes on the surface). It is a tubular network that comprises the *transport system of a cell*. It is fused to the nuclear membrane and extends through the cytoplasm to the cell membrane.

Mitochondrion (pl. mitochondria): These cell structures vary in terms of size and quantity. Some cells may have one mitochondrion, while others have thousands. This structure performs various functions such as *generating ATP*, and is also involved in *cell growth and death*. Mitochondria contain their own DNA that is separate from that contained in the nucleus.

MITOCHONDRIA FUNCTIONS

Four functions of mitochondria are: the production of **cell energy**, **cell signaling** (how communications are carried out within a cell, **cellular differentiation** (the process whereby a non-differentiated cell becomes transformed into a cell with a more specialized purpose), and **cell cycle and growth regulation** (the process whereby the cell gets ready to reproduce and reproduces). Mitochondria are numerous in eukaryotic cells. There may be hundreds or even thousands of mitochondria in a single cell. Mitochondria can be involved in many functions, their main one being *supplying the cell with energy.* Mitochondria consist of an inner and outer membrane. The inner membrane encloses the **matrix**, which contains the **mitochondrial DNA** (mtDNA) and ribosomes. Between the inner and outer membranes are **folds** (cristae). Chemical reactions occur here that release energy, control water levels in cells, and recycle and create proteins and fats. **Aerobic respiration** also occurs in the mitochondria.

> **Review Video: Mitochondria**
> Visit mometrix.com/academy and enter code: 444287

ANIMAL CELL STRUCTURE

Centrosome: This is comprised of the pair of **centrioles** located at right angles to each other and surrounded by protein. The centrosome is involved in *mitosis and the cell cycle.*

Centrioles: These are cylinder-shaped structures near the nucleus that are involved in *cellular division*. Each cylinder consists of nine groups of three **microtubules**. Centrioles occur in pairs.

Lysosome: This *digests proteins, lipids, and carbohydrates*, and also *transports undigested substances* to the cell membrane so they can be removed. The shape of a lysosome depends on the material being transported.

Cilia (singular: cilium): These are appendages extending from the surface of the cell, the movement of which *causes the cell to move*. They can also result in fluid being moved by the cell.

Flagella: These are tail-like structures on cells that use whip-like movements to *help the cell move*. They are similar to cilia, but are usually longer and not as numerous. A cell usually only has one or a few flagella.

NUCLEAR PARTS OF A CELL

- **Nucleus** (pl. nuclei): This is a small structure that contains the **chromosomes** and regulates the **DNA** of a cell. The nucleus is the defining structure of **eukaryotic cells**, and all eukaryotic cells have a nucleus. The nucleus is responsible for the passing on of genetic traits between generations. The nucleus contains a *nuclear envelope, nucleoplasm, a nucleolus, nuclear pores, chromatin, and ribosomes.*
- **Chromosomes**: These are highly condensed, threadlike rods of **DNA**. Short for **deoxyribonucleic acid**, DNA is the genetic material that *stores information about the plant or animal.*
- **Chromatin**: This consists of the DNA and protein that make up **chromosomes**.
- **Nucleolus**: This structure contained within the nucleus consists of protein. It is small, round, does not have a membrane, is involved in **protein synthesis**, and synthesizes and stores **RNA (ribonucleic acid)**.
- **Nuclear envelope**: This encloses the structures of the nucleus. It consists of inner and outer membranes made of **lipids**.
- **Nuclear pores**: These are involved in the exchange of material between the nucleus and the **cytoplasm**.
- **Nucleoplasm**: This is the liquid within the nucleus, and is similar to cytoplasm.

CELL MEMBRANES

The cell membrane, also referred to as the **plasma membrane**, is a thin semipermeable membrane of lipids and proteins. The cell membrane isolates the cell from its external environment while still enabling the cell to communicate with that outside environment. It consists of a **phospholipid bilayer**, or double layer, with the **hydrophilic ends** of the outer layer facing the external environment, the inner layer facing the inside of the cell, and the **hydrophobic ends** facing each other. **Cholesterol** in the cell membrane adds stiffness and flexibility. **Glycolipids** help the cell to recognize other cells of the organisms. The **proteins** in the cell membrane help give the cells shape. Special proteins help the cell communicate with its external environment. Other proteins transport molecules across the cell membrane.

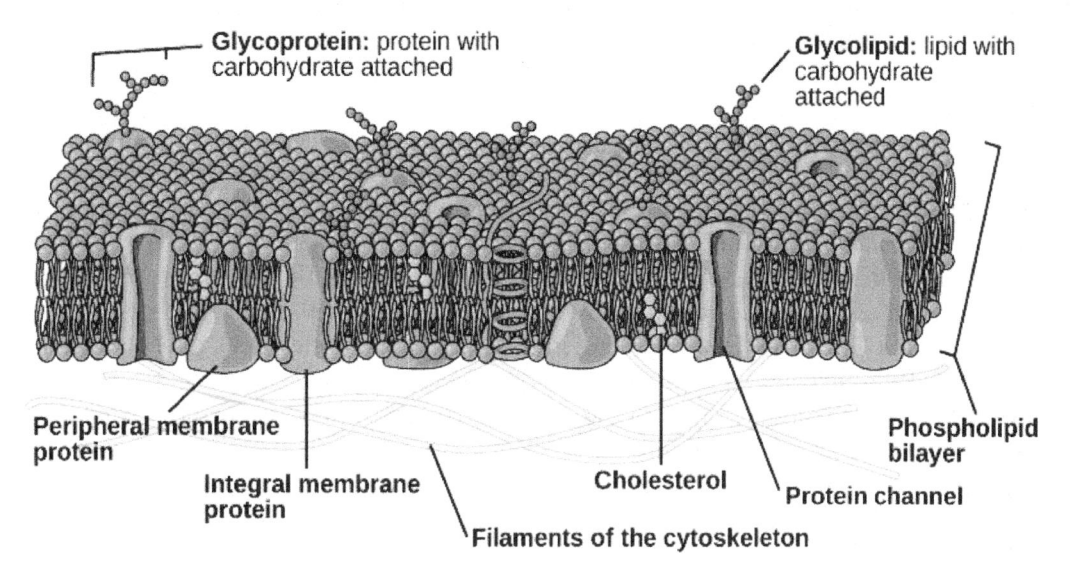

SELECTIVE PERMEABILITY

The cell membrane, or plasma membrane, has **selective permeability** with regard to size, charge, and solubility. With regard to molecule size, the cell membrane allows only small molecules to diffuse through it. **Oxygen** and **water** molecules are small and typically can pass through the cell membrane. The charge of the **ions** on the cell's surface also either attracts or repels ions. Ions with like charges are repelled, and ions with opposite charges are attracted to the cell's surface. Molecules that are soluble in **phospholipids** can usually pass through the cell membrane. Many molecules are not able to diffuse the cell membrane, and, if needed, those molecules must be moved through by active transport and **vesicles**.

CELL CYCLE

The term cell cycle refers to the process by which a cell **reproduces**, which involves *cell growth, the duplication of genetic material, and cell division*. Complex organisms with many cells use the cell cycle to replace cells as they lose their functionality and wear out. The entire cell cycle in animal cells can take 24 hours. The time required varies among different cell types. Human skin cells, for example, are constantly reproducing. Some other cells only divide infrequently. Once neurons are mature, they do not grow or divide. The two ways that cells can reproduce are through meiosis and mitosis. When cells replicate through **mitosis**, the "daughter cell" is an *exact replica* of the parent cell. When cells divide through **meiosis**, the daughter cells have *different genetic coding* than the parent cell. Meiosis only happens in specialized reproductive cells called **gametes**.

CELL DIFFERENTIATION

The human body is filled with many different types of cells. The process that helps to determine the cell type for each cell is known as **differentiation**. Another way to say this is when *a less-specialized cell becomes a more-specialized cell*. This process is controlled by the genes of each cell among a group of cells known as a **zygote**. Following the directions of the genes, a cell builds certain proteins and other pieces that set it apart as a specific type of cell.

An example occurs with **gastrulation**—an early phase in the embryonic development of most animals. During gastrulation, the cells are organized into three primary germ layers: **ectoderm**, **mesoderm**, and **endoderm**. Then, the cells in these layers differentiate into special tissues and organs. For example, the *nervous system* develops from the ectoderm. The *muscular system* develops from the mesoderm. Much of the *digestive system* develops from the endoderm.

MITOSIS

The primary events that occur during mitosis are:

- **Interphase**: The cell prepares for division by replicating its genetic and cytoplasmic material. Interphase can be further divided into G_1, S, and G_2.
- **Prophase**: The **chromatin** thickens into chromosomes and the **nuclear membrane** begins to disintegrate. Pairs of **centrioles** move to opposite sides of the cell and spindle fibers begin to form. The **mitotic spindle**, formed from cytoskeleton parts, moves chromosomes around within the cell.
- **Metaphase**: The spindle moves to the center of the cell and chromosome pairs align along the center of the spindle structure.
- **Anaphase**: The pairs of chromosomes, called sisters, begin to pull apart, and may bend. When they are separated, they are called **daughter chromosomes**. Grooves appear in the cell membrane.
- **Telophase**: The spindle disintegrates, the nuclear membranes reform, and the chromosomes revert to chromatin. In animal cells, the membrane is pinched. In plant cells, a new cell wall begins to form.
- **Cytokinesis**: This is the physical splitting of the cell (including the cytoplasm) into two cells. Some believe this occurs following telophase. Others say it occurs from anaphase, as the cell begins to furrow, through telophase, when the cell actually splits into two.

> **Review Video: Cellular Division: Mitosis and Meiosis**
> Visit mometrix.com/academy and enter code: 109813
>
> **Review Video: Mitosis**
> Visit mometrix.com/academy and enter code: 849894

MEIOSIS

Meiosis has the same phases as mitosis, but they happen twice. In addition, different events occur during some phases of meiosis than mitosis. The events that occur during the first phase of meiosis are interphase (I), prophase (I), metaphase (I), anaphase (I), telophase (I), and cytokinesis (I). During this first phase of meiosis, *chromosomes cross over, genetic material is exchanged, and tetrads of four chromatids are formed*. The nuclear membrane dissolves. Homologous pairs of chromatids are separated and travel to different poles. At this point, there has been one cell division resulting in two cells. Each cell goes through a second cell division, which consists of prophase (II), metaphase (II), anaphase (II), telophase (II), and cytokinesis (II). The result is *four daughter cells* with different sets of chromosomes. The daughter cells are **haploid**, which means they contain half the genetic material of the parent cell. The second phase of meiosis is similar to the process of mitosis. Meiosis encourages genetic diversity.

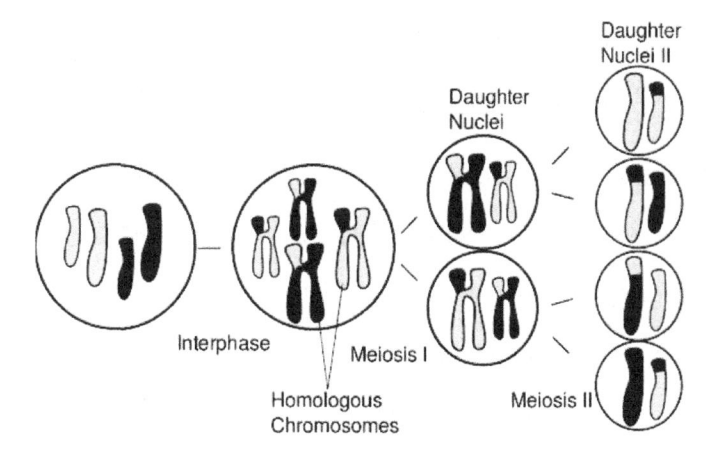

Tissues

Tissues are groups of cells that work together to perform a specific function. Tissues are divided into broad categories based on their function. Animal tissues may be divided into seven categories:

- **Epithelial** – Tissue in which cells are joined together tightly. *Skin* tissue is an example.
- **Connective** – Connective tissue may be dense, loose, or fatty. It protects and binds body parts. Connective tissues include *bone tissue, cartilage, tendons, ligaments, fat, blood, and lymph*.
- **Cartilage** – Cushions and provides structural support for body parts. It has a jelly-like base and is fibrous.
- **Blood** – Blood transports oxygen to cells and removes wastes. It also carries hormones and defends against disease.
- **Bone** – Bone is a hard tissue that supports and protects softer tissues and organs. Its marrow produces red blood cells.
- **Muscle** – Muscle tissue helps support and move the body. The three types of muscle tissue are *smooth, cardiac, and skeletal*.
- **Nervous** – Nerve tissue is located in the *brain, spinal cord, and nerves*. Cells called neurons form a network through the body that control responses to changes in the external and internal environment. Some send signals to muscles and glands to trigger responses.

Organs

Organs are groups of tissues that work together to perform specific functions. Complex animals have several organs that are grouped together in multiple **systems**. For example, the **heart** is specifically designed to pump blood throughout an organism's body. The heart is composed mostly of muscle tissue in the myocardium, but it also contains connective tissue in the blood and membranes, nervous tissue that controls the heart rate, and epithelial tissue in the membranes. Gills in fish and lungs in reptiles, birds, and mammals are specifically designed to exchange gases. In birds, crops are designed to store food and gizzards are designed to grind food.

Organ systems are groups of organs that work together to perform specific functions. In mammals, there are 11 major organ systems: **integumentary system, respiratory system, cardiovascular system, endocrine system, nervous system, immune system, digestive system, excretory system, muscular system, skeletal system**, and **reproductive system**.

TERMS OF DIRECTION

Medial means *nearer to the midline* of the body. In anatomical position, the little finger is medial to the thumb.

Lateral is the opposite of medial. It refers to structures *further away from the body's midline*, at the sides. In anatomical position, the thumb is lateral to the little finger.

Proximal refers to structures *closer to the center* of the body. The hip is proximal to the knee.

Distal refers to structures *further away from the center* of the body. The knee is distal to the hip.

Anterior refers to structures in *front*.

Posterior refers to structures *behind*.

Cephalad and **cephalic** are adverbs meaning towards the *head*. **Cranial** is the adjective, meaning of the *skull*.

Caudad is an adverb meaning towards the *tail* or posterior. **Caudal** is the adjective, meaning of the *hindquarters*.

Superior means *above*, or closer to the head.

Inferior means *below*, or closer to the feet.

THE THREE PRIMARY BODY PLANES

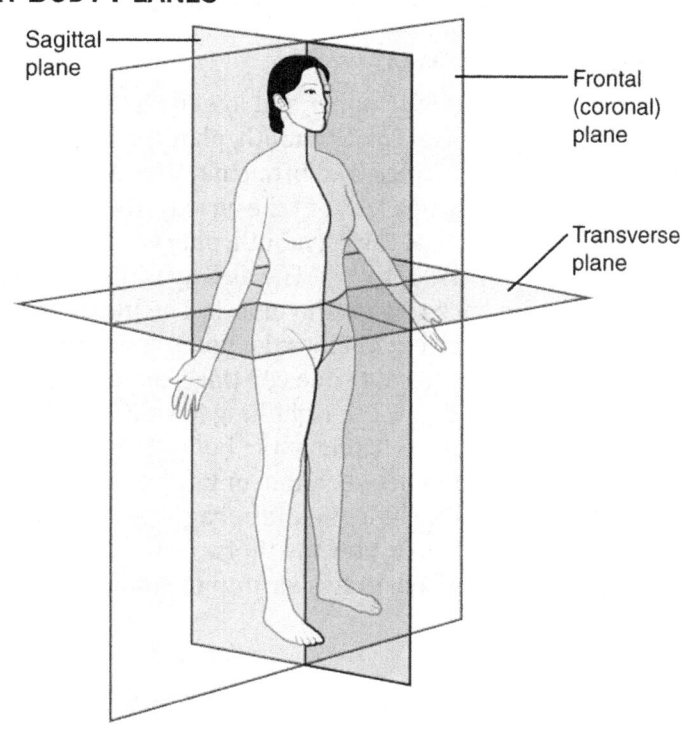

The **transverse (or horizontal) plane** divides the patient's body into imaginary upper (*superior*) and lower (*inferior or caudal*) halves.

The **sagittal plane** divides the body, or any body part, vertically into right and left sections. The sagittal plane runs parallel to the midline of the body.

The **coronal (or frontal) plane** divides the body, or any body structure, vertically into front and back (*anterior* and *posterior*) sections. The coronal plane runs vertically through the body at right angles to the midline.

Respiratory System

STRUCTURE OF THE RESPIRATORY SYSTEM

The respiratory system can be divided into the upper and lower respiratory system. The **upper respiratory system** includes the nose, nasal cavity, mouth, pharynx, and larynx. The **lower respiratory system** includes the trachea, lungs, and bronchial tree. Alternatively, the components of the respiratory system can be categorized as part of the airway, the lungs, or the respiratory muscles. The **airway** includes the nose, nasal cavity, mouth, pharynx (throat), larynx (voice box), trachea (windpipe), bronchi, and bronchial network. The airway is lined with **cilia** that trap microbes and debris and sweep them back toward the mouth. The **lungs** are structures that house the **bronchi** and bronchial network, which extend into the lungs and terminate in millions of **alveoli** (air sacs). The walls of the alveoli are only one cell thick, allowing for the exchange of gases with the blood capillaries that surround them. The right lung has three lobes. The left lung has only two lobes, leaving room for the heart on the left side of the body. The lungs are surrounded by a **pleural membrane**, which reduces friction between the lungs and walls of the thoracic cavity when breathing. The respiratory muscles include the **diaphragm** and the **intercostal muscles**. The diaphragm is a dome-shaped muscle that separates the thoracic and abdominal cavities; as it contracts, it expands the thoracic cavity which draws air into the lungs. The intercostal muscles are located between the ribs.

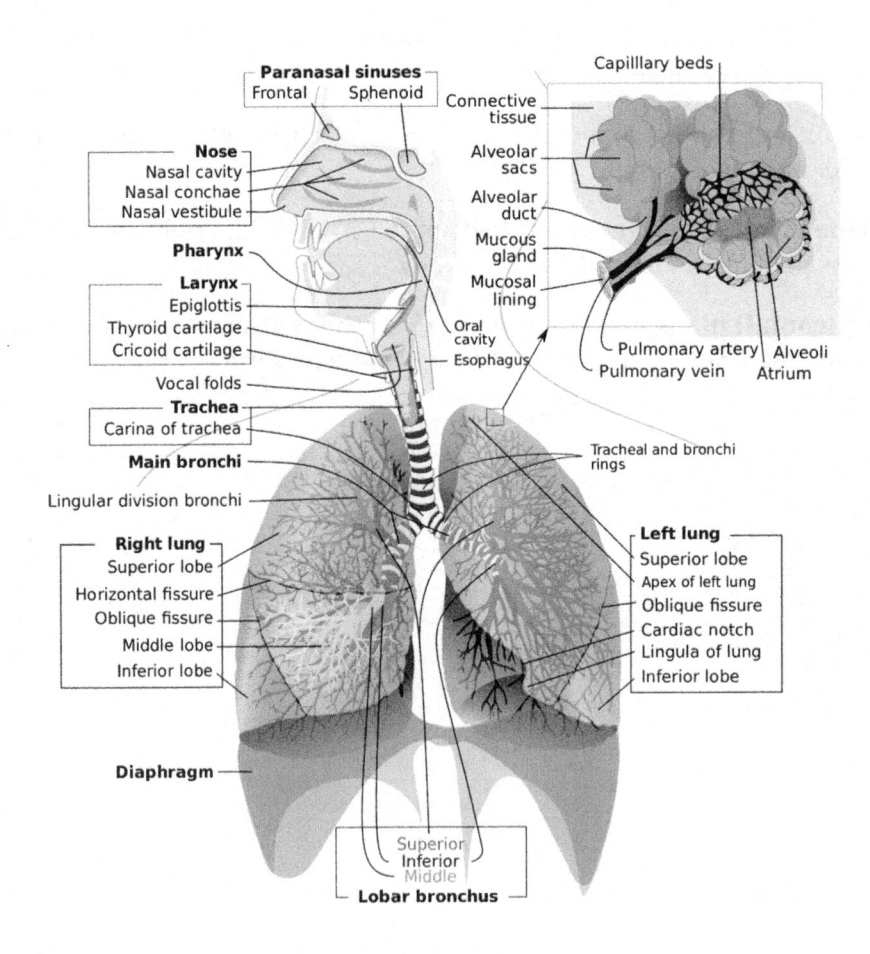

FUNCTIONS OF THE RESPIRATORY SYSTEM

The main function of the respiratory system is to supply the body with **oxygen** and rid the body of **carbon dioxide**. This exchange of gases occurs in millions of tiny **alveoli**, which are surrounded by blood capillaries. The respiratory system also filters air. Air is warmed, moistened, and filtered as it passes through the nasal passages before it reaches the lungs. The respiratory system also allows for speech. As air passes through the throat, it moves through the **larynx** (voice box), which vibrates and produces sound, before it enters the **trachea** (windpipe). Cough production allows foreign particles which have entered the nasal passages or airways to be expelled from the respiratory system. The respiratory system functions in the sense of smell using **chemoreceptors** that are located in the nasal cavity and respond to airborne chemicals. The respiratory system also helps the body maintain acid-base **homeostasis**. Hyperventilation can increase blood pH during **acidosis** (low pH). Slowing breathing during **alkalosis** (high pH) helps lower blood pH.

> **Review Video: Respiratory System**
> Visit mometrix.com/academy and enter code: 783075

BREATHING PROCESS

During the breathing process, the **diaphragm** and the **intercostal muscles** contract to expand the lungs.

During **inspiration** or inhalation, the diaphragm contracts and moves down, increasing the size of the chest cavity. The intercostal muscles contract and the ribs expand, increasing the size of the **chest cavity**. As the volume of the chest cavity increases, the pressure inside the chest cavity decreases. Because the outside air is under a greater amount of pressure than the air inside the lungs, air rushes into the lungs.

When the diaphragm and intercostal muscles relax, the size of the chest cavity decreases, forcing air out of the lungs (**expiration** or exhalation). The breathing process is controlled by the portion of the brain stem called the **medulla oblongata**. The medulla oblongata monitors the level of carbon dioxide in the blood and signals the breathing rate to increase when these levels are too high.

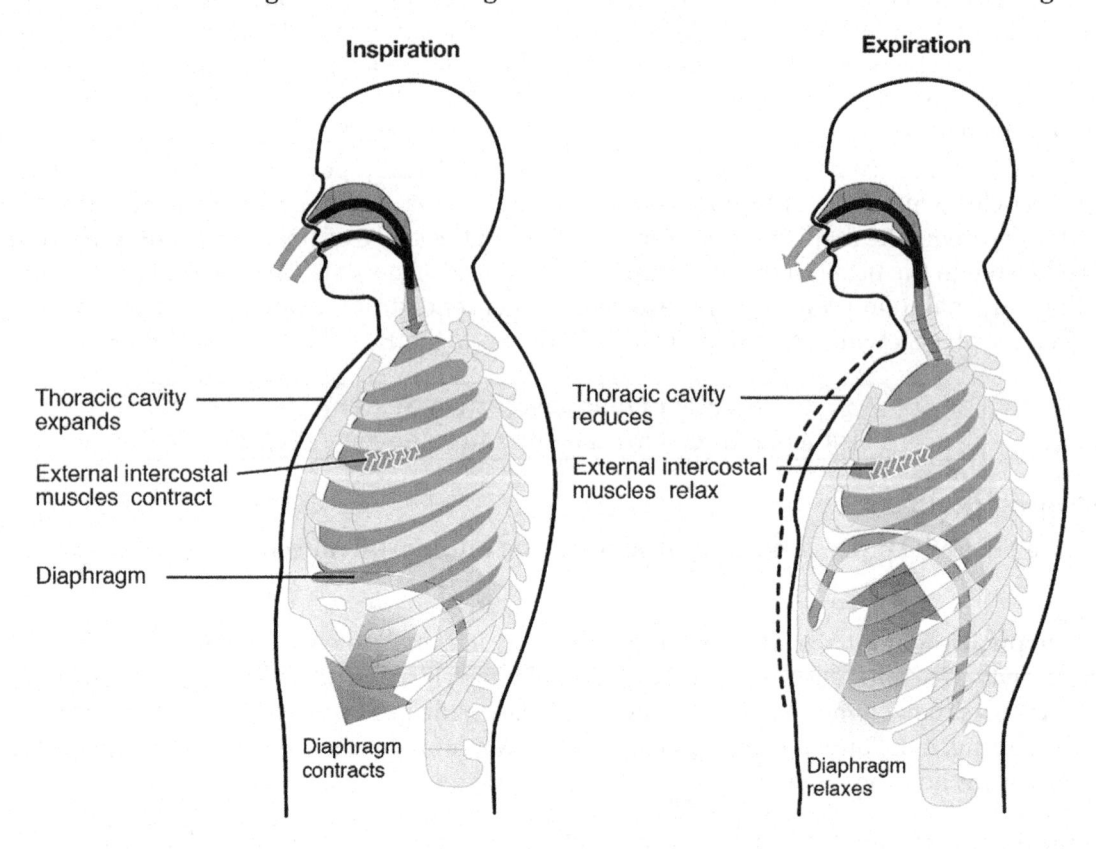

Cardiovascular System

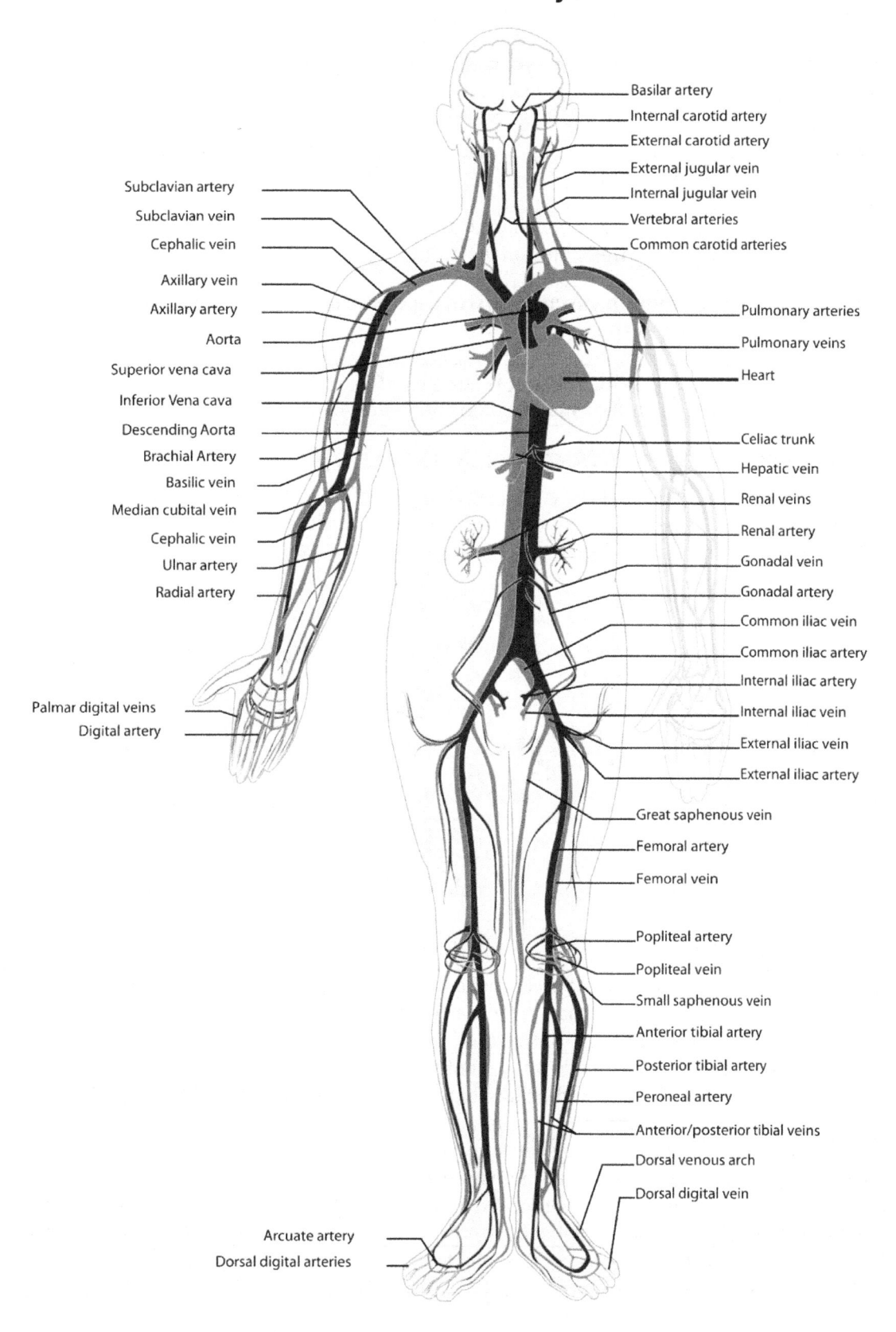

The **circulatory system** is responsible for the internal transport of substances to and from the cells. The circulatory system consists of the following parts:

- **Blood**: Blood is composed of water, solutes, and other elements in a fluid connective tissue.
- **Blood vessels**: Vessels are tubules of different sizes that transport blood in a closed system to tissues throughout the body.
- **Heart**: The heart is a muscular pump providing the pressure necessary to keep blood flowing throughout the circulatory system.

As the blood moves through the system from larger tubules through smaller ones, the rate slows. The flow of blood in the **capillary beds**, the smallest tubules, is quite slow.

A supplementary system, the **lymph vascular system**, cleans excess fluids and proteins and returns them to the circulatory system.

> **Review Video: What is the Circulatory System?**
> Visit mometrix.com/academy and enter code: 376581

ARTERIAL AND VENOUS SYSTEMS (ARTERIES, ARTERIOLES, VENULES, VEINS)

The walls of all blood vessels (except the capillaries) consist of three layers: the innermost **tunica intima**, the **tunica media** consisting of smooth muscle cells and elastic fibers, and the outer **tunica adventitia**.

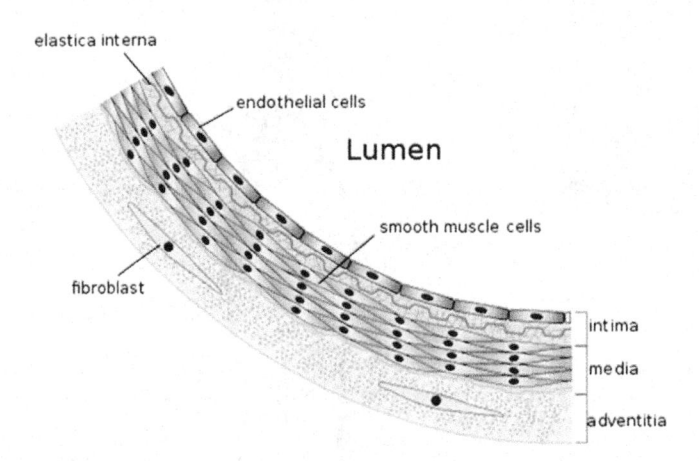

Vessel	Structure	Function
Elastic arteries	Includes the aorta and major branches Tunica media has more elastin than any other vessels Largest vessels in the arterial system	Stretch when blood is forced out of the heart, and recoil under low pressure
Muscular arteries	Includes the arteries that branch off of the elastic arteries Tunica media has a higher proportion of smooth muscle cells, and fewer elastic fibers as compared to elastic arteries	Regulate blood flow by vasoconstriction / vasodilation
Arterioles	Tiny vessels that lead to the capillary beds Tunica media is thin, but composed almost entirely smooth muscle cells	Primary vessels involved in vasoconstriction / vasodilation Control blood flow to capillaries
Venules	Tiny vessels that exit the capillary beds Thin, porous walls; few muscle cells and elastic fibers	Empty blood into larger veins

Vessel	Structure	Function
Veins	Thin tunica media and tunica intima Wide lumen Valves prevent backflow of blood	Carry blood back to the heart

BLOOD

Blood helps maintain a healthy internal environment in animals by carrying raw materials to cells and removing waste products. It helps stabilize internal pH and hosts cells of the immune system.

An adult human has about five quarts of blood. Blood is composed of **red blood cells, white blood cells, platelets**, and **plasma**. Plasma constitutes more than half of the blood volume. It is mostly water and serves as a solvent. Plasma contains plasma proteins, ions, glucose, amino acids, hormones, and dissolved gases. **Platelets** are fragments of stem cells and serve an important function in blood clotting.

Red blood cells transport **oxygen** to cells. Red blood cells form in the bone marrow and can live for about four months. These cells are constantly being replaced by fresh ones, keeping the total number relatively stable. They lack a nucleus.

Part of the immune system, white blood cells defend the body against **infection** and remove wastes. The types of white blood cells include lymphocytes, neutrophils, monocytes, eosinophils, and basophils.

HEART

The **heart** is a muscular pump made of cardiac muscle tissue. Heart chamber contraction and relaxation is coordinated by electrical signals from the self-exciting **sinoatrial node** and the **atrioventricular node**. **Atrial contraction** fills the ventricles and **ventricular contraction** forces blood into arteries leaving the heart. This sequence is called the **cardiac cycle**. Valves keep blood moving through the heart in a single direction and prevent any backwash as it flows through its four chambers.

Deoxygenated blood from the body flows through the heart in this order:

1. The **superior vena cava** brings blood from the upper body; the **inferior vena cava** brings blood from the lower body.
2. Right atrium
3. Tricuspid valve (right atrioventricular [AV] valve)
4. Right ventricle
5. Pulmonary valve
6. Left and right pulmonary artery (note: these arteries carry deoxygenated blood)
7. Lungs (where gas exchange occurs)

Oxygenated blood returns to the body through:

1. Left and right pulmonary veins (note: these veins carry oxygenated blood)
2. Left atrium
3. Mitral valve (left atrioventricular [AV] valve)
4. Left ventricle
5. Aortic valve
6. Aortic arch
7. Aorta

The left and right sides of the heart are separated by the septum. The heart has its own circulatory system with its own **coronary arteries**.

CARDIAC CYCLE

The **first phase** of the cardiac cycle is the ventricular filling phase. During this phase, the pressure in the ventricle is lower than the pressure in the atrium which forces open the atrioventricular valve and allows blood to pass from the atrium to the ventricle. Also, during the time, the pressure in the blood vessels leading from the ventricle (the aorta or pulmonary artery) is greater than ventricular pressure that forces the semilunar valves closed. The **second phase** of the cardiac cycle is ventricular contraction. The ventricle contracts during this phase, increasing the pressure within the ventricle. The atrial pressure is now lower than ventricular pressure, which pushes the atrioventricular valves closed. Initially, the semilunar valves are also closed. When the pressure in the ventricle rises above pressure in the blood vessel leading away from the heart (the aorta or the pulmonary artery), the semilunar valves are forced open and ventricular ejection begins. The **third phase** of the cardiac cycle is ventricular relaxation. Ventricular pressure decreases when blood is ejected from the ventricles into blood vessels leading away from the heart. When the pressure falls below the pressure in the blood vessel (the aorta or the pulmonary artery), the semilunar valves are forced closed. When the ventricle relaxes and the pressure falls below the pressure in the atrium, the atrioventricular valves are opened and the period of ventricular filling begins again.

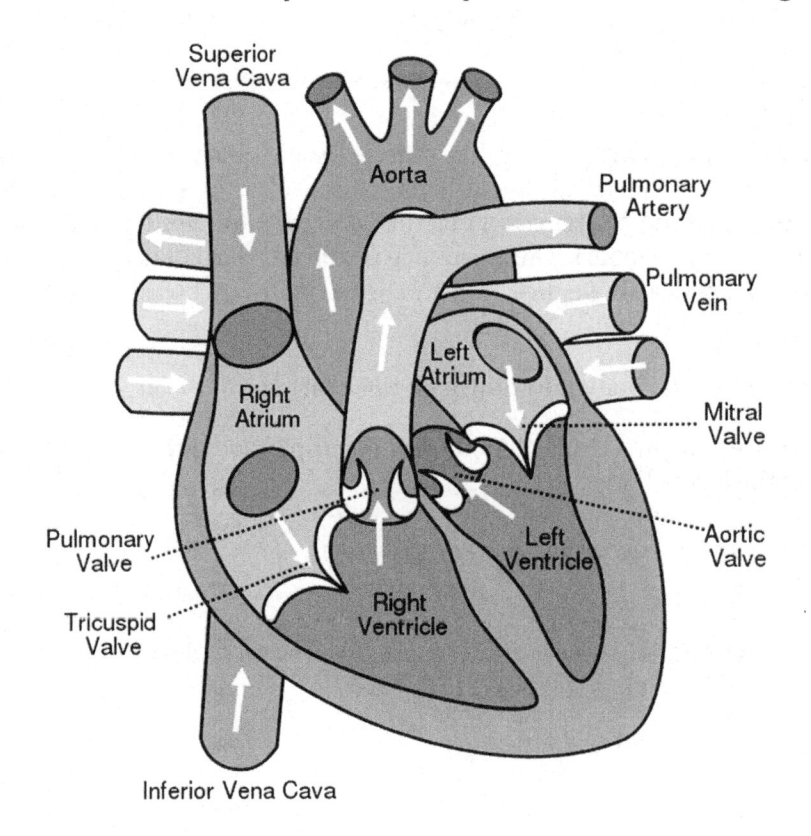

TYPES OF CIRCULATION

The **circulatory system** includes coronary circulation, pulmonary circulation, and systemic circulation. **Coronary circulation** is the flow of blood to the heart tissue. Blood enters the **coronary arteries**, which branch off the aorta, supplying major arteries, which enter the heart with oxygenated blood. The deoxygenated blood returns to the right atrium through the **cardiac veins**, which empty into the **coronary sinus**. **Pulmonary circulation** is the flow of blood between the heart and the lungs. Deoxygenated blood flows from the right ventricle to the lungs through **pulmonary arteries**. Oxygenated blood flows back to the left atrium through the **pulmonary veins**. **Systemic circulation** is the flow of blood to the entire body with the exception of coronary circulation and pulmonary circulation. Blood exits the left ventricle through the aorta, which branches into the *carotid arteries, subclavian arteries, common iliac arteries, and the renal artery*. Blood returns to the heart through the *jugular veins, subclavian veins, common iliac veins, and renal veins*, which empty into the **superior** and **inferior venae cavae**. Included in systemic circulation is **portal circulation**, which is the flow of blood from the digestive system to the liver and then to the heart, and **renal circulation**, which is the flow of blood between the heart and the kidneys.

BLOOD PRESSURE

Blood pressure is the fluid pressure generated by the cardiac cycle.

Arterial blood pressure functions by transporting oxygen-poor blood into the lungs and oxygen-rich blood to the body tissues. **Arteries** branch into smaller arterioles which contract and expand based on signals from the body. **Arterioles** are where adjustments are made in blood delivery to specific areas based on complex communication from body systems.

Capillary beds are diffusion sites for exchanges between blood and interstitial fluid. A capillary has the thinnest wall of any blood vessel, consisting of a single layer of **endothelial cells**.

Capillaries merge into venules, which in turn merge with larger diameter tubules called **veins**. Veins transport blood from body tissues *back to the heart*. Valves inside the veins facilitate this transport. The walls of veins are thin and contain smooth muscle and also function as blood volume reserves.

LYMPHATIC SYSTEM

The main function of the **lymphatic system** is to *return excess tissue fluid to the bloodstream*. This system consists of transport vessels and lymphoid organs. The lymph vascular system consists of **lymph capillaries**, **lymph vessels**, and **lymph ducts**. The major functions of the lymph vascular system are:

- The return of excess fluid to the blood.
- The return of protein from the capillaries.
- The transport of fats from the digestive tract.
- The disposal of debris and cellular waste.

Lymphoid organs include the lymph nodes, spleen, appendix, adenoids, thymus, tonsils, and small patches of tissue in the small intestine. **Lymph nodes** are located at intervals throughout the lymph vessel system. Each node contains **lymphocytes** and **plasma cells**. The **spleen** filters blood stores of red blood cells and macrophages. The **thymus** secretes hormones and is the major site of lymphocyte production.

SPLEEN

The spleen is in the upper left of the abdomen. It is located behind the stomach and immediately below the diaphragm. It is about the size of a thick paperback book and weighs just over half a pound. It is made up of **lymphoid tissue**. The blood vessels are connected to the spleen by **splenic sinuses** (modified capillaries). The following **peritoneal ligaments** support the spleen:

- The **gastrolienal ligament** connects the stomach to the spleen.
- The **lienorenal ligament** connects the kidney to the spleen.
- The middle section of the **phrenicocolic ligament** (connects the left colic flexure to the thoracic diaphragm).

The main functions of the spleen are to *filter unwanted materials* from the blood (including old red blood cells) and to help *fight infections*. Up to ten percent of the population has one or more accessory spleens that tend to form at the **hilum** of the original spleen.

Gastrointestinal System

The digestive system uses the following processes to convert protein, fats, and carbohydrates into usable energy for the body:

- **Movement**: Movement mixes and passes nutrients through the system and eliminates waste.
- **Secretion**: Enzymes, hormones, and other substances necessary for digestion are secreted into the digestive tract.
- **Digestion**: Digestion includes the chemical breakdown of nutrients into smaller units that enter the internal environment.
- **Absorption**: Nutrients pass through plasma membranes into the blood or lymph and then to the body.

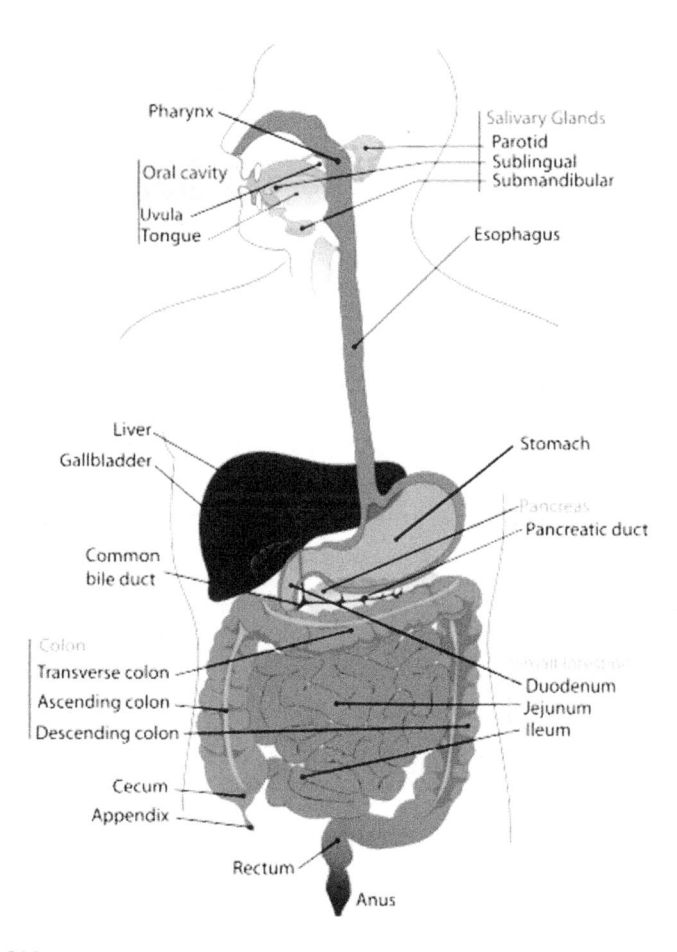

MOUTH AND STOMACH

Digestion begins in the mouth with the chewing and mixing of nutrients with **saliva**. Only humans and other mammals actually chew their food. **Salivary glands** are stimulated and secrete saliva. Saliva contains **enzymes** that initiate the breakdown of starch in digestion. Once swallowed, the food moves down the **pharynx** into the **esophagus** en route to the stomach.

The **stomach** is a flexible, muscular sac. It has three main functions:

- Mixing and storing food
- Dissolving and degrading food via secretions
- Controlling passage of food into the small intestine

Protein digestion begins in the stomach. Stomach acidity helps break down the food and make nutrients available for absorption. Smooth muscle moves the food by **peristalsis**, contracting and relaxing to move nutrients along. Smooth muscle contractions move nutrients into the small intestine where the **absorption** process begins.

Liver

The liver is the largest solid organ of the body. It is also the largest gland. It weighs about three pounds in an adult and is located below the diaphragm on the right side of the abdomen. The liver is made up of four **lobes**: right, left, quadrate, and caudate lobes. The liver is secured to the diaphragm and abdominal walls by five **ligaments**. They are called the falciform (which forms a membrane-like barrier between the right and left lobes), coronary, right triangular, left triangular, and round ligaments.

The liver processes blood once it has received nutrients from the intestines via the **hepatic portal vein**. The **hepatic artery** supplies oxygen-rich blood from the abdominal aorta so that the organ can function. Blood leaves the liver through the **hepatic veins**. The liver's functional units are called **lobules** (made up of layers of liver cells). Blood enters the lobules through branches of the portal vein and hepatic artery. The blood then flows through small channels called **sinusoids**.

The liver is responsible for performing many vital functions in the body including:

- Production of **bile**
- Production of certain **blood plasma proteins**
- Production of **cholesterol** (and certain proteins needed to carry fats)
- Storage of excess glucose in the form of **glycogen** (that can be converted back to glucose when needed)
- Regulation of **amino acids**
- Processing of **hemoglobin** (to store iron)
- Conversion of ammonia (that is poisonous to the body) to **urea** (a waste product excreted in urine)
- **Purification** of the blood (clears out drugs and other toxins)
- Regulation of **blood clotting**
- Controlling infections by boosting **immune factors** and removing bacteria.

The nutrients (and drugs) that pass through the liver are converted into forms that are appropriate for the body to use.

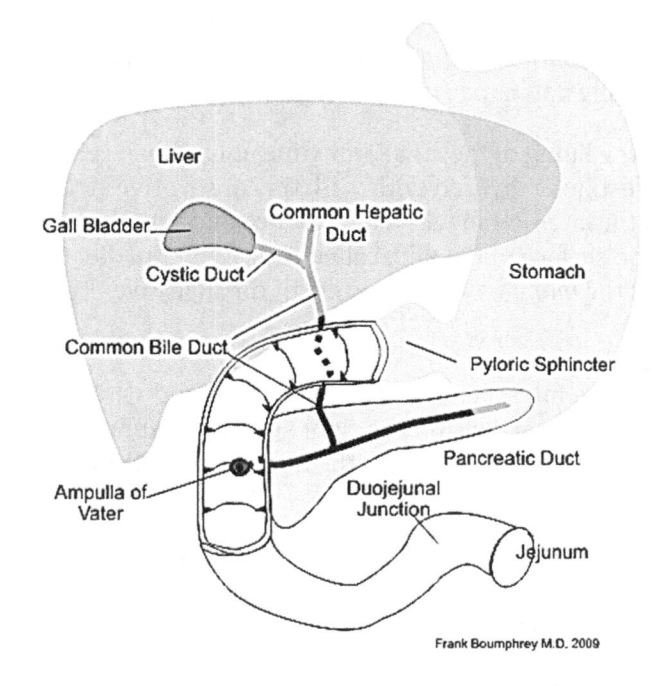

PANCREAS

The pancreas is six to ten inches long and located at the back of the abdomen behind the stomach. It is a long, tapered organ. The wider (right) side is called the **head** and the narrower (left) side is called the **tail**. The head lies near the **duodenum** (the first part of the small intestine) and the tail ends near the **spleen**. The body of the pancreas lies between the head and the tail. The pancreas is made up of exocrine and endocrine tissues. The **exocrine tissue** secretes digestive enzymes from a series of ducts that collectively form the main pancreatic duct (that runs the length of the pancreas). The **main pancreatic duct** connects to the common bile duct near the duodenum. The **endocrine tissue** secretes hormones (such as insulin) into the bloodstream. Blood is supplied to the pancreas from the *splenic artery, gastroduodenal artery, and the superior mesenteric artery*.

DIGESTIVE ROLE OF PANCREAS

The pancreas assists in the digestion of foods by secreting **enzymes** (to the small intestine) that help to break down many foods, especially fats and proteins.

The precursors to these enzymes (called **zymogens**) are produced by groups of exocrine cells (called **acini**). They are converted, through a chemical reaction in the gut, to the active enzymes (such as **pancreatic lipase** and **amylase**) once they enter the small intestine. The pancreas also secretes large amounts of **sodium bicarbonate** to neutralize the stomach acid that reaches the small intestine.

The **exocrine** functions of the pancreas are controlled by hormones released by the stomach and small intestine (duodenum) when food is present. The exocrine secretions of the pancreas flow into the main pancreatic duct (**Wirsung's duct**) and are delivered to the duodenum through the pancreatic duct.

SMALL INTESTINE

In the digestive process, most nutrients are absorbed in the **small intestine**. Enzymes from the pancreas, liver, and stomach are transported to the small intestine to aid digestion. These enzymes act on *fats, carbohydrates, nucleic acids, and proteins*. **Bile** is a secretion of the liver and is particularly useful in breaking down fats. It is stored in the **gall bladder** between meals.

By the time food reaches the lining of the small intestine, it has been reduced to small molecules. The lining of the small intestine is covered with **villi**, tiny absorptive structures that greatly increase the surface area for interaction with chyme (the semi-liquid mass of partially digested food). Epithelial cells at the surface of the villi, called **microvilli**, further increase the ability of the small intestine to serve as the *main absorption organ* of the digestive tract.

LARGE INTESTINE

Also called the **colon**, the large intestine concentrates, mixes, and stores waste material. A little over a meter in length, the colon ascends on the right side of the abdominal cavity, cuts across transversely to the left side, then descends and attaches to the **rectum**, a short tube for waste disposal.

When the rectal wall is distended by waste material, the nervous system triggers an impulse in the body to expel the waste from the rectum. A muscle **sphincter** at the end of the **anus** is stimulated to facilitate the expelling of waste matter.

The speed at which waste moves through the colon is influenced by the volume of fiber and other undigested material present. Without adequate bulk in the diet, it takes longer to move waste along, sometimes with negative effects. Lack of bulk in the diet has been linked to a number of disorders.

> **Review Video: Gastrointestinal System**
> Visit mometrix.com/academy and enter code: 378740

Nervous System

The human nervous system senses, interprets, and issues commands as a response to conditions in the body's environment. This process is made possible by a complex communication system of cells called **neurons**.

Messages are sent across the plasma membrane of neurons through a process called **action potential**. These messages occur when a neuron is stimulated past a necessary threshold. These stimulations occur in a sequence from the stimulation point of one neuron to its contact with another neuron. At the point of contact, called a **chemical synapse**, a substance is released that stimulates or inhibits the action of the adjoining cell. A network of nerves composed of neurons fans out across the body and forms the framework for the nervous system. The direction the information flows depends on the specific organizations of nerve circuits and pathways.

> **Review Video: The Nervous System**
> Visit mometrix.com/academy and enter code: 708428

THE SOMATIC NERVOUS SYSTEM AND THE REFLEX ARC

The somatic nervous system (**SNS**) controls the five senses and the voluntary movement of skeletal muscle. So, this system has all of the neurons that are connected to sense organs. Efferent (motor) and afferent (sensory) nerves help the somatic nervous system operate the senses and the movement of skeletal muscle. **Efferent nerves** bring signals from the central nervous system to the sensory organs and the muscles. **Afferent nerves** bring signals from the sensory organs and the muscles to the central nervous system. The somatic nervous system also performs involuntary movements which are known as reflex arcs.

A **reflex**, the simplest act of the nervous system, is an automatic response without any conscious thought to a stimulus via the reflex arc. The **reflex arc** is the simplest nerve pathway, which bypasses the brain and is controlled by the spinal cord. For example, in the classic knee-jerk response (patellar tendon reflex), the stimulus is the reflex hammer hitting the tendon, and the response is the muscle contracting, which jerks the foot upward. The stimulus is detected by sensory receptors, and a message is sent along a **sensory** (afferent) neuron to one or more **interneurons** in the spinal cord. The interneuron(s) transmit this message to a **motor** (efferent) neuron, which carries the message to the correct **effector** (muscle).

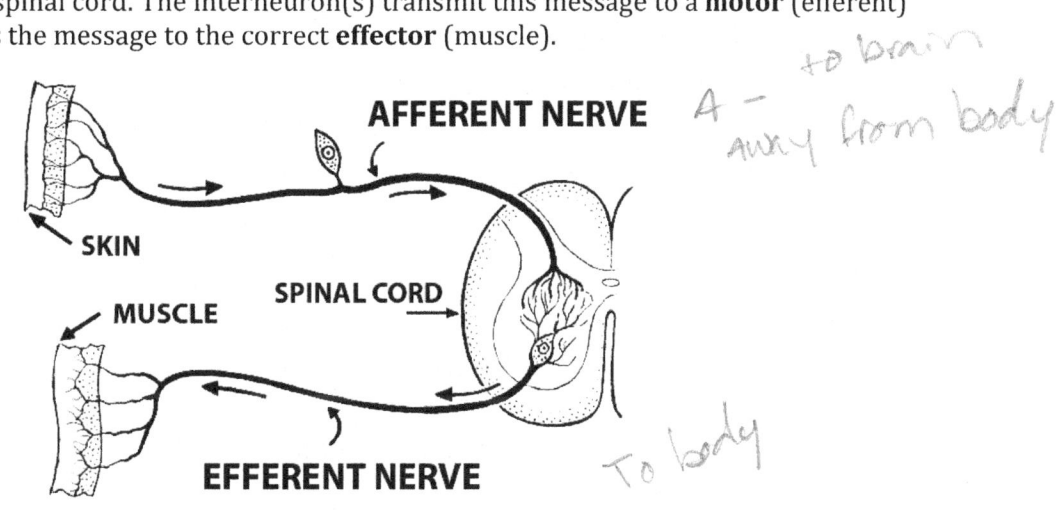

Muscular System

There are three types of muscle tissue: **skeletal**, **cardiac**, and **smooth**. There are more than 600 muscles in the human body. All muscles have these three properties in common:

- **Excitability**: All muscle tissues have an electric gradient that can reverse when stimulated.
- **Contraction**: All muscle tissues have the ability to contract, or shorten.
- **Elongate**: All muscle tissues share the capacity to elongate, or relax.

> **Review Video: Muscular System**
> Visit mometrix.com/academy and enter code: 967216

TYPES OF MUSCULAR TISSUE

The three types of muscular tissue are skeletal muscle, smooth muscle, and cardiac muscle.

Skeletal muscles are *voluntary* muscles that work in pairs to move various parts of the skeleton. Skeletal muscles are composed of **muscle fibers** (cells) that are bound together in parallel **bundles**. Skeletal muscles are also known as **striated muscle** due to their striped appearance under a microscope.

Smooth muscle tissues are *involuntary* muscles that are found in the walls of internal organs such as the stomach, intestines, and blood vessels. Smooth muscle tissues or **visceral tissue** is nonstriated. Smooth muscle cells are shorter and wider than skeletal muscle fibers. Smooth muscle tissue is also found in sphincters or valves that control various openings throughout the body.

Cardiac muscle tissue is *involuntary* muscle that is found only in the heart. Like skeletal muscle cells, cardiac muscle cells are also striated.

Only skeletal muscle interacts with the skeleton to move the body. When they contract, the muscles transmit **force** to the attached bones. Working together, the muscles and bones act as a system of levers which move around the joints. A small contraction of a muscle can produce a large movement. A limb can be extended and rotated around a joint due to the way the muscles are arranged.

SKELETAL MUSCLE CONTRACTION

Skeletal muscles consist of numerous muscle fibers. Each muscle fiber contains a bundle of **myofibrils**, which are composed of multiple repeating contractile units called **sarcomeres**.

Myofibrils contain two protein **microfilaments**: a thick filament and a thin filament. The thick filament is composed of the protein **myosin**. The thin filament is composed of the protein **actin**. The dark bands (**striations**) in skeletal muscles are formed when thick and thin filaments overlap. Light bands occur where the thin filament is overlapped. Skeletal muscle attraction occurs when the thin filaments slide over the thick filaments, shortening the sarcomere.

When an **action potential** (electrical signal) reaches a muscle fiber, **calcium ions** are released. According to the sliding filament model of muscle contraction, these calcium ions bind to the myosin and actin, which assists in the binding of the **myosin heads** of the thick filaments to the

actin molecules of the thin filaments. **Adenosine triphosphate** released from glucose provides the energy necessary for the contraction.

Structure of a Skeletal Muscle

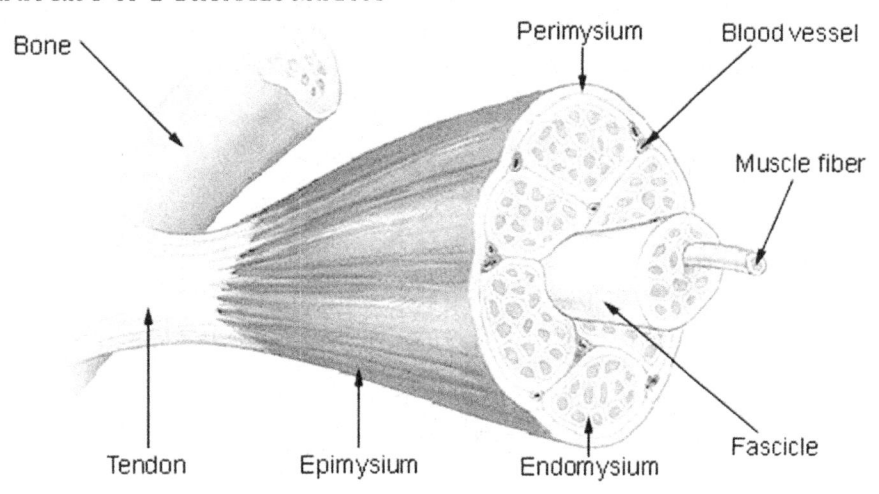

Labels: Bone, Perimysium, Blood vessel, Muscle fiber, Fascicle, Endomysium, Epimysium, Tendon

MAJOR MUSCLES OF THE BODY

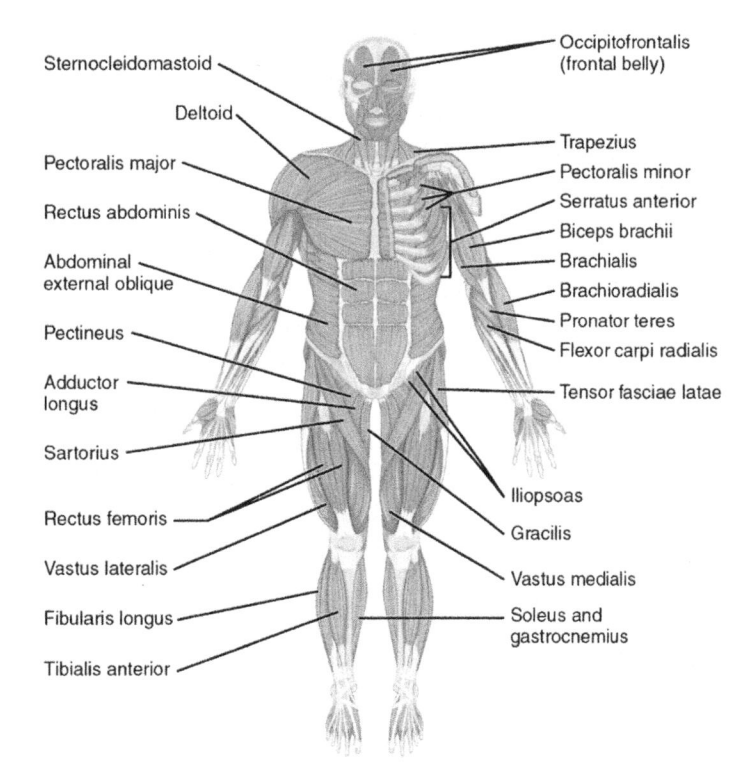

Labels: Sternocleidomastoid, Deltoid, Pectoralis major, Rectus abdominis, Abdominal external oblique, Pectineus, Adductor longus, Sartorius, Rectus femoris, Vastus lateralis, Fibularis longus, Tibialis anterior, Occipitofrontalis (frontal belly), Trapezius, Pectoralis minor, Serratus anterior, Biceps brachii, Brachialis, Brachioradialis, Pronator teres, Flexor carpi radialis, Tensor fasciae latae, Iliopsoas, Gracilis, Vastus medialis, Soleus and gastrocnemius

Major muscles of the body.
Right side: superficial; left side: deep (anterior view)

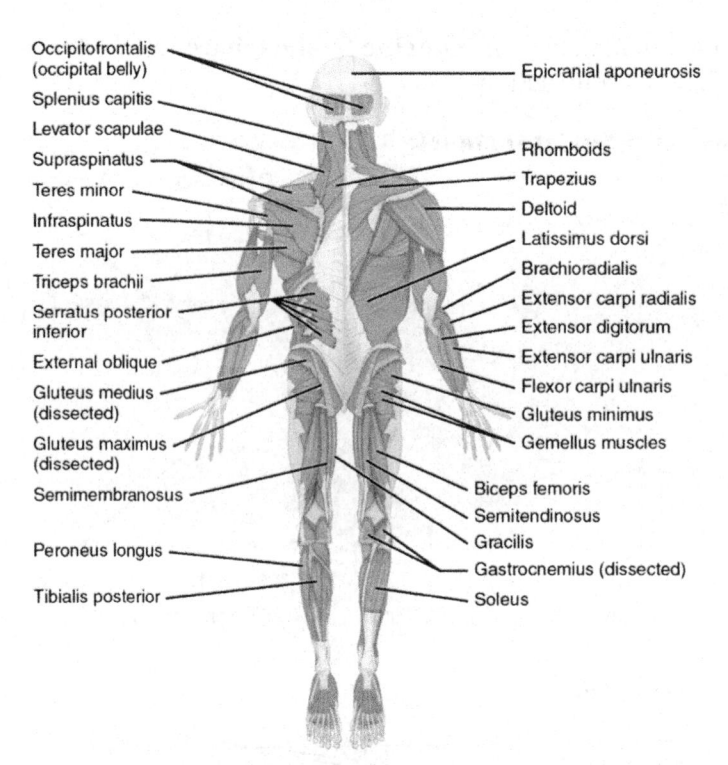

Major muscles of the body.
Right side: superficial; left side:
deep (posterior view)

Reproductive System

MALE REPRODUCTIVE SYSTEM

The functions of the male reproductive system are to produce, maintain, and transfer **sperm** and **semen** into the female reproductive tract and to produce and secrete **male hormones**.

The external structure includes the penis, scrotum, and testes. The **penis**, which contains the **urethra**, can fill with blood and become erect, enabling the deposition of semen and sperm into the female reproductive tract during sexual intercourse. The **scrotum** is a sack of skin and smooth muscle that houses the testes and keeps the testes outside the body wall at a cooler, proper temperature for **spermatogenesis**. The **testes**, or testicles, are the male gonads, which produce sperm and testosterone.

The internal structure includes the epididymis, vas deferens, ejaculatory ducts, urethra, seminal vesicles, prostate gland, and bulbourethral glands. The **epididymis** stores the sperm as it matures. Mature sperm moves from the epididymis through the **vas deferens** to the **ejaculatory duct**. The **seminal vesicles** secrete alkaline fluids with proteins and mucus into the ejaculatory duct also. The **prostate gland** secretes a milky white fluid with proteins and enzymes as part of the semen. The **bulbourethral**, or Cowper's, glands secrete a fluid into the urethra to neutralize the acidity in the urethra, which would damage sperm.

Additionally, the hormones associated with the male reproductive system include **follicle-stimulating hormone (FSH)**, which stimulates spermatogenesis; **luteinizing hormone (LH)**, which stimulates testosterone production; and **testosterone**, which is responsible for the male sex characteristics. FSH and LH are gonadotropins, which stimulate the gonads (male testes and female ovaries). FSH and LH are gonadotropins, which stimulate the gonads (male testes and female ovaries).

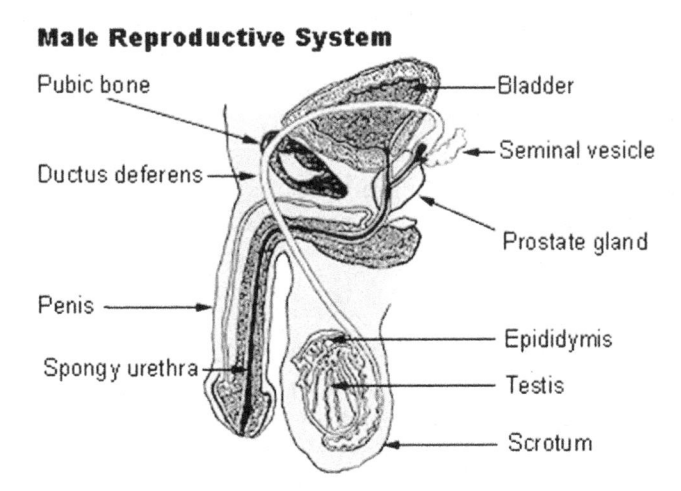

Male Reproductive System

FEMALE REPRODUCTIVE SYSTEM

The functions of the female reproductive system are to produce **ova** (oocytes or egg cells), transfer the ova to the **fallopian tubes** for fertilization, receive the sperm from the male, and provide a protective, nourishing environment for the developing **embryo**.

The external portion of the female reproductive system includes the labia majora, labia minora, Bartholin's glands, and clitoris. The **labia majora** and the **labia minora** enclose and protect the vagina. The **Bartholin's glands** secrete a lubricating fluid. The **clitoris** contains erectile tissue and nerve endings for sensual pleasure.

The internal portion of the female reproductive system includes the ovaries, fallopian tubes, uterus, and vagina. The **ovaries**, which are the female gonads, produce the ova and secrete **estrogen** and **progesterone**. The **fallopian tubes** carry the mature egg toward the uterus. Fertilization typically occurs in the fallopian tubes. If fertilized, the egg travels to the **uterus**, where it implants in the uterine wall. The uterus protects and nourishes the developing embryo until birth. The **vagina** is a muscular tube that extends from the **cervix** of the uterus to the outside of the body. The vagina receives the semen and sperm during sexual intercourse and provides a birth canal when needed.

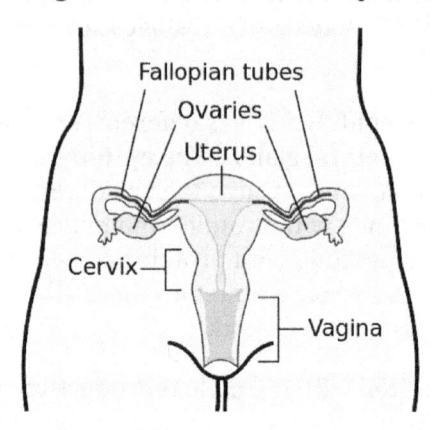

FEMALE REPRODUCTIVE CYCLE

The female reproductive cycle is characterized by changes in both the ovaries and the uterine lining (endometrium).

The ovarian cycle has three phases: the follicular phase, ovulation, and the luteal phase. During the **follicular phase**, FSH stimulates the maturation of the follicle, which then secretes estrogen. Estrogen helps to regenerate the uterine lining that was shed during menstruation. **Ovulation**, the release of a secondary oocyte from the ovary, is induced by a surge in LH. The **luteal phase** begins with the formation of the corpus luteum from the remnants of the follicle. The corpus luteum secretes progesterone and estrogen, which inhibit FSH and LH. Progesterone also maintains the thickness of the endometrium. Without the implantation of a fertilized egg, the corpus luteum begins to regress, and the levels of estrogen and progesterone drop. FSH and LH are no longer inhibited, and the cycle renews.

The uterine cycle also consists of three phases: the proliferative phase, secretory phase, and menstrual phase. The **proliferative phase** is characterized by the regeneration of the uterine lining. During the **secretory phase**, the endometrium becomes increasingly vascular, and nutrients are secreted to prepare for implantation. Without implantation, the endometrium is shed during **menstruation**.

PREGNANCY, PARTURITION, LACTATION

Pregnancy: When a blastocyst implants in the uterine lining, it releases hCG. This hormone prevents the corpus luteum from degrading, and it continues to produce estrogen and progesterone. These hormones are necessary to maintain the uterine lining. By the second trimester, the placenta secretes enough of its own estrogen and progesterone to sustain pregnancy and the levels continue to increase throughout pregnancy, while hCG hormone levels decrease.

Parturition: The precise mechanism for the initiation of parturition (birth) is unclear. Birth is preceded by increased levels of fetal glucocorticoids, which act on the placenta to increase estrogen and decrease progesterone. Stretching of the cervix stimulates the release of oxytocin from the posterior pituitary gland. Oxytocin and estrogen stimulate the release of prostaglandins, and prostaglandins and oxytocin increase uterine contractions. This positive feedback mechanism results in the birth of the fetus.

Lactation: During pregnancy, levels of the hormone prolactin increase, but its effect on the mammary glands is inhibited by estrogen and progesterone. After parturition, the levels of these hormones decrease, and prolactin is able to stimulate the production of milk. Suckling stimulates the release of oxytocin, which results in the ejection of milk.

Integumentary System

The integumentary system, which consists of the skin including the sebaceous glands, sweat glands, hair, and nails, serves a variety of functions associated with protection, secretion, and communication. In the functions associated with protection, the integumentary system protects the body from **pathogens** including bacteria, viruses, and various chemicals. In the functions associated with secretion, **sebaceous glands** secrete **sebum** (oil) that waterproofs the skin, and **sweat glands** are associated with the body's homeostatic relationship of **thermoregulation**. Sweat glands also serve as excretory organs and help rid the body of metabolic wastes. In the functions associated with communication, **sensory receptors** distributed throughout the skin send information to the brain regarding pain, touch, pressure, and temperature. In addition to protection, secretion, and communication, the skin manufactures **vitamin D** and can absorb certain chemicals such as specific medications.

> **Review Video: Integumentary System**
> Visit mometrix.com/academy and enter code: 655980

LAYERS OF THE SKIN

The layers of the skin from the surface of the skin inward are the epidermis and dermis. The subcutaneous layer lying below the dermis is also part of the integumentary system. The **epidermis** is the most superficial layer of the skin. The epidermis, which consists entirely of **epithelial cells**, does not contain any blood vessels. The deepest portion of the epidermis is the **stratum basale**, which is a single layer of cells that continually undergo division. As more and more cells are produced, older cells are pushed toward the surface. Most epidermal cells are keratinized. **Keratin** is a waxy protein that helps to waterproof the skin. As the cells die, they are sloughed off. The **dermis** lies directly beneath the epidermis. The dermis consists mostly of connective tissue. The dermis contains blood vessels, sensory receptors, hair follicles, sebaceous glands, and sweat glands. The dermis also contains **elastin** and **collagen fibers**. The **subcutaneous layer** or **hypodermis** is actually not a layer of the skin. The subcutaneous layer consists of connective tissue, which binds the skin to the underlying muscles. Fat deposits in the subcutaneous layer help to cushion and insulate the body.

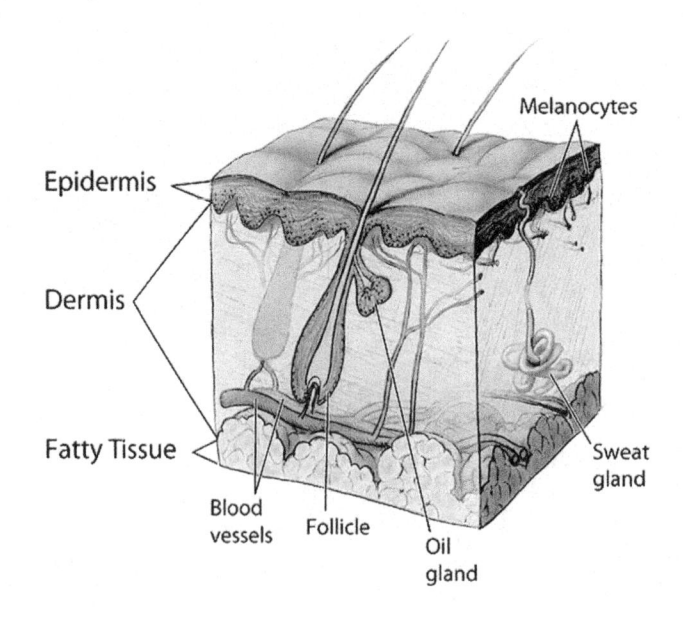

The types of cells found in the epidermis and dermis:

Cell Type	Location	Description
Keratinocytes	Epidermis	The most common type of cell in the epidermis
		Arise from stem cells in the stratum basale
		They flatten and die as they move toward the surface of the skin
		Produce keratin - a fibrous protein that hardens the cell and helps make the skin water resistant
Melanocytes	Epidermis	Produces melanin - a pigment that gives skin its color and protects against UV radiation
Langerhans cells	Epidermis	Antigen-presenting cells of the immune system (phagocytes)
		More common in stratum spinosum than other layers of epidermis
Merkel cells	Epidermis	Cutaneous receptors, detect light touch. Located in stratum basale
Fibroblasts	Dermis	Secrete collagen, elastin, glycosaminoglycans, and other components of the extracellular matrix
Adipocytes	Dermis	Fat cells
Macrophages	Dermis	Phagocytic cells that engulf potential pathogens
Mast cells	Dermis	Antigen-presenting cells that play a role in the inflammatory response (release histamine)

SKIN'S INVOLVEMENT IN TEMPERATURE HOMEOSTASIS

The skin is involved in **temperature homeostasis** or thermoregulation through the activation of the sweat glands. By **thermoregulation**, the body maintains a stable body temperature as one component of a stable internal environment. The temperature of the body is controlled by a negative feedback system consisting of a receptor, control center, and effector. The **receptors** are sensory cells located in the dermis of the skin. The **control center** is the **hypothalamus**, which is located in the brain. The **effectors** include the *sweat glands, blood vessels, and muscles* (shivering). The evaporation of sweat across the surface of the skin cools the body to maintain its tolerance range. **Vasodilation** of the blood vessels near the surface of the skin also releases heat into the environment to lower body temperature. Shivering is associated with the muscular system.

SEBACEOUS GLANDS VS. SWEAT GLANDS

Sebaceous glands and sweat glands are exocrine glands found in the skin. **Exocrine glands** secrete substances into **ducts**. In this case, the secretions are through the ducts to the surface of the skin.

Sebaceous glands are **holocrine glands**, which secrete sebum. **Sebum** is an oily mixture of lipids and proteins. Sebaceous glands are connected to hair follicles and secrete sebum through the hair pore. Sebum inhibits water loss from the skin and protects against bacterial and fungal infections.

Sweat glands are either eccrine glands or apocrine glands. **Eccrine glands** are not connected to hair follicles. They are activated by elevated body temperature. Eccrine glands are located throughout the body and can be found on the forehead, neck, and back. Eccrine glands secrete a salty solution of electrolytes and water containing sodium chloride, potassium, bicarbonate, glucose, and antimicrobial peptides.

Eccrine glands are activated as part of the body's thermoregulation. **Apocrine glands** secrete an oily solution containing fatty acids, triglycerides, and proteins. Apocrine glands are located in the armpits, groin, palms, and soles of the feet. Apocrine glands secrete this oily sweat when a person experiences stress or anxiety. Bacteria feed on apocrine sweat and expel aromatic fatty acids, producing body odor.

Endocrine System

The endocrine system is responsible for secreting the **hormones** and other molecules that help regulate the entire body in both the short and the long term. There is a close working relationship between the endocrine system and the nervous system. The **hypothalamus** and the **pituitary gland** coordinate to serve as a **neuroendocrine control center**.

Hormone secretion is triggered by a variety of signals, including hormonal signs, chemical reactions, and environmental cues. Only cells with particular **receptors** can benefit from hormonal influence. This is the "key in the lock" model for hormonal action. **Steroid hormones** trigger gene activation and protein synthesis in some target cells. **Protein hormones** change the activity of existing enzymes in target cells. Hormones such as **insulin** work quickly when the body signals an urgent need. Slower acting hormones afford longer, gradual, and sometimes permanent changes in the body.

Endocrine glands are intimately involved in a myriad of reactions, functions, and secretions that are crucial to the well-being of the body. The eight major endocrine glands and their functions include the following:

- **Adrenal cortex**: Monitors blood sugar level; helps in lipid and protein metabolism
- **Adrenal medulla**: Controls cardiac function; raises blood sugar and controls the size of blood vessels
- **Thyroid gland**: Helps regulate metabolism and functions in growth and development
- **Parathyroid**: Regulates calcium levels in the blood
- **Pancreas islets**: Raises and lowers blood sugar; active in carbohydrate metabolism
- **Thymus gland**: Plays a role in immune responses
- **Pineal gland**: Has an influence on daily biorhythms and sexual activity
- **Pituitary gland**: Plays an important role in growth and development

> **Review Video: Endocrine System**
> Visit mometrix.com/academy and enter code: 678939

HORMONES OF THE HYPOTHALAMUS AND PITUITARY

The **hypothalamus** is the link between the nervous system and the endocrine system. It is located in the brain, superior to the pituitary and inferior to the thalamus. The hypothalamus communicates with the pituitary by secreting "releasing hormones" (RH) and "inhibiting hormones" (IH). Hormones of the hypothalamus include:

Hormone	Action
GnRH - gonadotropin RH	Stimulates anterior pituitary to release LH and FSH
GHRH - growth hormone RH	Stimulates anterior pituitary to release GH
GHIH - growth hormone IH (somatostatin)	Inhibits the release of GH from the anterior pituitary
TRH - thyrotropin RH	Stimulates anterior pituitary to release thyrotropin (TSH)
PRH - prolactin RH	Stimulates anterior pituitary to release prolactin
PIH - prolactin IH (dopamine)	Inhibits the release of prolactin from the anterior pituitary
CRH - corticotropin RH	Stimulates anterior pituitary to release ACTH
Oxytocin	Targets the uterus - stimulates contractions. Targets the mammary glands - milk secretion
ADH - antidiuretic hormone (vasopressin)	Targets the kidneys and blood vessels - increases water retention

The **pituitary** is nicknamed the "master gland" because many of the hormones it secretes act on other endocrine glands. It is located within the sella turcica of the sphenoid bone, beneath the hypothalamus. This pea-sized gland hangs from a thin stalk called the infundibulum, and it consists of an anterior and posterior lobe - each with a different function.

Source	Hormone	Action
Pituitary gland (anterior)	TSH - thyroid stimulating hormone (thyrotropin)	Targets the thyroid - stimulates the secretion of thyroid hormones
	ACTH - adrenocorticotropic hormone	Targets the adrenal cortex - stimulates the release of glucocorticoids and mineralocorticoids
	GH - growth hormone	Targets muscle and bone - stimulates growth
	FSH - follicle stimulating hormone	Targets the gonads - stimulates the maturation of sperm cells and ovarian follicles
	LH - luteinizing hormone	Targets the gonads - stimulates the production of sex hormones; surge stimulates ovulation in females
	PRL - prolactin	Targets the mammary glands - stimulates production of milk
Pituitary gland (posterior)	Oxytocin (produced in hypothalamus; stored and released by posterior pituitary)	Targets the uterus - stimulates contractions
		Targets the mammary glands - stimulates milk secretion
	ADH - antidiuretic hormone (vasopressin) (produced in hypothalamus; stored and released by posterior pituitary)	Targets the kidneys and blood vessels - increases water retention

Hormone Sources of the Head and Neck

Source/Description	Hormone	Action
Pineal gland Situated between the two hemispheres of the brain where the two halves of the thalamus join.	Melatonin	Targets the brain - regulates daily rhythm (wake and sleep)
Thyroid gland Butterfly-shaped gland; the point of attachment between the two lobes is called the isthmus. The isthmus is on the anterior portion of the trachea, with the lobes wrapping partially around the trachea.	T_3 - triiodothyronine	Targets most cells - stimulates cellular metabolism
	T_4 - thyroxine	Targets most cells - stimulates cellular metabolism
	Calcitonin	Targets bone and kidneys - lowers blood calcium
Parathyroid gland Four small glands that are embedded in the posterior aspect of the thyroid.	PTH - Parathyroid hormone	Targets bone and kidneys - raises blood calcium

Hormone Sources of the Abdomen

Source/Description	Hormone	Action
Thymus gland Located between the sternum and the heart, embedded in the mediastinum. It slowly decreases in size after puberty.	Thymosin	Targets lymphatic tissues - stimulates the production of T-cells
Pancreas The head of the pancreas is situated in the curve of the duodenum and the tail points toward the left side of the body. The pancreas is mostly posterior to the stomach.	Insulin	Targets the liver, muscle, and adipose tissue - decreases blood glucose
	Glucagon	Targets the liver - increases blood glucose
	GHIH - growth hormone IH (somatostatin)	Inhibits the secretion of insulin and glucagon
Adrenal medulla Located on top of the kidneys. The adrenal medulla is the inner part of the gland.	Epinephrine and norepinephrine	Target heart, blood vessels, liver, and lungs - increase heart rate, increase blood sugar (fight or flight response)
Adrenal cortex The adrenal cortex is the outer portion of the adrenal gland.	Mineralocorticoids (aldosterone)	Target the kidneys - increase the retention of Na^+ and excretion of K^+
	Glucocorticoids	Target most tissues - released in response to long-term stressors, increase blood glucose (but not as quickly as glucagon)
	Androgens	Target most tissues - stimulate development of secondary sex characteristics

Source/Description	Hormone	Action
GI tract	Gastrin	Targets the stomach - stimulates the release of HCl
	Secretin	Targets the pancreas and liver - stimulates the release of digestive enzymes and bile
	CCK - cholecystokinin	Targets the pancreas and liver - stimulates the release of digestive enzymes and bile
Kidneys	Erythropoietin	Targets the bone marrow - stimulates the production of red blood cells
	Calcitriol	Targets the intestines - increases the reabsorption of Ca^{2+}
Heart	ANP - atrial natriuretic peptide	Targets the kidneys and adrenal cortex - reduces reabsorption of Na^+, lowers blood pressure
Adipose Tissue	Leptin	Targets the brain - suppresses appetite

HORMONE SOURCES OF THE REPRODUCTIVE SYSTEM

Source/Description	Hormone	Action
Ovaries The ovaries rest in depressions in the pelvic cavity on each side of the uterus. (Note that ovaries produce testosterone in small amounts.)	Estrogen	Target the uterus, ovaries, mammary glands, brain, and other tissues - stimulate uterine lining growth, regulate menstrual cycle, facilitate the development of secondary sex characteristics
	Progesterone	Targets mainly the uterus and mammary glands - stimulates uterine lining growth, regulates menstrual cycle, required for maintenance of pregnancy
	Inhibin	Targets the anterior pituitary - inhibits the release of FSH
Placenta Attached to the wall of the uterus during pregnancy	Estrogen, progesterone, and inhibin	(See above)
	Human chorionic gonadotropin (hCG)	Targets the ovaries - stimulates the production of estrogen and progesterone
Testes Located within the scrotum, behind the penis.	Testosterone	Targets the testes and many other tissues - promotes spermatogenesis, secondary sex characteristics
	Inhibin	(See above)

Urinary System

The urinary system is capable of eliminating excess substances while preserving the substances needed by the body to function. The **urinary system** consists of the kidneys, urinary ducts, and bladder.

Components of the Urinary System

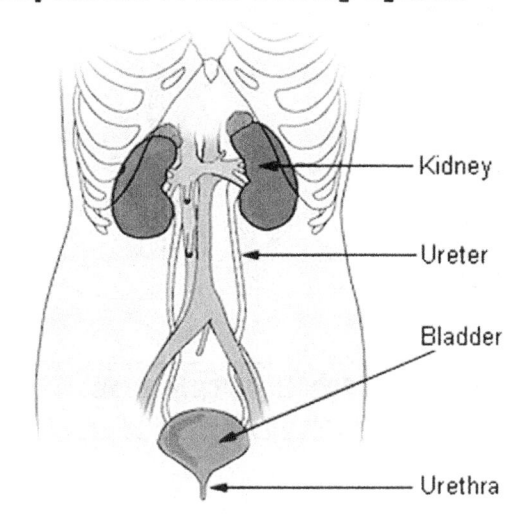

[Diagram showing Kidney, Ureter, Bladder, Urethra]

> **Review Video: Urinary System**
> Visit mometrix.com/academy and enter code: 601053

KIDNEYS

The kidneys are bean-shaped organs that are located at the back of the abdominal cavity just under the diaphragm. Each **kidney** (the labelled diagram on the left) consists of the renal cortex (outer layer), renal medulla (inner layer), and renal pelvis, which collects waste products from the nephrons and funnels them to the ureter.

The **renal cortex** (1) is composed of approximately one million **nephrons** (6 and the labelled diagram on the right), which are the tiny, individual filters of the kidneys. Each nephron contains a cluster of capillaries called a **glomerulus** (8) surrounded by the cup-shaped **Bowman's capsule** (9), which leads to a **tubule** (10).

The kidneys receive blood from the **renal arteries (3)**, which branch off the aorta. In general, the kidneys filter the blood (F), reabsorb needed materials (R), and secrete (S) and excrete (E) wastes and excess water in the urine. More specifically, blood flows from the renal arteries into **arterioles** (7) into the glomerulus, where it is filtered. The **glomerular filtrate** enters the **proximal convoluted tubule**, where water, glucose, ions, and other organic molecules are reabsorbed back into the bloodstream through the **renal vein** (4). Reabsorption and secretion occur between the tubules and the **peritubular capillaries** (12).

Additional substances such as urea and drugs are removed from the blood in the **distal convoluted tubule**. Also, the pH of the blood can be adjusted in the distal convoluted tubule by the secretion of **hydrogen ions**. Finally, the unabsorbed materials flow out from the collecting tubules located in the **renal medulla** (2) to the **renal pelvis** as urine. Urine is drained from the kidneys through the

ureters (5) to the **urinary bladder**, where it is stored until expulsion from the body through the **urethra**.

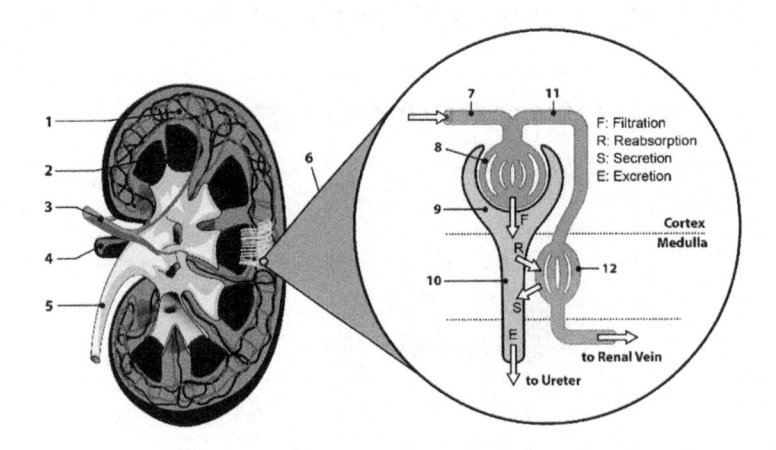

Review Video: Urinary System
Visit mometrix.com/academy and enter code: 601053

Immune System

The immune system protects the body against invading **pathogens** including bacteria, viruses, fungi, and protists. The immune system includes the **lymphatic system** (lymph, lymph capillaries, lymph vessel, and lymph nodes) as well as the **red bone marrow** and numerous **leukocytes**, or white blood cells. Tissue fluid enters the **lymph capillaries**, which combine to form **lymph vessels**. Skeletal muscle contractions move the lymph one way through the lymphatic system to lymphatic ducts, which dump back into the venous blood supply and the **lymph nodes**, which are situated along the lymph vessels, and filter the lymph of pathogens and other matter. The lymph nodes are concentrated in the neck, armpits, and groin areas. Outside the lymphatic vessel system lies the **lymphatic tissue,** including the tonsils, adenoids, thymus, spleen, and Peyer's patches. The **tonsils**, located in the pharynx, protect against pathogens entering the body through the mouth and throat. The **thymus** serves as a maturation chamber for immature T cells that are formed in the bone marrow. The **spleen** cleans the blood of dead cells and pathogens. **Peyer's patches**, which are located in the small intestine, protect the digestive system from pathogens.

> **Review Video: Immune System**
> Visit mometrix.com/academy and enter code: 622899

The body's general immune defenses include:

- **Skin** – An intact epidermis and dermis form a formidable barrier against bacteria.
- **Ciliated Mucous Membranes** – Cilia sweep pathogens out of the respiratory tract.
- **Glandular Secretions** – Secretions from exocrine glands destroy bacteria.
- **Gastric Secretions** – Gastric acid destroys pathogens.
- **Normal Bacterial Populations** – Compete with pathogens in the gut and vagina.

In addition, **phagocytes** and inflammation responses mobilize white blood cells and chemical reactions to stop infection. These responses include localized redness, tissue repair, and fluid-seeping healing agents. Additionally, **plasma proteins** act as the complement system to repel bacteria and pathogens.

Three types of white blood cells form the foundation of the body's immune system:

- **Macrophages** – Phagocytes that alert T cells to the presence of foreign substances.
- **T Lymphocytes** – These directly attack cells infected by viruses and bacteria.
- **B Lymphocytes** – These cells target specific bacteria for destruction.

Memory cells, **suppressor T cells**, and **helper T cells** also contribute to the body's defense. Immune responses can be **antibody-mediated** when the response is to an antigen, or **cell-mediated** when the response is to already infected cells. These responses are controlled and measured counterattacks that recede when the foreign agents are destroyed. Once an invader has attacked the body, if it returns it is immediately recognized and a secondary immune response occurs. This secondary response is rapid and powerful, much more so than the original response. These memory lymphocytes circulate throughout the body for years, alert to a possible new attack.

TYPES OF LEUKOCYTES

Leukocytes, or white blood cells, are produced in the red bone marrow. Leukocytes can be classified as **monocytes** (macrophages and dendritic cells), **granulocytes** (neutrophils, basophils, and eosinophils), **T lymphocytes**, **B lymphocytes**, or **natural killer cells**.

Macrophages found traveling in the lymph or fixed in lymphatic tissue are the largest, long-living phagocytes that engulf and destroy pathogens. **Dendritic cells** present antigens (foreign particles) to T cells. **Neutrophils** are short-living phagocytes that respond quickly to invaders. **Basophils** alert the body of invasion. **Eosinophils** are large, long-living phagocytes that defend against multicellular invaders.

T lymphocytes or T cells include helper T cells, killer T cells, suppressor T cells, and memory T cells. **Helper T cells** help the body fight infections by producing antibodies and other chemicals. **Killer T cells** destroy cells that are infected with a virus or pathogen and tumor cells. **Suppressor T cells** stop or "suppress" the other T cells when the battle is over. **Memory T cells** remain in the blood on alert in case the invader attacks again. **B lymphocytes**, or B cells, produce antibodies.

ANTIGEN AND TYPICAL IMMUNE RESPONSE

Antigens are substances that stimulate the **immune system**. Antigens are typically proteins on the surfaces of bacteria, viruses, and fungi.

Substances such as drugs, toxins, and foreign particles can also be antigens. The human body recognizes the antigens of its own cells, but it will attack cells or substances with unfamiliar antigens.

Specific **antibodies** are produced for each antigen that enters the body. In a typical immune response, when a pathogen or foreign substance enters the body, it is engulfed by a **macrophage**, which presents fragments of the antigen on its surface. A **helper T cell** joins the macrophage, and the killer (cytotoxic) T cells and B cells are activated. **Killer T cells** search out and destroy cells presenting the same antigens. **B cells** differentiate into plasma cells and memory cells.

Plasma cells produce antibodies specific to that pathogen or foreign substance. **Antibodies** bind to antigens on the surface of pathogens and mark them for destruction by other phagocytes. **Memory cells** remain in the blood stream to protect against future infections from the same pathogen.

ACTIVE AND PASSIVE IMMUNITY

At birth, an **innate immune system** protects an individual from pathogens. When an individual encounters infection or has an immunization, the individual develops an **adaptive immunity** that reacts to pathogens. So, this adaptive immunity is acquired. Active and passive immunities can be acquired naturally or artificially.

A **naturally acquired active immunity** is natural because the individual is exposed and builds immunity to a pathogen *without an immunization*. An **artificially acquired active immunity** is artificial because the individual is exposed and builds immunity to a pathogen *by a vaccine*.

A **naturally acquired passive immunity** is natural because it happens *during pregnancy* as antibodies move from the mother's bloodstream to the bloodstream of the fetus. The antibodies can also be transferred from a mother's breast milk. During infancy, these antibodies provide temporary protection until childhood.

An **artificially acquired passive immunity** is an *immunization* that is given in recent outbreaks or emergency situations. This immunization provides quick and short-lived protection to disease by the use of antibodies that can come from another person or animal.

> **Review Video: Immune System**
> Visit mometrix.com/academy and enter code: 622899

Skeletal System

Axial Skeleton and the Appendicular Skeleton

The human skeletal system, which consists of 206 bones along with numerous tendons, ligaments, and cartilage, is divided into the axial skeleton and the appendicular skeleton.

The **axial skeleton** consists of 80 bones and includes the vertebral column, rib cage, sternum, skull, and hyoid bone. The **vertebral column** consists of 33 vertebrae classified as cervical vertebrae, thoracic vertebrae, lumbar vertebrae, and sacral vertebrae. The **rib cage** includes 12 paired ribs, 10 pairs of true ribs and two pairs of floating ribs, and the **sternum**, which consists of the manubrium, corpus sterni, and xiphoid process. The **skull** includes the cranium and facial bones. The **ossicles** are bones in the middle ear. The **hyoid bone** provides an attachment point for the tongue muscles. The axial skeleton protects vital organs including the brain, heart, and lungs.

The **appendicular skeleton** consists of 126 bones including the pectoral girdle, pelvic girdle, and appendages. The **pectoral girdle** consists of the scapulae (shoulder blades) and clavicles (collarbones). The **pelvic girdle** attaches to the sacrum at the sacroiliac joint. The upper appendages (arms) include the humerus, radius, ulna, carpals, metacarpals, and phalanges. The lower appendages (legs) include the femur, patella, fibula, tibia, tarsals, metatarsals, and phalanges.

> **Review Video: Skeletal System**
> Visit mometrix.com/academy and enter code: 256447

Adult Human Skeleton

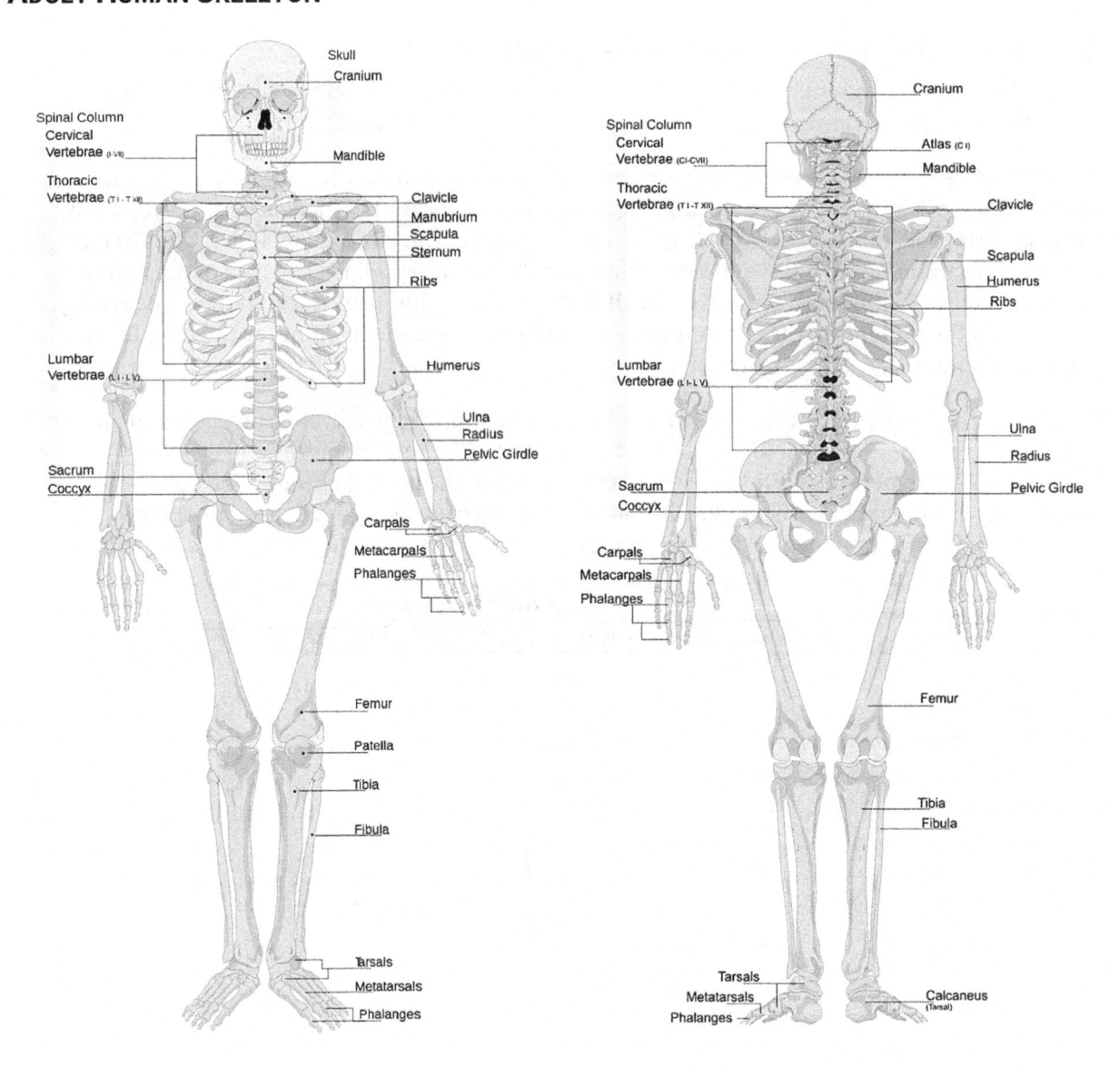

Joint Structures

Joints are the locations where two or more elements of the skeleton connect. They can be classified according to range of motion, as well as the material that holds the joint together.

Functional classification

Class	Description	Range of Motion	Examples
Synarthrosis	Either fibrous or cartilaginous	Immovable	Skull sutures, teeth/mandible
Amphiarthrosis	Either fibrous or cartilaginous	Slight	Intervertebral discs, distal tibiofibular joint
Diarthrosis	Always synovial	Free movement	Wrist, knee, shoulder

Structural classification

Class	Description	Types, Range of Motion	Examples
Fibrous	Held together by fibrous connective tissue	**Suture**: immovable	skull
		Gomphosis: immovable	teeth/mandible
		Syndesmosis: slightly movable	distal tibiofibular joint
Cartilaginous	Held together by cartilage	**Synchondrosis**: hyaline cartilage, nearly immovable	first rib/sternum
		Symphysis: fibrocartilage, slightly movable	intervertebral discs, pubic symphysis
Synovial	The most common type of joint; characterized by a joint cavity filled with synovial fluid	**Pivot**: allows rotation	atlantoaxial joint
		Hinge: allows movement in one plane	knee
		Saddle: allows pivoting in two planes and axial rotation	first metacarpal/ trapezium
		Gliding: allows sliding	carpals
		Condyloid: allows pivoting in two planes but no axial rotation	radiocarpal joint
		Ball and socket: have the highest range of motion	hip

FUNCTIONS OF THE SKELETAL SYSTEM

The skeletal system serves many functions including providing structural support, providing movement, providing protection, producing blood cells, and storing substances such as fat and minerals. The skeletal system provides the body with structure and support for the muscles and organs. The axial skeleton transfers the weight from the upper body to the lower appendages. The skeletal system provides movement with **joints** and the muscular system. Bones provide attachment points for muscles. Joints including **hinge joints**, **ball-and-socket joints**, **pivot joints**, **ellipsoid joints**, **gliding joints**, and **saddle joints**. Each muscle is attached to two bones: the origin and the insertion. The **origin** remains immobile, and the **insertion** is the bone that moves as the muscle contracts and relaxes. The skeletal system serves to protect the body. The **cranium** protects the brain. The **vertebrae** protect the spinal cord. The **rib cage** protects the heart and lungs. The **pelvis** protects the reproductive organs. The **red marrow** manufactures red and white blood cells. All bone marrow is red at birth, but adults have approximately one-half red bone marrow and one-half yellow bone marrow. **Yellow bone marrow** stores fat. Also, the skeletal system provides a reservoir to store the minerals **calcium** and **phosphorus**.

The skeletal system has an important role in the following body functions:

- **Movement** – The action of skeletal muscles on bones moves the body.
- **Mineral Storage** – Bones serve as storage facilities for essential mineral ions.
- **Support** – Bones act as a framework and support system for the organs.
- **Protection** – Bones surround and protect key organs in the body.
- **Blood Cell Formation** – Red blood cells are produced in the marrow of certain bones.

Bones are classified as long, short, flat, or irregular. They are a connective tissue with a base of pulp containing **collagen** and living cells. Bone tissue is constantly regenerating itself as the mineral composition changes. This allows for special needs during growth periods and maintains calcium levels for the body. Bone regeneration can deteriorate in old age, particularly among women, leading to **osteoporosis**.

The flexible and curved **backbone** is supported by muscles and ligaments. **Intervertebral discs** are stacked one above another and provide cushioning for the backbone. Trauma or shock may cause these discs to **herniate** and cause pain. The sensitive **spinal cord** is enclosed in a cavity which is well protected by the bones of the vertebrae.

Joints are areas of contact adjacent to bones. **Synovial joints** are the most common, and are freely moveable. These may be found at the shoulders and knees. **Cartilaginous joints** fill the spaces between some bones and restrict movement. Examples of cartilaginous joints are those between vertebrae. **Fibrous joints** have fibrous tissue connecting bones and no cavity is present.

COMPACT AND SPONGY BONE

Compact Bone & Spongy (Cancellous) Bone

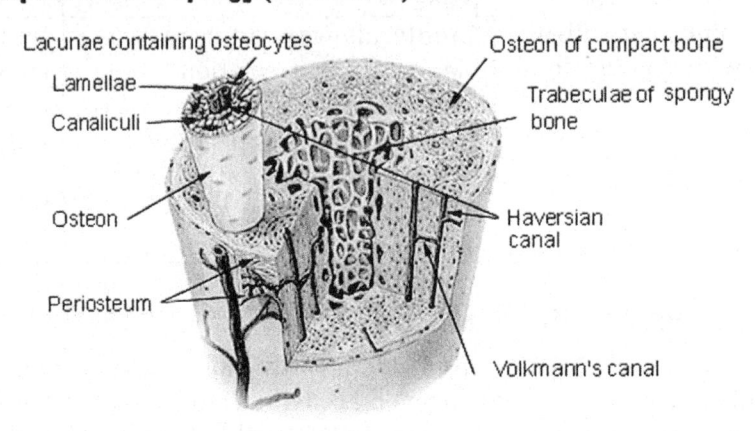

Two types of connective bone tissue include compact bone and spongy bone.

Compact, or **cortical**, bone, which consists of tightly packed cells, is strong, dense, and rigid. Running vertically throughout compact bone are the **Haversian canals**, which are surrounded by concentric circles of bone tissue called **lamellae**. The spaces between the lamellae are called the **lacunae**. These lamellae and canals along with their associated arteries, veins, lymph vessels, and nerve endings are referred to collectively as the **Haversian system**.

The Haversian system provides a reservoir for calcium and phosphorus for the blood. Also, bones have a thin outside layer of compact bone, which gives them their characteristic smooth, white appearance.

Spongy, or **cancellous**, bone consists of **trabeculae**, which are a network of girders with open spaces filled with red bone marrow.

Compared to compact bone, spongy bone is lightweight and porous, which helps reduce the bone's overall weight. The red marrow manufactures red and white blood cells. In long bones, the **diaphysis** consists of compact bone surrounding the marrow cavity and spongy bone containing red marrow in the **epiphyses**. Bones have varying amounts of compact bone and spongy bone depending on their classification.

KNAT Practice Test #1

Want to take this practice test in an online interactive format?
Check out the bonus page, which includes interactive practice questions and
much more: **http://www.mometrix.com/bonus948/knat**

Reading Comprehension

Questions 1-4 pertain to the following passage:

It is most likely that you have never had diphtheria. You probably don't even know anyone who has suffered from this disease. In fact, you may not even know what diphtheria is. Similarly, diseases like whooping cough, measles, mumps, and rubella may all be unfamiliar to you. In the nineteenth and early twentieth centuries, these illnesses struck hundreds of thousands of people in the United States each year, mostly children, and tens of thousands of people died. The names of these diseases were frightening household words. Today, they are all but forgotten. That change happened largely because of vaccines.

You probably have been vaccinated against diphtheria. You may even have been exposed to the bacterium that causes it, but the vaccine prepared your body to fight off the disease so quickly that you were unaware of the infection. Vaccines take advantage of your body's natural ability to learn how to combat many disease-causing germs, or microbes. What's more, your body remembers how to protect itself from the microbes it has encountered before. Collectively, the parts of your body that remember and repel microbes are called the immune system. Without the proper functioning of the immune system, the simplest illness—even the common cold—could quickly turn deadly.

On average, your immune system needs more than a week to learn how to fight off an unfamiliar microbe. Sometimes, that isn't enough time. Strong microbes can spread through your body faster than the immune system can fend them off. Your body often gains the upper hand after a few weeks, but in the meantime you are sick. Certain microbes are so virulent that they can overwhelm or escape your natural defenses. In those situations, vaccines can make all the difference.

Traditional vaccines contain either parts of microbes or whole microbes that have been altered so that they don't cause disease. When your immune system confronts these harmless versions of the germs, it quickly clears them from your body. In other words, vaccines trick your immune system in order to teach your body important lessons about how to defeat its opponents.

1. What is the main idea of the passage?
   a. The nineteenth and early twentieth centuries were a dark period for medicine.
   b. You have probably never had diphtheria.
   c. Traditional vaccines contain altered microbes.
   d. Vaccines help the immune system function properly.

155

2. Which statement is *not* a detail from the passage?
   a. Vaccines contain microbe parts or altered microbes.
   b. The immune system typically needs a week to learn how to fight a new disease.
   c. The symptoms of disease do not emerge until the body has learned how to fight the microbe.
   d. A hundred years ago, children were at the greatest risk of dying from now-treatable diseases.

3. What is the meaning of the word *virulent* as it is used in the third paragraph?
   a. tiny
   b. malicious
   c. contagious
   d. annoying

4. What is the author's primary purpose in writing the essay?
   a. to entertain
   b. to persuade
   c. to inform
   d. to analyze

Questions 5-8 pertain to the following passage:

Foodborne illnesses are contracted by eating food or drinking beverages contaminated with bacteria, parasites, or viruses. Harmful chemicals can also cause foodborne illnesses if they have contaminated food during harvesting or processing. Foodborne illnesses can cause symptoms ranging from upset stomach to diarrhea, fever, vomiting, abdominal cramps, and dehydration. Most foodborne infections are undiagnosed and unreported, though the Centers for Disease Control and Prevention estimates that every year about 76 million people in the United States become ill from pathogens in food. About 5,000 of these people die.

Harmful bacteria are the most common cause of foodborne illness. Some bacteria may be present at the point of purchase. Raw foods are the most common source of foodborne illnesses because they are not sterile; examples include raw meat and poultry contaminated during slaughter. Seafood may become contaminated during harvest or processing. One in 10,000 eggs may be contaminated with Salmonella inside the shell. Produce, such as spinach, lettuce, tomatoes, sprouts, and melons, can become contaminated with Salmonella, Shigella, or Escherichia coli (E. coli). Contamination can occur during growing, harvesting, processing, storing, shipping, or final preparation. Sources of produce contamination vary, as these foods are grown in soil and can become contaminated during growth, processing, or distribution. Contamination may also occur during food preparation in a restaurant or a home kitchen. The most common form of contamination from handled foods is the calicivirus, also called the Norwalk-like virus.

When food is cooked and left out for more than two hours at room temperature, bacteria can multiply quickly. Most bacteria don't produce an odor or change in color or texture, so they can be impossible to detect. Freezing food slows or stops bacteria's growth, but does not destroy the bacteria. The microbes can become reactivated when the food is thawed. Refrigeration also can slow the growth of some bacteria. Thorough cooking is required to destroy the bacteria.

5. **What is the subject of the passage?**
   a. foodborne illnesses
   b. the dangers of uncooked food
   c. bacteria
   d. proper food preparation

6. **Which statement is *not* a detail from the passage?**
   a. Every year, more than 70 million Americans contract some form of foodborne illness.
   b. Once food is cooked, it cannot cause illness.
   c. Refrigeration can slow the growth of some bacteria.
   d. The most common form of contamination in handled foods is calicivirus.

7. **What is the meaning of the word *pathogens* as it is used in the first paragraph?**
   a. diseases
   b. vaccines
   c. disease-causing substances
   d. foods

8. **What is the meaning of the word *sterile* as it is used in the second paragraph?**
   a. free of bacteria
   b. healthy
   c. delicious
   d. impotent

Questions 9-12 pertain to the following passage:

There are a number of health problems related to bleeding in the esophagus and stomach. Stomach acid can cause inflammation and bleeding at the lower end of the esophagus. This condition, usually associated with the symptom of heartburn, is called esophagitis, or inflammation of the esophagus. Sometimes a muscle between the esophagus and stomach fails to close properly and allows the return of food and stomach juices into the esophagus, which can lead to esophagitis. In another unrelated condition, enlarged veins (varices) at the lower end of the esophagus rupture and bleed massively. Cirrhosis of the liver is the most common cause of esophageal varices. Esophageal bleeding can be caused by a tear in the lining of the esophagus (Mallory-Weiss syndrome). Mallory-Weiss syndrome usually results from vomiting, but may also be caused by increased pressure in the abdomen from coughing, hiatal hernia, or childbirth. Esophageal cancer can cause bleeding.

The stomach is a frequent site of bleeding. Infections with Helicobacter pylori (H. pylori), alcohol, aspirin, aspirin-containing medicines, and various other medicines (such as nonsteroidal anti-inflammatory drugs [NSAIDs]—particularly those used for arthritis) can cause stomach ulcers or inflammation (gastritis). The stomach is often the site of ulcer disease. Acute or chronic ulcers may enlarge and erode through a blood vessel, causing bleeding. Also, patients suffering from burns, shock, head injuries, cancer, or those who have undergone extensive surgery may develop stress ulcers. Bleeding can also occur from benign tumors or cancer of the stomach, although these disorders usually do not cause massive bleeding.

9. What is the main idea of the passage?
a. The digestive system is complex.
b. Of all the digestive organs, the stomach is the most prone to bleeding.
c. Both the esophagus and the stomach are subject to bleeding problems. ✓
d. Esophagitis afflicts the young and old alike.

10. Which statement is *not* a detail from the passage?
a. Alcohol can cause stomach bleeding.
b. Ulcer disease rarely occurs in the stomach.
c. Benign tumors rarely result in massive bleeding.
d. Childbirth is one cause of Mallory-Weiss syndrome.

11. What is the meaning of the word *rupture* as it is used in the first paragraph?
a. tear
b. collapse
c. implode
d. detach

12. What is the meaning of the word *erode* as it is used in the second paragraph?
a. avoid
b. divorce
c. contain
d. wear away

Questions 13-16 pertain to the following passage:

We met Kathy Blake while she was taking a stroll in the park . . . by herself. What's so striking about this is that Kathy is completely blind, and she has been for more than 30 years.

The diagnosis from her doctor was retinitis pigmentosa, or RP. It's an incurable genetic disease that leads to progressive visual loss. Photoreceptive cells in the retina slowly start to die, leaving the patient visually impaired.

"Life was great the year before I was diagnosed," Kathy said. "I had just started a new job; I just bought my first new car. I had just started dating my now-husband. Life was good. The doctor had told me that there was some good news and some bad news. 'The bad news is you are going to lose your vision; the good news is we don't think you are going to go totally blind.' Unfortunately, I did lose all my vision within about 15 years."

Two years ago, Kathy got a glimmer of hope. She heard about an artificial retina being developed in Los Angeles. It was experimental, but Kathy was the perfect candidate.

Dr. Mark Humayun is a retinal surgeon and biomedical engineer. "A good candidate for the artificial retina device is a person who is blind because of retinal blindness," he said. "They've lost the rods and cones, the light-sensing cells of the eye, but the rest of the circuitry is relatively intact. In the simplest rendition, this device basically takes a blind person and hooks them up to a camera."

It may sound like the stuff of science fiction . . . and just a few years ago it was. A camera is built into a pair of glasses, sending radio signals to a tiny chip in the back of the retina. The chip, small enough to fit on a fingertip, is implanted surgically and stimulates the nerves that lead to the vision center of the brain. Kathy is one of twenty patients who have undergone surgery and use the device.

It has been about two years since the surgery, and Kathy still comes in for weekly testing at the University of Southern California's medical campus. She scans back and forth with specially made, camera-equipped glasses until she senses objects on a screen and then touches the objects. The low-resolution image from the camera is still enough to make out the black stripes on the screen. Impulses are sent from the camera to the 60 receptors that are on the chip in her retina. So, what is Kathy seeing?

"I see flashes of light that indicate a contrast from light to dark—very similar to a camera flash, probably not quite as bright because it's not hurting my eye at all," she replied.

Humayun underscored what a breakthrough this is and how a patient adjusts. "If you've been blind for 30 or 50 years, (and) all of a sudden you get this device, there is a period of learning," he said. "Your brain needs to learn. And it's literally like seeing a baby crawl—to a child walk—to an adult run."

While hardly perfect, the device works best in bright light or where there is a lot of contrast. Kathy takes the device home. The software that runs the device can be upgraded. So, as the software is upgraded, her vision improves. Recently, she was outside with her husband on a moonlit night and saw something she hadn't seen for a long time.

"I scanned up in the sky (and) I got a big flash, right where the moon was, and pointed it out. I can't even remember how many years ago it's been that I would have ever been able to do that."

This technology has a bright future. The current chip has a resolution of 60 pixels. Humayun says that number could be increased to more than a thousand in the next version.

"I think it will be extremely exciting if they can recognize their loved ones' faces and be able to see what their wife or husband or their grandchildren look like, which they haven't seen," said Humayun.

Kathy dreams of a day when blindness like hers will be a distant memory. "My eye disease is hereditary," she said. "My three daughters happen to be fine, but I want to know that if my grandchildren ever have a problem, they will have something to give them some vision."

13. What is the primary subject of the passage?
a. a new artificial retina
b. Kathy Blake
c. hereditary disease
d. Dr. Mark Humayun

14. What is the meaning of the word *progressive* as it is used in the second paragraph?
a. selective
b. gradually increasing
c. diminishing
d. disabling

15. Which statement is *not* a detail from the passage?
    a. The use of an artificial retina requires a special pair of glasses.
    b. Retinal blindness is the inability to perceive light.
    c. Retinitis pigmentosa is curable.
    d. The artificial retina performs best in bright light.

16. What is the author's intention in writing the essay?
    a. to persuade
    b. to entertain
    c. to analyze
    d. to inform

Questions 17-22 pertain to the following passage:

The immune system is a network of cells, tissues, and organs that defends the body against attacks by foreign invaders. These invaders are primarily microbes—tiny organisms such as bacteria, parasites, and fungi—that can cause infections. Viruses also cause infections, but are too primitive to be classified as living organisms. The human body provides an ideal environment for many microbes. It is the immune system's job to keep the microbes out or destroy them.

The immune system is amazingly complex. It can recognize and remember millions of different enemies, and it can secrete fluids and cells to wipe out nearly all of them. The secret to its success is an elaborate and dynamic communications network. Millions of cells, organized into sets and subsets, gather and transfer information in response to an infection. Once immune cells receive the alarm, they produce powerful chemicals that help to regulate their own growth and behavior, enlist other immune cells, and direct the new recruits to trouble spots.

Although scientists have learned much about the immune system, they continue to puzzle over how the body destroys invading microbes, infected cells, and tumors without harming healthy tissues. New technologies for identifying individual immune cells are now allowing scientists to determine quickly which targets are triggering an immune response. Improvements in microscopy are permitting the first-ever observations of living B cells, T cells, and other cells as they interact within lymph nodes and other body tissues.

In addition, scientists are rapidly unraveling the genetic blueprints that direct the human immune response, as well as those that dictate the biology of bacteria, viruses, and parasites. The combination of new technology with expanded genetic information will no doubt reveal even more about how the body protects itself from disease.

17. What is the main idea of the passage?
    a. Scientists fully understand the immune system.
    b. The immune system triggers the production of fluids.
    c. The body is under constant invasion by malicious microbes.
    d. The immune system protects the body from infection.

18. Which statement is *not* a detail from the passage?
    a. Most invaders of the body are microbes.
    b. The immune system relies on excellent communication.
    c. Viruses are extremely sophisticated.
    d. The cells of the immune system are organized.

19. What is the meaning of the word *ideal* as it is used in the first paragraph?
    a. thoughtful
    b. confined
    c. hostile
    d. perfect

20. Which statement is *not* a detail from the passage?
    a. Scientists can now see T cells.
    b. The immune system ignores tumors.
    c. The ability of the immune system to fight disease without harming the body remains mysterious.
    d. The immune system remembers millions of different invaders.

21. What is the meaning of the word *enlist* as it is used in the second paragraph?
    a. call into service
    b. write down
    c. send away
    d. put across

22. What is the author's primary purpose in writing the essay?
    a. to persuade
    b. to analyze
    c. to inform
    d. to entertain

Writing

Questions 1-5 are based on the following passage.

¹In Ruth Campbell's book *Exploring the Titanic*, the events of the famous ship's only journey and sinking are brought to life. ²The Titanic was built in 1912, and it was the largest passenger steamship at the time. ³On what would be its first and only journey, the ship departed from Southampton in England and were supposed to arrive in New York City. ⁴The ship hit an iceberg late at night on April 14, 1912, and sank less than three hours later.

⁵Titanic was designed by some of the best engineers and had the latest technology of the time. ⁶The ship was made to carry over three and a half thousand passengers and crew members, but had only twenty lifeboats. ⁷There were not enough lifeboats for all of the people onboard, and as a result, only seven hundred six people survived.

⁸One interesting thing about Titanic is that the ship was divided into classes. ⁹The most expensive tickets were first class, and first-class passengers had the biggest and most luxerious rooms. ¹⁰Because of this arrangement the majority of the survivors came from first class. ¹¹They were able to reach the deck fastest to get a seat on a lifeboat. ¹²The third-class rooms were located the farthest below deck, and the majority of the third-class passengers did not survive.

¹³Ruth Campbell's book was very interesting but also sad because the story of Titanic is true. ¹⁴However, Campbell ended the book by talking about the positive things that have happened because of this tragedy. ¹⁵Most importantly, passenger ships are now required to carry enough lifeboats for all passengers onboard. ¹⁶Titanic had more passenger compartments than any ship that had been built. ¹⁷It was a good book, and it conveyed a good message that in history mistakes should teach us lessons to keep us from repeating them.

1. Which sentence contains an error in subject-verb agreement?

   a. Sentence 3
   b. Sentence 7
   c. Sentence 10
   d. Sentence 12

2. Which of the following changes corrects an error in punctuation?

   a. Remove the comma after *onboard* in sentence 7.
   b. Add a comma after *arrangement* in sentence 10.
   c. Remove the hyphen between *third* and *class* in sentence 12.
   d. Add a comma after *things* in sentence 14.

3. Which of the following sentences interrupts the flow of its paragraph by including off-topic information and should be moved or deleted?

   a. Sentence 4
   b. Sentence 7
   c. Sentence 13
   d. Sentence 16

4. Which word in the third paragraph is incorrect?

   a. The word *expensive* in sentence 9
   b. The word *luxerious* in sentence 9
   c. The word *arrangement* in sentence 10
   d. The word *passengers* in sentence 12

5. Where should the following sentence be added to the third paragraph?

   The first-class rooms were the closest to the ship's deck.

   a. After sentence 9.
   b. After sentence 10.
   c. After sentence 11.
   d. After sentence 12.

Questions 6-10 are based on the following passage.

¹Basketball is arguably, one of the most popular and most exciting sports of our time. ²Behind this fast-paced sport, however, is a rich history. ³There have been many changes made to the game over the years, but the essence remains the same. ⁴From it's humble beginnings in 1891, basketball has grown to have worldwide following.

⁵One thing that sets the history of basketball apart from other major sports is the fact that it was created by just one man. ⁶In 1891, Dr. James Naismith, a teacher and Presbyterian Minister, needed an indoor game to keep college students at the Springfield, Massachusetts, YMCA Training School busy during long winter days. ⁷This need prompted the creation of basketball, which was originally played by tossing a soccer ball into an empty peach basket nailed to the gym wall. ⁸There was two teams but only one basket in the original game.

⁹Because of the simplicity of basketball, the game had spread across the nation within 30 years of its invention in Massachusetts. ¹⁰As more teams formed, the need for a league became apparent. ¹¹On June 6, 1946, the Basketball Association of America (BAA) was formed. ¹²The smaller National Basketball League (NBL) formed soon after. ¹³The NBA played its first full season in 1948-49 and is still going strong today.

¹⁴Though much has changed in our world in the last hundred years, the popularity of the sport of basketball has remained strong. ¹⁵From a simple YMCA gym to the multi-million-dollar empire it is today, the appeal of the sport has endured. ¹⁶Although many changes have been made over the years, the essence of basketball has remained constant. ¹⁷Its rich history and simplicity ensure that basketball will always be a popular sport around the world.

6. Which of the following changes corrects an error in punctuation?

   a. Remove the comma after *arguably* in sentence 1.
   b. Add a comma after *sports* in sentence 5.
   c. Remove the hyphen between *multi* and *million* in sentence 15.
   d. Remove the comma after *years* in sentence 16.

7. Which of the following sentences repeats information from earlier in the passage and should be deleted for redundancy?
   a. Sentence 5
   b. Sentence 8
   c. Sentence 12
   d. Sentence 16

8. Which word in the passage is incorrect?
   a. The word *it's* in sentence 4
   b. The word *prompted* in sentence 7.
   c. The word *apparent* in sentence 10.
   d. The word *popularity* in sentence 14.

9. Which sentence contains an error in subject-verb agreement?
   a. Sentence 3
   b. Sentence 7
   c. Sentence 8
   d. Sentence 16

10. Where should the following sentence be added to the third paragraph?

    In 1948, the BAA absorbed the NBL, and the National Basketball Association (NBA) was born.

    a. After sentence 10.
    b. After sentence 11.
    c. After sentence 12.
    d. After sentence 13.

Questions 11-16 are based on the following passage.

¹The islands of New Zealand are among the most remote of all the Pacific islands. ²New Zealand is an archipelago, with two large islands and a number of smaller ones. ³Its climate is far cooler than the rest of Polynesia. ⁴According to Maori legends, it was colonized in the early fifteenth century by a wave of Polynesian voyagers who traveled southward in their canoes and settled on North Island. ⁵At this time, New Zealand will already be known to the Polynesians, who had probably first landed there some 400 years earlier.

⁶The Polynesian southward migration was limited by the availability of food. ⁷Traditional Polynesian tropical crops such as taro and breadfruit would grow on North Island, but the climate of the South Island was too cold for them. ⁸Coconuts would not grow on either island. ⁹The first settlers were forced to rely on hunting gathering, and fishing. ¹⁰Especially on the South Island, most settlements remained close to the sea. ¹¹These flightless birds were easy prey for the settlers, and within a few centuries they had been hunted to extinction. ¹²Fish, shellfish, and the roots of the fern were other important sources of food, but even these began to diminish in quantity as the human population increased. ¹³The Maori had few other sources of meat: dogs, smaller birds, and rats. ¹⁴Archaeological evidence show that human flesh was also eaten, and that tribal warfare increased markedly after the moa disappeared.

¹⁵By far the most important farmed crop in precolonial New Zealand was the sweet potato. ¹⁶This tuber was hearty enough to grow throughout the islands, and could be stored to provide food during the winter months, when other food-gathering activities were difficult. ¹⁷Maori tribes often

lived in encampments called *pa*, which were fortified with earthen embancments and usually located near the best sweet potato farmlands. ¹⁸Sweet potatoes have higher starch content than the crops the Maori grew on their native islands. ¹⁹The availability of the sweet potato made possible a significant increase in the human population and allowed the Maori to grow and thrive in relative peace in New Zealand for centuries.

11. Which of the following changes corrects an error in verb usage?
  a. In sentence 5, change *will already be* to *was already*.
  b. In sentence 7, change *was too cold* to *would be too cold*.
  c. In sentence 12, change *began to diminish* to *began diminishing*.
  d. In sentence 16, change *was hearty* to *is hearty*.

12. Which word in the passage is incorrect?
  a. The word *voyagers* in sentence 4
  b. The word *extinction* in sentence 11
  c. The word *Archaeological* in sentence 14
  d. The word *embancments* in sentence 17

13. Which sentence contains an error in subject-verb agreement?
  a. Sentence 4
  b. Sentence 12
  c. Sentence 14
  d. Sentence 18

14. Which of the following changes corrects an error in punctuation?
  a. Remove the comma after *archipelago* in sentence 2.
  b. Add a comma after *hunting* in sentence 9.
  c. Change the colon after *meat* to a semicolon in sentence 13.
  d. Remove the hyphen between *food* and *gathering* in sentence 16.

15. Where should the following sentence be added to the passage?

  At the time of the Polynesian incursion, enormous flocks of moa birds had their rookeries on the island shores.

  a. After sentence 6.
  b. After sentence 10.
  c. After sentence 12.
  d. After sentence 17.

16. Which of the following sentences interrupts the flow of its paragraph by including off-topic information and should be deleted?
  a. Sentence 7
  b. Sentence 12
  c. Sentence 15
  d. Sentence 18

Questions 17-21 are based on the following passage.

¹After Orville and Wilbur Wright flew the first successful airplane in 1903, the age of flying slowly began. ²Many new pilots learned how to fly in World War I, which the United States joined in 1917. ³During the war, the American public loved hearing stories, about the daring pilots and their

air fights. ⁴After the war ended though, many Americans thought that men and women belonged on the ground and not in the air.

⁵In the years after the war and through the Roaring Twenties, many of America's pilots found themselves without jobs. ⁶Some of them gave up flying altogether. ⁷Pilot Eddie Rickenbacker, who used to be called America's Ace of Aces, became a car salesman. ⁸But other pilots, however, found new and creative things to do with their airplanes.

⁹Pilot Casey Jones used his airplane to help get news across the country. ¹⁰When a big news story broke, Jones flew news photos to newspapers in different cities. ¹¹Another pilot, Roscoe Turner traveled around the country with a lion cub in his plane. ¹²The cub was the mascot of an oil company, and Turner convinced the company that flying the cub around would be a good advertisement. ¹³The Humane Society wasn't very happy about this idea, and they convinced Turner to make sure the lion cub always wore a parachute. ¹⁴In the 1920s, the U.S. Postal Service developed airmail. ¹⁵Prior to this, the post traveled on trains and can take weeks to reach a destination, but transporting the post by airplane allowed that time to be cut dramatically.

¹⁶Flying was dangerous work in those early days, because the aircraft of the time didn't have sophisticated instruments or much safety equipment. ¹⁷Many pilots had to bale out and use their parachutes when their planes iced up in the cold air or had other trouble. ¹⁸Despite all of the dangers and challenges of early aviation, these brave pioneers continued to make use of their ability to fly to advance the state of human civilization.

17. Which of the following changes corrects an error in verb usage?
    a. In sentence 2, change *learned* to *learn*.
    b. In sentence 5, change *found* to *founded*.
    c. In sentence 9, change *used* to *would have used*.
    d. In sentence 15, change *can* to *could*.

18. Which word used in the passage is unnecessary and should be deleted?
    a. The word *after* in sentence 1
    b. The word *altogether* in sentence 6.
    c. The word *but* in sentence 8.
    d. The word *because* in sentence 16.

19. Which of the following changes corrects an error in punctuation?
    a. Remove the comma after *stories* in sentence 3.
    b. Remove the comma after *Aces* in sentence 7.
    c. Add a comma after *cub* in sentence 12.
    d. Add a comma after *out* in sentence 17.

20. Which of the following sentences could be deleted from the third paragraph without disrupting the flow of the passage?
    a. Sentence 10
    b. Sentence 12
    c. Sentence 13
    d. Sentence 15

21. Which word in the passage is incorrect?
   a. The word *salesman* in sentence 7
   b. The word *broke* in sentence 10
   c. The word *mascot* in sentence 12
   d. The word *bale* in sentence 17

Mathematics

1. 474 + 2038 =
    a. 2512
    b. 2412
    c. 2521
    d. 2502

2. 3703 − 1849 =
    a. 1954
    b. 1854
    c. 1974
    d. 1794

3. 229 × 738 =
    a. 161,622
    b. 167,670
    c. 169,002
    d. 171,451

4. Round to the nearest whole number: 435 ÷ 7 =
    a. 16
    b. 62
    c. 74
    d. 86

5. Report all decimal places: 3.7 + 7.289 + 4 =
    a. 14.989
    b. 5.226
    c. 15.0
    d. 15.07

6. 27 − 3.54 =
    a. 24.56
    b. 23.46
    c. 33.3
    d. 24.54

7. Karen goes to the grocery store with $40. She buys a carton of milk for $1.85, a loaf of bread for $3.20, and a bunch of bananas for $3.05. How much money does she have left?
    a. $30.95
    b. $31.90
    c. $32.10
    d. $34.95

8. Round your answer to the hundredths place: 28 ÷ 0.6 =
    a. 46.67
    b. 0.021
    c. 17.50
    d. 16.8

9. Express the answer in simplest form: $\frac{3}{8} + \frac{2}{8} =$

   a. $\frac{1}{8}$
   b. $\frac{1}{2}$
   c. $\frac{5}{8}$
   d. $\frac{5}{16}$

10. Present the sum as a mixed number in simplest form: $1\frac{1}{2} + \frac{12}{9} =$

   a. $2\frac{3}{5}$
   b. $1\frac{3}{4}$
   c. $3\frac{1}{3}$
   d. $2\frac{5}{6}$

11. Aaron worked $2\frac{1}{2}$ hours on Monday, $3\frac{3}{4}$ hours on Tuesday, and $7\frac{2}{3}$ hours on Thursday. How many hours did he work in all?

   a. $10\frac{5}{6}$
   b. $12\frac{1}{2}$
   c. $13\frac{1}{4}$
   d. $13\frac{11}{12}$

12. Express the answer in simplest form: Dean has brown, white, and black socks. One-third of his socks are white; one-sixth of his socks are black. What fraction of his socks are brown?

   a. $\frac{1}{3}$
   b. $\frac{2}{6}$
   c. $\frac{1}{2}$
   d. $\frac{3}{4}$

13. Express your answer as a mixed number in simplest form: $4\frac{1}{3} \times \frac{2}{7} =$

   a. $6\frac{1}{3}$
   b. $3\frac{7}{10}$
   c. $\frac{8}{21}$
   d. $1\frac{5}{21}$

14. Express the answer as a mixed number or fraction in simplest form: $\frac{5}{8} \div \frac{1}{5} =$

    a. $\frac{1}{8}$
    b. $2\frac{3}{4}$
    c. $3\frac{1}{3}$
    d. $3\frac{1}{8}$

15. Round to the nearest whole number: Bill got $\frac{7}{9}$ of the answers right on his chemistry test. On a scale of 1 to 100, what numerical grade would he receive?

    a. 77
    b. 78
    c. 79
    d. 80

16. Change the fraction to a decimal and round to the hundredths place: $4\frac{3}{7} =$

    a. 4.37
    b. 4.43
    c. 4.56
    d. 4.78

17. Change the decimal to the simplest equivalent proper fraction: 0.07 =

    a. $\frac{7}{10}$
    b. $\frac{0.07}{10}$
    c. $\frac{7}{100}$
    d. $\frac{70}{100}$

18. Change the fraction to the simplest possible ratio: $\frac{8}{14} =$

    a. 2:3
    b. 4:7
    c. 4:6
    d. 3:5

19. Solve for x:

    3:2 :: 24:x

    a. 16
    b. 12
    c. 2
    d. 22

20. Change the decimal to a percent: 0.64 =

    a. 0.64%
    b. 64%
    c. 6.4%
    d. 0.064%

21. Change the percent to a decimal: 38% =
    a. 3.8
    b. 0.038
    c. 38.0
    d. 0.38

22. Change the percent to a decimal: 126% =
    a. 126.0
    b. 0.0126
    c. 0.126
    d. 1.26

23. Change the fraction to a percent and round to the nearest whole number: $\frac{9}{13}$ =
    a. 33%
    b. 69%
    c. 72%
    d. 78%

24. Round to the nearest percentage point: Gerald made 13 out of the 22 shots he took in the basketball game. What was his shooting percentage?
    a. 13%
    b. 22%
    c. 59%
    d. 67%

25. Round to the tenths place: What is 6.4% of 32?
    a. 1.8
    b. 2.1
    c. 2.6
    d. 2.0

26. Roger's car gets an average of 25 miles per gallon. If his gas tank holds 16 gallons, about how far can he drive on a full tank?
    a. 41 miles
    b. 100 miles
    c. 320 miles
    d. 400 miles

27. Express the answer as a mixed number or fraction in simplest form: $2\frac{3}{9} \times \frac{1}{3}$ =
    a. $\frac{7}{8}$
    b. $2\frac{3}{7}$
    c. $\frac{12}{27}$
    d. $\frac{7}{9}$

28. What is the numerical value of the Roman number XVII?
   a. 22
   b. 17
   c. 48
   d. 57

Science

1. What is the typical result of mitosis in humans?
    a. two diploid cells
    b. two haploid cells
    c. four diploid cells
    d. four haploid cells

2. Which of the following is *not* a product of the Krebs cycle?
    a. carbon dioxide
    b. oxygen
    c. adenosine triphosphate (ATP)
    d. energy carriers

3. What kind of bond connects sugar and phosphate in DNA?
    a. hydrogen
    b. ionic
    c. covalent
    d. overt

4. Which hormone is produced by the pineal gland?
    a. insulin
    b. testosterone
    c. melatonin
    d. epinephrine

5. What is the name for a cell that does *not* contain a nucleus?
    a. eukaryote
    b. bacteria
    c. prokaryote
    d. cancer

6. What is the longest phase in the life of a cell?
    a. prophase
    b. interphase
    c. anaphase
    d. metaphase

7. Which of the following is a protein?
    a. cellulose
    b. hemoglobin
    c. estrogen
    d. ATP

8. Which of the following structures is *not* involved in translation?
    a. tRNA
    b. mRNA
    c. ribosome
    d. DNA

9. Which of the following is necessary for cell diffusion?
   a. water
   b. membrane
   c. ATP
   d. gradient

10. Which part of aerobic respiration uses oxygen?
    a. osmosis
    b. Krebs cycle
    c. glycolysis
    d. electron transport system

11. Where is the parathyroid gland located?
    a. neck
    b. back
    c. side
    d. brain

12. Which structure of the nervous system carries action potential in the direction of a synapse?
    a. cell body
    b. axon
    c. neuron
    d. myelin

13. Which structure controls the hormones secreted by the pituitary gland?
    a. hypothalamus
    b. adrenal gland
    c. testes
    d. pancreas

14. Which of the following hormones decreases the concentration of blood glucose?
    a. insulin
    b. glucagon
    c. growth hormone
    d. glucocorticoids

15. Which structure in the brain is responsible for arousal and maintenance of consciousness?
    a. The midbrain
    b. The reticular activating system
    c. The diencephalon
    d. The limbic system

16. Which layer of the heart contains striated muscle fibers for contraction of the heart?
    a. Pericardium
    b. Epicardium
    c. Endocardium
    d. Myocardium

17. Which granulocyte is most likely to be elevated during an allergic response?
   a. Neutrophil
   b. Monocyte
   c. Eosinophil
   d. Basophil

18. Cricoid cartilage is found on the:
   a. alveoli
   b. bronchioles
   c. bronchi
   d. trachea

19. What is the proper order of the divisions of the small intestine as food passes through the gastrointestinal tract?
   a. Ileum, duodenum, jejunum
   b. Duodenum, Ileum, jejunum
   c. Duodenum, jejunum, ileum
   d. Ileum, jejunum, duodenum

20. Which range represents the normal pH of the body fluids?
   a. 7.05 to 7.15
   b. 7.15 to 7.25
   c. 7.25 to 7.35
   d. 7.35 to 7.45

Answer Key and Explanations for Test #1

Reading Comprehension

1. D: The main idea of this passage is that vaccines help the immune system function properly. Identifying main ideas is one of the key skills tested on the exam. One of the common traps that many test-takers fall into is assuming that the first sentence of the passage will express the main idea. Although this will be true for some passages, often the author will use the first sentence to attract interest or to make an introductory, but not central, point. On this question, if you assume that the first sentence contains the main idea, you will incorrectly choose answer B. Finding the main idea of a passage requires patience and thoroughness; you cannot expect to know the main idea until you have read the entire passage. In this case, a diligent reading will show you that answer choices A, B, and C express details from the passage, but only answer choice D is a comprehensive summary of the author's message.

2. C: This passage does not state that the symptoms of disease will not emerge until the body has learned to fight the disease. The reading comprehension section of the exam will include several questions that require you to identify details from a passage. The typical structure of these questions is to ask you to identify the answer choice that contains a detail not included in the passage. This question structure makes your work a little more difficult, because it requires you to confirm that the other three details are in the passage. In this question, the details expressed in answer choices A, B, and D are all explicit in the passage. The passage never states, however, that the symptoms of disease do not emerge until the body has learned how to fight the disease-causing microbe. On the contrary, the passage implies that a person may become quite sick and even die before the body learns to effectively fight the disease.

3. B: In the third paragraph, the word *virulent* means "malicious." The reading comprehension section of the exam will include several questions that require you to define a word as it is used in the passage. Sometimes the word will be one of those used in the vocabulary section of the exam; other times, the word in question will be a slightly difficult word used regularly in academic and professional circles. In some cases, you may already know the basic definition of the word. Nevertheless, you should always go back and look at the way the word is used in the passage. The exam will often include answer choices that are legitimate definitions for the given word, but which do not express how the word is used in the passage. For instance, the word *virulent* could in some circumstances mean contagious. However, since the passage is not talking about transfer of the disease, but the effects of the disease once a person has caught it, malicious is the more appropriate answer.

4. C: The author's primary purpose in writing this essay is to inform. The reading comprehension section of the exam will include a few questions that ask you to determine the purpose of the author. The answer choices are always the same: The author's purpose is to entertain, to persuade, to inform, or to analyze. When an author is *writing to entertain*, he or she is not including a great deal of factual information; instead, the focus is on vivid language and interesting stories. *Writing to persuade* means "trying to convince the reader of something." When a writer is just trying to provide the reader with information, without any particular bias, he or she is *writing to inform*. Finally, *writing to analyze* means to consider a subject already well known to the reader. For instance, if the above passage took an objective look at the pros and cons of various approaches to fighting disease, we would say that the passage was a piece of analysis. Because the purpose of this passage is to present new information to the reader in an objective manner, it is clear that the author's intention is to inform.

5. A: The subject of this passage is foodborne illnesses. Identifying the subject of a passage is similar to identifying the main idea. Do not assume that the first sentence of the passage will declare the subject. Oftentimes, an author will approach his or her subject by first describing some related, familiar subject. In this passage, the author does introduce the subject of the passage in the first sentence. However, it is only by reading the rest of the passage that you can determine the subject. One way to figure out the subject of a passage is to identify the main idea of each paragraph, and then identify the common thread in each.

6. B: This passage never states that cooked food cannot cause illness. Indeed, the first sentence of the third paragraph states that harmful bacteria can be present on cooked food that is left out for two or more hours. This is a direct contradiction of answer choice B. If you can identify an answer choice that is clearly contradicted by the text, you can be sure that it is not one of the ideas advanced by the passage. Sometimes the correct answer to this type of question will be something that is contradicted in the text; on other occasions, the correct answer will be a detail that is not included in the passage at all.

7. C: In the first paragraph, the word *pathogens* means "disease-causing substances." The vocabulary you are asked to identify in the reading comprehension section of the exam will tend to be health related. The makers of the exam are especially interested in your knowledge of the terminology used by doctors and nurses. Some of these words, however, are rarely used in normal conversation, so they may be unfamiliar to you. The best way to determine the meaning of an unfamiliar word is to examine how it is used in context. In the last sentence of the first paragraph, it is clear that pathogens are some substances that cause disease. Note that the pathogens are not diseases themselves; we would not say that an uncooked piece of meat "has a disease," but rather that consuming it "can cause a disease." For this reason, answer choice C is better than answer choice A.

8. A: In the second paragraph, the word *sterile* means "free of bacteria." This question provides a good example of why you should always refer to the word as it is used in the text. The word *sterile* is often used to describe "a person who cannot reproduce." If this definition immediately came to mind when you read the question, you might have mistakenly chosen answer D. However, in this passage the author describes raw foods as *not sterile*, meaning that they contain bacteria. For this reason, answer choice A is the correct response.

9. C: The main idea of the passage is that both the esophagus and the stomach are subject to bleeding problems. The structure of this passage is simple: The first paragraph discusses bleeding disorders of the esophagus, and the second paragraph discusses bleeding disorders of the stomach. Remember that statements can be true, and can even be explicitly stated in the passage, and can yet not be the main idea of the passage. The main idea given in answer choice A is perhaps true, but is too general to be classified as the main idea of the passage.

10. B: The passage never states that ulcer disease rarely occurs in the stomach. On the contrary, in the second paragraph the author states that ulcer disease *can* affect the blood vessels in the stomach. The three other answer choices can be found within the passage. The surest way to answer a question like this is to comb through the passage, looking for each detail in turn. This is a time-consuming process, however, so you may want to follow any initial intuition you have. In other words, if you are suspicious of one of the answer choices, see if you can find it in the passage.

Often you will find that the detail is expressly contradicted by the author, in which case you can be sure that this is the right answer.

11. A: In the first paragraph, the word *rupture* means "tear." All of the answer choices are action verbs that suggest destruction. In order to determine the precise meaning of rupture, then, you must examine its usage in the passage. The author is describing a condition in which damage to a vein causes internal bleeding. Therefore, it does not make sense to say that the vein has *collapsed* or *imploded*, as neither of these verbs suggests a ripping or opening in the side of the vein. Similarly, the word *detach* suggests an action that seems inappropriate for a vein. It seems quite possible, however, for a vein to *tear*: Answer choice A is correct.

12. D: In the second paragraph, the word *erode* means "wear away." Your approach to this question should be the same as for question 11. Take a look at how the word is used in the passage. The author is describing a condition in which ulcers degrade a vein to the point of bleeding. Obviously, it is not appropriate to say that the ulcer has *avoided*, *divorced*, or *contained* the vein. It *is* sensible, however, to say that the ulcer has *worn away* the vein.

13. A: The primary subject of the passage is a new artificial retina. This question is a little tricky, because the author spends so much time talking about the experience of Kathy Blake. As a reader, however, you have to ask yourself whether Mrs. Blake or the new artificial retina is more essential to the story. Would the author still be interested in the story if a different person had the artificial retina? Probably. Would the author have written about Mrs. Blake if she hadn't gotten the artificial retina? Almost certainly not. Really, the story of Kathy Blake is just a way for the author to make the artificial retina more interesting to the reader. Therefore, the artificial retina is the primary subject of the passage.

14. B: In the second paragraph, the word *progressive* means "gradually increasing." The root of the word is *progress*, which you may know means "advancement toward a goal." With this in mind, you may be reasonably certain that answer choice B is correct. It is never a bad idea to examine the context, however. The author is describing *progressive visual loss*, so you might be tempted to select answer choice C or D, since they both suggest loss or diminution. Remember, however, that the adjective *progressive* is modifying the noun *loss*. Since the *loss* is increasing, the correct answer is B.

15. C: The passage never states that retinitis pigmentosa (RP) is curable. This question may be somewhat confusing, since the passage discusses a new treatment for RP. However, the passage never declares that researchers have come up with a cure for the condition; rather, they have developed a new technology that allows people who suffer from RP to regain some of their vision. This is not the same thing as curing RP. Kathy Blake and others like her still have RP, though they have been assisted by this new technology.

16. D: The author's intention in writing this essay is to inform. You may be tempted to answer that the author's intention is to entertain. Indeed, the author expresses his message through the story of Kathy Blake. This story, however, is not important by itself. It is clearly included as a way of explaining the new camera glasses. If the only thing the reader learned from the passage was the story of Kathy Blake, the author would probably be disappointed. At the same time, the author is not really trying to persuade the reader of anything. There is nothing controversial about these new glasses: Everyone is in favor of them. The mission of the author, then, is simply to inform the reader.

17. D: The main idea of the passage is that the immune system protects the body from infection. The author repeatedly alludes to the complexity and mystery of the immune system, so it cannot be true that scientists fully understand this part of the body. It is true that the immune system triggers the production of fluids, but this description misses the point. Similarly, it is true that the body is under constant invasion by malicious microbes; however, the author is much more interested in the body's response to these microbes. For this reason, the best answer choice is D.

18. C: The passage never states that viruses are extremely sophisticated. In fact, the passage explicitly states the opposite. However, in order to know this, you need to understand the word *primitive*. The passage says that viruses are too primitive, or early in their development, to be classified as living organisms. A primitive organism is simple and undeveloped—exactly the opposite of sophisticated. If you do not know the word *primitive*, you can still answer the question by finding all three of the other answer choices in the passage.

19. D: In the first paragraph, the word *ideal* means "perfect." Do not be confused by the similarity of the word *ideal* to *idea* and mistakenly select answer choice A. Take a look at the context in which the word is used. The author is describing how many millions of microbes can live inside the human body. It would not make sense, then, for the author to be describing the body as a *hostile* environment for microbes. Moreover, whether or not the body is a confined environment would not seem to have much bearing on whether it is good for microbes. Rather, the paragraph suggests that the human body is a perfect environment for microbes.

20. B: The passage never states that the immune system ignores tumors. Indeed, at the beginning of the third paragraph, the author states that scientists remain puzzled by the body's ability to fight tumors. This question is a little tricky, because it is common knowledge that many tumors prove fatal to the human body. However, you should not take this to mean that the body does not at least try to fight tumors. In general, it is best to seek out direct evidence in the text rather than to rely on what you already know. You will have enough time on the exam to fully examine and research each question.

21. A: In the second paragraph, the word *enlist* means "call into service." The use of this word is an example of figurative language, the use of a known image or idea to elucidate an idea that is perhaps unfamiliar to the reader. In this case, the author is describing the efforts of the immune system as if they were a military campaign. The immune system *enlists* other cells, and then directs these *recruits* to areas where they are needed. You are probably familiar with *enlistment* and *recruitment* as they relate to describe military service. The author is trying to draw a parallel between the enlistment of young men and women and the enlistment of immune cells. For this reason, "call into service" is the best definition for *enlist*.

22. C: The author's primary purpose in writing this essay is to inform. As you may have noticed, the essays included in the reading comprehension section of the exam were most often written to inform. This should not be too surprising; after all, the most common intention of any writing on general medical subjects is to provide information rather than to persuade, entertain, or analyze. This does not mean that you can automatically assume that "to inform" will be the answer for every question of this type. However, if you are in doubt, it is probably best to select this answer. In this case, the passage is written in a clear, declarative style with no obvious prejudice on the part of the author. The primary intention of the passage seems to be providing information about the immune system to a general audience.

Writing

1. A: The subject of sentence 3 is *ship*. The sentence has a compound verb, "departed...and were supposed to arrive..." The second part of the compound verb should read, "was supposed to arrive" to match the singular subject.

2. B: Sentence 10 begins with the introductory phrase, "Because of this arrangement," which should be set off from the rest of the sentence with a comma.

3. D: Sentence 16 contains information about the design of Titanic and should either be moved to paragraph 2, where it would fit better topically, or be deleted from the passage altogether.

4. B: In sentence 9, this word should be spelled *luxurious*. All the other words are spelled and used correctly.

5. A: Note that sentence 10 (Because of this arrangement the majority of the survivors came from first class.) begins with the transitional phrase, "Because of this arrangement." None of the information given in sentence 9 provides a reason for the survivors being primarily first-class passengers. The sentence that is to be inserted, however, does provide an explanation.

6. A: The comma placed after *arguably* in sentence 1 is not called for here. It unnecessarily interrupts the flow of the sentence.

7. D: Sentence 16 expresses exactly the same thought as sentence 3 from the first paragraph. It does not provide any new information and is not necessary for the conclusion of the passage. It should be removed.

8. A: In sentence 4, the possessive pronoun *its* should be used instead of the contraction *it's*. All the other words are spelled and used correctly.

9. C: The verb *was* must be plural to match its closest subject *teams*.

10. C: Sentences 11 and 12 introduce the BAA and the NBL, but not the NBA. Sentence 13 discusses the inaugural season of the NBA without discussing its origin. Placing the proposed sentence, which explains how the NBA was formed by a merger from the BAA and NBL, after sentence 12 is the most logical option.

11. A: In sentence 5, the verb phrase *will already be* describes a situation that is to exist in the future, but the sentence is discussing something that already exists: The Polynesians' awareness of New Zealand.

12. D: In sentence 17, this word should be spelled *embankment*. All the other words are spelled and used correctly.

13. C: In sentence 14, the singular subject *evidence* is currently paired with the plural verb *show*. It needs to be paired with a singular verb, such as *shows*.

14. B: Sentence 9 provides a list of activities used by the settlers to acquire food. Items in this list must be separated by commas.

15. B: Sentence 11 begins by referring to "these flightless birds." Sentence 10 does not mention any birds, so placing the proposed sentence, which describes flocks of birds, between these two sentences is ideal.

16. D: The focus of the final paragraph is how the sweet potato allowed the Maori to produce enough food to survive without fighting one another for the limited resources. Sentence 18 interjects an unnecessary piece of information about the nutritional composition of the sweet potato, which interrupts the flow of paragraph and distracts from its purpose.

17. D: In sentence 15, the subject *post* has a compound verb: "traveled...and can take..." Both verbs need to having match tenses, so *can* should be changed to *could*.

18. C: Sentence 8 does introduce information that is in contrast with what was stated in the previous sentence, but the sentence currently uses two different transitional words to signal that contrast: *but* and *however*. Only one of these signaling words is necessary.

19. A: The comma after *stories* in sentence 3 is unnecessary and should be removed. None of the other suggested changes would improve the passage.

20. C: The third paragraph consists of three anecdotes about the jobs that pilots were able to find in the years following World War I. Each anecdote is introduced and then clarified or explained more fully. Sentence 13 provides extraneous information about the Humane Society's response to one of those jobs. All the other sentences listed here provide information that is necessary to explain the purpose or context of these jobs.

21. D: In sentence 17, the correct word is *bail* to use in the phrase *bail out*, meaning to jump out of the plane while it is in the air. As a verb, the word *bale* is primarily used to describe the gathering of hay or other similar material into a tightly wrapped roll (a bale).

Mathematics

1. A: The answer is 2512. To solve this problem, you must know how to add numbers with multiple digits. It may be easier for you to complete this problem if you align the numbers vertically. The crucial thing when setting up the vertical problem is to make sure that the place values are lined up correctly. In this problem, the larger number (2038) should be placed on top, such that the 8 is over the 4, the 3 is over the 7, and so on. Then add the place value farthest to the right. In this case, the 4 and the 8 that we find in the ones place have a sum of 12; the 2 is placed in the final sum, and the 1 is carried over to the next place value to the left, the tens. The tens place is the next to be added: 3 plus 7 equal 10, with the addition of the carried 1 making 11. Again, the first 1 is carried over to the next place value. The problem proceeds on in this vein.

2. B: The answer is 1854. To solve this problem, you must know how to subtract one multiple-digit number from another. As with the above addition problems, the most important step in this kind of problem is to set up the proper vertical alignment. In subtraction problems, the larger number must always be on top, and there can be only two terms in all (an addition problem can have an infinite number of terms). In this problem, the ones places should be aligned such that the 3 in 3703 is above the 9 in 1849. This problem also requires you to understand what to do when you have a larger value on the bottom of a subtraction problem. In this case, the 3 on the top of the ones place is smaller than the 9 beneath it, so it must borrow 1 from the number to its left. Unfortunately, there is a 0 to the left of the three, so we must extract a 1 from the next place over again. The 7 in 3703 becomes a 6, the 0 becomes a 10 only to have 1 taken away, leaving it as a 9. The 3 in the ones place becomes 13, from which we can now subtract the 9.

3. C: The answer is 169,002. To solve this problem, you must know how to multiply numbers with several digits. These problems often intimidate students because they produce such large numbers, but they are actually quite simple. As with the above addition and subtraction problems, the crucial first step is to align the terms vertically such that the 8 in 738 is above the 9 in 229. In multiplication, it is a good idea to put the larger number on top, although it is only essential to do so when one of the terms has more place values than the other. In a multiple-digit multiplication problem, every digit gets multiplied by every other digit: First the 9 in 229 is multiplied by the three digits in 738, moving from right to left. Only the digit in the ones place is brought down; the digit in the tens place is placed above the digit to the immediate left and added to the product of the next multiplication. In this problem, then, the 9 and 8 produce 72: The 2 is placed below, and the 7 is placed above the 3 in 738. Then the 9 and the 3 are multiplied and produce 27, to which the 7 is added, making 34. The 4 comes down, the 3 goes above the first 2 in 229, and the process continues. The product of 9 multiplied by 738 is placed below and is added to the products of 2 and 738 and 2 and 738, respectively. For each successive product, the first digit goes one place value to the left. So, in other words, 0 is placed under the 2. These three products are added together to calculate the final product of 738 and 229.

4. B: The answer is 62. To solve this problem, you must know how to divide a multiple-digit number by a single-digit number. To begin with, set up the problem as $7\overline{)435}$. Then determine the number of times that 7 will go into 43 (one way to do this is to multiply 7 by various numbers until you find a product that is either 43 exactly or no more than 6 fewer than 43). In this case, you will find that 7 goes into 43 six times. Place the 6 above the 3 in 435 and multiply the 6 by 7. The product, 42, should be subtracted from 43, leaving a difference of 1. Since 7 cannot go into 1, bring down the 5 to create 15. The 7 will go into 15 twice, so place a 2 to the right of the 6 on top of the problem. At this point, you should recognize that only answer choice B can be correct. If you proceed further, however, you will find that 435 must become 435.0 so that the 0 can be brought down to make a large enough number to be divided by 7. Once a decimal point is introduced to the dividend, a decimal point must be placed directly above it in the quotient. If you continue working this problem, you will end up with an answer of 62.14.... Note that the instructions tell you only to round to the nearest whole number. Once you have solved to the tenths place, there is no need to continue.

5. A: The answer is 14.989. To solve this problem, you must know how to add a series of numbers when some of the numbers include decimals. As with addition problems 1 and 2, the most important first step is to set up the proper vertical alignment. This step is even more important when working with decimals. Be sure that all of the decimal points are in alignment; in other words, the 7 in 3.7 should be above the 2 in 7.289. Since the final term, 4, is a whole number, we assume a 0 in the tenths place. Similarly, you may assume zeros in the hundredths and thousandths places, if you prefer to have a digit in every relevant place. Then beginning at the rightmost place value (in this case, the thousandths), add the terms together as you would with whole numbers. The decimal point of the sum should be aligned with the decimal points of the terms.

6. B: The answer is 23.46. To solve this problem, you must know how to subtract a number with a decimal from a whole number. At first glance, this problem seems complex, but it is actually quite simple once you set it up in vertical form. Remember that the decimal point must remain aligned and that a decimal point can be assumed after the 7 in 27. In order to solve this problem, you should assume zeros for the tenths and hundredths places of 27. The problem is solved as 27.00 − 3.54. Obviously, in order to solve this problem, you will have to borrow from the 7 in 27.00. The normal rules for borrowing in subtraction still apply when working with decimals. Be sure to keep the decimal point of the difference aligned with the decimal points of the terms.

7. B: The answer is $31.90. To solve this problem, you must know how to solve word problems involving decimal subtraction. In this scenario, Karen starts out with a certain amount of money and spends some of it on groceries. To calculate how much money she has left, simply subtract the money spent from the original figure: 40 − 1.85 − 3.20 − 3.05. There is no reason to include the dollar sign in your calculations, so long as you remember that it exists. You cannot subtract the costs of these items at the same time, so you must either subtract them one by one or add them up and subtract the sum from 40. Either way will generate the right answer.

8. A: The answer is 46.67. To solve this problem, you must know how to divide a whole number by a decimal. To begin with, set the problem up in the form $0.6\overline{)28}$. You cannot perform division when the divisor is less than one, however, so shift the decimal point one place to the right. For every action in the divisor, an identical action must be taken in the dividend: Shift the decimal point (which can be assumed after the 8 in 28) in the dividend as well. The problem is now $6\overline{)280}$. This problem can now be solved just like problems 7 and 8. Remember to round your answer to the hundredths place for this problem (this means you will need to solve to the thousandths place). With a knowledge of place value, you can immediately eliminate answer choices B and D, since they are solved to the nearest thousandth and tenth place, respectively.

9. C: The answer is $\frac{5}{8}$. To solve this problem, you must know how to add fractions with like denominators. This kind of operation is actually quite simple. The denominator of the sum remains the same; the calculation is performed by adding the numerators. On problems like this, the makers of the exam will probably try to fool you by including one possible answer in which the denominators have been added; in this problem, for instance, you would end up with answer choice D if you added both numerator and denominator. Do not assume that you have answered the question correctly because your calculations match one of the answer choices. Always check your work.

10. D: The answer is $2\frac{5}{6}$. To solve this problem, you must know how to add mixed numbers and improper fractions. To begin with, convert the mixed number (a mixed number includes a whole number and a fraction) into an improper fraction (a fraction in which the numerator is larger than the denominator). This is done by multiplying the whole number by the denominator and adding the product to the numerator: 1 × 2 + 1 = 3. The problem is now $\frac{3}{2} + \frac{12}{9}$. Then find the lowest common denominator by listing some multiples of 2 and 9. The lowest common multiple is 18, so you must convert both terms: $\frac{3}{2} \times \frac{9}{9} = \frac{27}{18}$, and $\frac{12}{9} \times \frac{2}{2} = \frac{24}{18}$. The problem is now $\frac{27}{18} + \frac{24}{18} = \frac{51}{18}$. This fraction can be reduced by dividing both the numerator and the denominator by 3: $\frac{51 \div 3}{18 \div 3} = \frac{17}{6}$. This improper fraction can be converted to the mixed number $2\frac{5}{6}$.

11. D: The answer is $13\frac{11}{12}$. This problem requires you to understand addition involving mixed numbers. The calculation required by this problem is straightforward: In order to derive the number of hours Aaron worked, add up the three mixed numbers. To make this possible, you will need to find the least common multiple of 2, 4, and 3 so that you can establish a common denominator. The lowest common denominator for this problem is 12. You can either add up the whole numbers separately from the fractions or convert the mixed numbers into improper fractions and add them in that form. Either way will yield the correct answer.

12. C: The answer is $\frac{1}{2}$. To solve this problem, you must know how to solve word problems requiring fraction addition and subtraction. You are given the proportions of Dean's socks that are white and black. The best approach to this problem is adding together the two known quantities and subtracting the sum from 1. First you need to find a common denominator for $\frac{1}{3}$ and $\frac{1}{6}$. The lowest common multiple of these two numbers is 6, so convert $\frac{1}{3}$ by multiplying the numerator and denominator by 2. The new equation will be $\frac{2}{6} + \frac{1}{6} = \frac{3}{6}$. This sum is equivalent to $\frac{1}{2}$, meaning that half of Dean's socks are either white or black. The other half, then, are brown. If you need to perform the calculation, however, it will look like this: $\frac{2}{2} - \frac{1}{2} = \frac{1}{2}$.

13. D: The answer is $1\frac{5}{21}$. To solve this problem, you must know how to multiply mixed numbers and fractions. Unlike fraction addition and subtraction, fraction multiplication does not require a common denominator. However, it is necessary to convert mixed numbers into improper fractions. This is done by multiplying the whole number by the denominator and adding the product to the numerator: in this case, 4 × 3 + 1 = 13. So, the problem is now $\frac{13}{3} \times \frac{2}{7}$. Fraction multiplication is performed by multiplying numerator by numerator and denominator by denominator: $\frac{13 \times 2}{3 \times 7} = \frac{26}{21}$. This improper fraction can be converted into a mixed number by dividing numerator by denominator, which gives $1\frac{5}{21}$.

14. D: The answer is $3\frac{1}{8}$. To solve this problem, you must know how to divide fractions. The process of dividing fractions is similar to that of multiplying fractions, except that the second term must first be inverted, or replaced with its reciprocal. Once this is done, the numerator is multiplied by the numerator, and the denominator is multiplied by the denominator. This problem can be solved by multiplying $\frac{5}{8}$ by the reciprocal of $\frac{1}{5}$, which is $\frac{5}{1}$ or 5: $\frac{5\times 5}{8\times 1} = \frac{25}{8}$. Finally, convert this improper fraction into a mixed number according to the usual procedure.

15. B: The answer is 78. To solve this problem, you must know how to convert a fraction into a ratio. In this problem, you are being asked to convert the fraction into a value on a scale from 1 to 100, which is basically like being asked to convert it into a percentage. To do so, divide the numerator by the denominator. The answer will be a repeating seven: 0.777.... Calculate to the thousandths place in order to determine the value. Because the digit in the thousandths place is a 7, you will round up the digit to the left to establish the final answer, 78.

16. B: The answer is 4.43. To solve this problem, you must know how to convert mixed numbers into decimals. Perhaps the easiest way to perform this operation is to convert the mixed number into an improper fraction and then divide the numerator by the denominator. Convert the mixed number into an improper fraction by multiplying the whole number by the denominator and adding the product to the numerator: 4 × 7 + 3 = 31, so the improper fraction is $\frac{31}{7}$. Next divide 31 by 7, according to the same procedure used in problems 7 and 8. Remember that when you have to add 0 to 31 in order to continue your calculations, you must put a decimal point directly above in the quotient. Also, since the problem asks you to round to the hundredths place, you must solve the problem to the nearest thousandth.

17. C: The answer is $\frac{7}{100}$. To solve this problem, you must know how to convert decimals into fractions. Remember that all of the numbers to the right of a decimal point represent values less than one. So, a decimal number such as this will not include any whole numbers when it is converted into a fraction. The 7 is in the hundredths place, so the number is properly expressed as $\frac{7}{100}$. The fraction cannot be simplified because 7 and 100 do not share any factors besides one.

18. B: The answer is 4:7. To solve this problem, you must know how to convert fractions into ratios. A ratio expresses the relationship between two numbers. For instance, the ratio 2:3 suggests that for every 2 of one thing, there will be 3 of the other. If we applied this ratio to the length and width of a rectangle, for instance, we would be saying that for every 2 units of length, the rectangle must have 3 units of width. A fraction is just one way to express a ratio: The fraction $\frac{8}{14}$ is equivalent to the ratio 8:14. To simplify the ratio, divide both sides by the greatest common factor, 2. The simplest form of this ratio is 4:7.

19. A: The answer is 16. To solve this problem, you must understand proportions. A proportion is a comparison between two or more equivalent ratios. A simple proportion is 1:2 :: 2:4, which can be expressed in words as "1 is to 2 as 2 is to 4." Just as 2 is twice 1, 4 is twice 2. Problem 37 asks you to identify a missing term in a proportion. One way to do this is to set up the problem as a set of equivalent fractions and solve for the variable: $\frac{3}{2} = \frac{24}{x}$. To solve this equation, cross-multiply. You will end up with 3x = 48. Divide both sides by 3 to find that x = 16.

20. B: The answer is 64%. To solve this problem, you must know how to convert a decimal into a percent. A percentage is a number expressed in terms of hundredths. When we say, for instance, that a candidate received 55% of the vote, we mean that she received 55 out of every 100 votes cast. When we say that the sales tax is 6%, we mean that for every 100 cents in the price another 6 cents are added to the final cost. To convert a decimal into a percentage, multiply it by 100 or just shift the decimal point two places to the right. In this case, by moving the decimal point two places to the right you can derive the correct answer, 64%.

185

21. D: The answer is 0.38. To solve this problem, you must know how to convert percentages into decimals. This is done by shifting the decimal point two places to the right. This operation is the same as dividing the percentage by 100. In this problem, assume that the decimal is after the eight in 38%. The equivalent decimal, then, is 0.38.

22. D: The answer is 1.26. To solve this problem, you must know how to convert percentages into decimals. Remember that a percentage is really just an expression of a value in terms of hundredths. That is, 25% is the same as 25 out of 100. To convert a percentage into a decimal, shift the decimal point two places to the left. In this case, the decimal point is assumed to be after the six in 126%. By shifting the decimal point two places to the left, you find that the equivalent decimal is 1.26.

23. B: The answer is 69%. To solve this problem, you must know how to convert fractions into percentages. This is done by dividing the numerator by the denominator. In this case, the problem is set up as $13\overline{)9.0}$, because a decimal point and 0 are required to make the calculation possible.

Although the decimal point is there, you should still treat 9.0 as if it were 90 when performing your division. Since 13 will go into 90 six times, you can place a 6 above the 0 in 9.0. Remember that your quotient will have a decimal point in the identical place; that is, directly to the left of the 6. If you continue your calculations, you will derive an answer of 0.692... However, once you derive that first 6, you should be able to select the correct answer choice. Remember that percentage is the same as hundredths; in other words, 69% is the same as sixty-nine hundredths.

24. C: The answer is 59%. To solve this problem, you must know how to convert a fraction into a percentage. Gerald made 13 out of 22 shots, a performance that can also be expressed by the fraction 13/22. To convert this fraction into a percentage, divide the numerator by the denominator: $22\overline{)13}$. Once you derive the initial 5 in the quotient, you can be fairly certain that answer choice C is correct. Whenever possible, try to take these kinds of shortcuts to save yourself some time. Although the exam gives you plenty of time to complete all of the questions, by saving a little time here and there you can give yourself more opportunities to work through the harder problems.

25. D: The answer is 2.0. To solve this problem, you must know how to find equivalencies involving percentages. This problem can be solved with the same strategy used in problem 48. To begin with, set up the following equation: $\frac{6.4}{100} = \frac{x}{32}$. Next cross-multiply: 6.4 × 32 = 100x. This produces 204.8 = 100x, which is solved for x by dividing both sides of the equation by 100. The value of x is 2.048, which is rounded to 2.0. Or change the percent to a decimal, 0.064, and multiply by 32 to obtain 2.048 and round to 2.0.

26. D: The answer is 400 miles. This problem requires you to understand word problems involving mileage rates and multiplication. The problem states that the car gets an average 25 miles per gallon; in other words, every gallon of fuel powers the car for approximately 25 miles. If the car holds 16 gallons of gas, then, and each of these gallons provides 25 miles of travel, you can set up the following equation: 25 miles/gallon × 16 gallons = 400 miles. Since the first term has gallons in the denominator and the second term has gallons in what would be the numerator (if it were expressed as 16 gallons/1), these units cancel each other out and leave only miles.

27. D: The answer is $\frac{7}{9}$. This problem requires you to understand multiplication of mixed numbers and fractions. The process is the same as for the previous problem: First, reduce the fractional part of the mixed number to $\frac{1}{3}$. Then convert $2\frac{1}{3}$ into the mixed number $\frac{7}{3}$. Next, multiply numerator by numerator and denominator by denominator to get the answer: $\frac{7}{3} \times \frac{1}{3} = \frac{7}{9}$.

28. B: The answer is 17. This problem requires you to know about Roman numerals. This system of numeration is still used in a number of professional contexts. The Roman numerals are as follows: I (1), V (5), X (10), L (50), C (100), D (500), and M (1000). You may also see the lowercase versions of these letters used. The order of the numerals is typically largest to smallest. However, when a smaller number is placed in front of a larger one, the smaller number is to be subtracted from the larger one that follows. For instance, the Roman numeral XIV is 14, as the 1 (I) is to be subtracted from the 5 (V). If the number had been written XVI, it would represent 16, as the 1 (I) is to be added to the 5 (V).

Science

1. A: The typical result of mitosis in humans is two diploid cells. *Mitosis* is the division of a body cell into two daughter cells. Each of the two produced cells has the same set of chromosomes as the parent. A diploid cell contains both sets of homologous chromosomes. A haploid cell contains only one set of chromosomes, which means that it only has a single set of genes. For the exam, you will need to know about all the different stages of cell division for both human and plant cells.

2. B: Oxygen is not one of the products of the Krebs cycle. The *Krebs cycle* is the second stage of cellular respiration. In this stage, a sequence of reactions converts pyruvic acid into carbon dioxide. This stage of cellular respiration produces the phosphate compounds that provide most of the energy for the cell. The Krebs cycle is also known as the citric acid cycle or the tricarboxylic acid cycle. The exam may require you to know all stages of cellular respiration: the process in which a plant cell converts carbon dioxide into oxygen.

3. C: The sugar and phosphate in DNA are connected by covalent bonds. A *covalent bond* is formed when atoms share electrons. It is very common for atoms to share pairs of electrons. Hydrogen bonds are used in DNA to bind complementary bases together, such as adenine with thymine or guanine with cytosine. An *ionic bond* is created when one or more electrons are transferred between atoms. *Ionic bonds*, also known as *electrovalent bonds*, are formed between ions with opposite charges. There is no such thing as an *overt bond* in chemistry. The exam will require you to understand and have some examples of these different types of bonds.

4. C: *Melatonin* is produced by the pineal gland. One of the primary functions of melatonin is regulation of the circadian cycle, which is the rhythm of sleep and wakefulness. *Insulin* helps regulate the amount of glucose in the blood. Without insulin, the body is unable to convert blood sugar into energy. *Testosterone* is the main hormone produced by the testes; it is responsible for the development of adult male sex characteristics. *Epinephrine*, also known as adrenaline, performs a number of functions: It quickens and strengthens the heartbeat and dilates the bronchioles. Epinephrine is one of the hormones secreted when the body senses danger.

5. C: Prokaryotic cells do not contain a nucleus. A *prokaryote* is simply a single-celled organism without a nucleus. It is difficult to identify the structures of a prokaryotic cell, even with a microscope. These cells are usually shaped like a rod, a sphere, or a spiral. A *eukaryote* is an organism containing cells with nuclei. Bacterial cells are prokaryotes, but since there are other kinds of prokaryotes, *bacteria* cannot be the correct answer to this question. *Cancer* cells are malignant, atypical cells that reproduce to the detriment of the organism in which they are located.

6. B: *Interphase* is the longest phase in the life of a cell. Interphase occurs between cell divisions. *Prophase* is the initial stage of mitosis. It is also the longest stage. During prophase, the chromosomes become visible, and the centrioles divide and position themselves on either side of the nucleus. *Anaphase* is the third phase of mitosis, in which chromosome pairs divide and take up positions on opposing poles. *Metaphase* is the second stage of mitosis. In it, the chromosomes align themselves across the center of the cell.

7. B: *Hemoglobin* is a protein. Proteins contain carbon, nitrogen, oxygen, and hydrogen. These substances are required for the growth and repair of tissue and the formation of enzymes. Hemoglobin is found in red blood cells and contains iron. It is responsible for carrying oxygen from the lungs to the various body tissues. *Adenosine triphosphate* (ATP) is a compound used by living organisms to store and use energy. *Estrogen* is a steroid hormone that stimulates the development of female sex characteristics. *Cellulose* is a complex carbohydrate that composes the better part of the cell wall.

8. D: Deoxyribonucleic acid (*DNA*) is not involved in translation. *Translation* is the process by which messenger RNA (*mRNA*) messages are decoded into polypeptide chains. Transfer RNA (*tRNA*) is a molecule that moves amino acids into the ribosomes during the synthesis of protein. Messenger RNA carries sets of instructions for the conversion of amino acids into proteins from the RNA to the other parts of the cell. *Ribosomes* are the tiny particles in the cell where proteins are put together. Ribosomes are composed of ribonucleic acid (RNA) and protein.

9. A: Water is required for cell diffusion. Diffusion is the movement of molecules from an area of high concentration to an area of lower concentration. This process takes place in the body in a number of different areas. For instance, nutrients diffuse from partially digested food through the walls of the intestine into the bloodstream. Similarly, oxygen that enters the lungs diffuses into the bloodstream through membranes at the end of the alveoli. In all these cases, the body has evolved special membranes that only allow certain materials through.

10. D: The *electron transport system* enacted during aerobic respiration requires oxygen. This is the last component of biological oxidation. *Osmosis* is the movement of fluid from an area of high concentration through a partially permeable membrane to an area of lower concentration. This process usually stops when the concentration is the same on either side of the membrane. *Glycolysis* is the initial step in the release of glucose energy. The *Krebs cycle* is the last phase of the process in which cells convert food into energy. It is during this stage that carbon dioxide is produced and hydrogen is extracted from molecules of carbon.

11. A: The parathyroid gland is located in the neck, directly behind the thyroid gland. It is responsible for the metabolism of calcium. It is part of the endocrine system. When the supply of calcium in blood diminishes to unhealthy levels, the parathyroid gland motivates the secretion of a hormone that encourages the bones to release calcium into the bloodstream. The parathyroid gland also regulates the amount of phosphate in the blood by stimulating the excretion of phosphates in the urine.

12. B: *Axons* carry action potential in the direction of synapses. Axons are the long, fiber-like structures that carry information from neurons. Electrical impulses travel along the body of the axons, some of which are up to a foot long. A *neuron* is a type of cell that is responsible for sending information throughout the body. There are several types of neurons, including muscle neurons, which respond to instructions for movement; sensory neurons, which transmit information about the external world; and interneurons, which relay messages between neurons. *Myelin* is a fat that coats the nerves and ensures the accurate transmission of information in the nervous system.

13. A: The *hypothalamus* controls the hormones secreted by the pituitary gland. This part of the brain maintains the body temperature and helps to control metabolism. The *adrenal glands*, which lie above the kidneys, secrete steroidal hormones, epinephrine, and norepinephrine. The *testes* are the male reproductive glands, responsible for the production of sperm and testosterone. The *pancreas* secretes insulin and a fluid that aids in digestion.

14. A: *Insulin* decreases the concentration of blood glucose. It is produced by the pancreas. *Glucagon* is a hormone produced by the pancreas. Glucagon acts in opposition to insulin, motivating an increase in the levels of blood sugar. *Growth hormone* is secreted by the pituitary gland. It is responsible for the growth of the body, specifically by metabolizing proteins, carbohydrates, and lipids. The *glucocorticoids* are a group of steroid hormones that are produced by the adrenal cortex. The glucocorticoids contribute to the metabolism of carbohydrates, proteins, and fats.

15. B: The reticular activating system (RAS) is primarily responsible for the arousal and maintenance of consciousness. The midbrain is a part of the brainstem, which has a crucial role in the regulation of autonomic functions like breathing and heart rate. The diencephalon consists of the hypothalamus and thalamus in the middle part of the brain between the cerebrum and midbrain. It plays a huge role in regulating and coordinating sensory information and hormonal secretion from the hypothalamus. The limbic system tends to the major instinctual drives like eating, sex, thirst, and aggression.

16. D: The myocardium is the layer of the heart that contains the muscle fibers responsible for contraction (Hint: myo- is the prefix for muscle). The endocardium and epicardium are the inner and outer layers of the heart wall, respectively. The pericardium is the sac in which the heart sits inside the chest cavity.

17. C: Eosinophils are most commonly recruited to deal with allergenic antigens. Monocytes, neutrophils, and basophils also deal with antigens during the immune response, but eosinophils are found to be elevated during an allergic response.

18. D: Cricoid cartilage refers to the thick rings of cartilage that surround the trachea, sitting right above the voice box. The purpose of these thick rings is to serve as additional support and protection for the delicate airway.

19. C: The duodenum is the first segment of the small intestine, connecting to the stomach on one end and to the jejunum on the other. The jejunum sits between the duodenum and the last section of small intestine, the ileum, which then connects to the large intestine.

20. D: There is a very narrow range of normal pH values in the human body, 7.35 to 7.45. Values lower than 7.35 indicate acidosis, and values higher than 7.45 indicate alkalosis. The human body can't function properly if the pH is outside of the normal range.

KNAT Practice Test #2

Reading Comprehension

Questions 1 to 8 pertain to the following passage:

Visual Perception

It is tempting to think that your eyes are simply mirrors that reflect whatever is in front of them. Researchers, however, have shown that your brain is constantly working to create the impression of a continuous, uninterrupted world.

For instance, in the last ten minutes, you have blinked your eyes around 200 times. You have probably not been aware of any of these interruptions in your visual world. Something you probably have not seen in a long time without the aid of a mirror is your nose. It is always right there, down in the bottom corner of your vision, but your brain filters it out so that you are not aware of your nose unless you purposefully look at it.

Nor are you aware of the artery that runs right down the middle of your retina. It creates a large blind spot in your visual field, but you never notice the hole it leaves. To see this blind spot, try the following: Cover your left eye with your hand. With your right eye, look at the O on the left. As you move your head closer to the O, the X will disappear as it enters the blind spot caused by your optical nerve.

O X

Your brain works hard to make the world look continuous!

1. The word <u>filters</u>, as used in this passage, most nearly means:
   a. Alternates
   b. Reverses
   c. Ignores
   d. Depends

2. The word <u>retina</u>, as used in this passage, most nearly means:
   a. Optical illusion
   b. Part of the eye
   c. Pattern
   d. Blindness

3. Which of the following statements can be inferred from this passage?
   a. Not all animals' brains filter out information
   b. Visual perception is not a passive process
   c. Blind spots cause accidents
   d. The eyes never reflect reality

191

4. **What is the author's purpose for including the two letters near the end of the passage?**
   a. To demonstrate the blind spot in the visual field
   b. To organize the passage
   c. To transition between the last two paragraphs of the passage
   d. To prove that the blind spot is not real

5. **What is the main purpose of this passage?**
   a. To persuade the reader to pay close attention to blind spots
   b. To explain the way visual perception works
   c. To persuade the reader to consult an optometrist if the O and X disappear
   d. To demonstrate that vision is a passive process

6. **Based on the passage, which of the following statements is true?**
   a. The brain cannot accurately reflect reality
   b. Glasses correct the blind spot caused by the optical nerve
   c. Vision is the least important sense
   d. The brain fills in gaps in the visual field

7. **The author mentions the nose to illustrate what point?**
   a. The brain filters out some visual information
   b. Not all senses work the same way
   c. Perception is a passive process
   d. The sense of smell filters out information

8. **Which of the following statements can be inferred from the second paragraph?**
   a. The brain filters out the sound created by the shape of the ears
   b. The brain does not perceive all activity in the visual field
   c. Closing one eye affects depth perception
   d. The brain evolved as a result of environmental factors

Questions 9 to 17 pertain to the following passage:

Oppositional Defiant Disorder

On a bad day, have you ever been irritable? Have you ever used a harsh tone or even been verbally disrespectful to your parents or teachers? Everyone has a short temper from time to time, but current statistics indicate that between 16% and 20% of a school's population suffer from a psychological condition known as Oppositional Defiance Disorder, or ODD.

ODD symptoms include difficulty complying with adult requests, excessive arguments with adults, temper tantrums, difficulty accepting responsibility for actions, low frustration tolerance, and behaviors intended to annoy or upset adults. Parents of children with ODD can often feel as though their whole relationship is based on conflict after conflict.

Unfortunately, ODD can be caused by a number of factors. Some students affected by ODD suffer abuse, neglect, and severe or unpredictable discipline at home. Others have parents with mood disorders or have experienced family violence. Various types of therapy are helpful in treating ODD, and some drugs can treat particular symptoms. However, no single cure exists.

The best advice from professionals is directed toward parents. Therapists encourage parents to avoid situations that usually end in power struggles, to try not to feed into oppositional behavior by reacting emotionally, to praise positive behaviors, and to discourage negative behaviors with timeouts instead of harsh discipline.

9. Which of the following statements can be inferred from paragraph 4?
   a. Parents of children with ODD are bad parents
   b. ODD is not a real psychological disorder
   c. Medication can worsen ODD
   d. Reacting emotionally to defiant behavior might worsen the behavior

10. Which of the following best describes the main idea of this passage?
   a. ODD has no cause
   b. ODD is a complex condition
   c. Parents with ODD should seek support
   d. Parents are the cause of ODD

11. As used in this passage, the word *oppositional* most nearly means:
   a. Uncooperative
   b. Violent
   c. Passive aggressive
   d. Altruistic

12. Which of the following can be inferred from paragraph one?
   a. Most children who speak harshly to their parents have ODD
   b. Most people exhibit symptoms of ODD occasionally
   c. Between 16% and 20% of the school population has been abused
   d. A short temper is a symptom of obsessive-compulsive disorder

13. As used in this passage, the phrase *feed into* most nearly means:
   a. Discourage
   b. Ignore
   c. Encourage
   d. Abuse

14. As used in this passage, the phrase *low frustration tolerance* most nearly means:
   a. Patience
   b. Low IQ
   c. Difficulty dealing with frustration
   d. The ability to cope with frustration

15. The author's purpose in writing this passage is to:
   a. Express frustration about ODD
   b. Prove that parents are the cause of ODD
   c. Inform the reader about this complex condition
   d. Persuade the reader to keep students with ODD out of public school

16. According to the passage, which of the following is a cause of ODD?
   a. Excessive television viewing
   b. Poor diet
   c. Severe or unpredictable punishment
   d. Low IQ

17. Based on the passage, which of the following statements seems most true?
   a. A variety of parenting techniques can be used to help children with ODD
   b. Children with ODD must be physically aggressive to be diagnosed
   c. Parents of children with ODD often engage in risk-taking activities
   d. Harsh disciplinary measures must be used to control children with ODD

Questions 18 to 20 pertain to the following passage:

About 17 million children and adults in the United States suffer from asthma, a condition that makes it hard to breathe. Today it is a problem that is treatable with modern medicine. In days gone by, there were many different superstitions about how to cure asthma. Some people thought that eating crickets with a little wine would help. Eating raw cat's meat might be the cure. Another idea was to try gathering some spiders' webs, rolling them into a ball, and then swallowing them. People also thought that if you ate a diet of only boiled carrots for two weeks, your asthma might go away. This carrot diet may have done some good for asthma patients since vitamin A in carrots is good for the lungs.

18. Which of the following would be a good title for the passage?
   a. Asthma in the United States
   b. Methods of treating asthma
   c. Old wives' tales
   d. Superstitions about asthma

19. The fact that 17 million children and adults in the United States suffer from asthma is probably the opening sentence of the passage because:
   a. It explains why people in times gone by might have found a need to try homemade cures
   b. It creates a contrast between today and the past
   c. It lets the reader know that many people have asthma
   d. It is a warning that anyone could get asthma

20. The main purpose of the passage is to:
   a. Describe herbal remedies
   b. Explain some of the measures for treating asthma from long ago
   c. Define superstitions
   d. Extol the virtues of modern medicine

Questions 21 and 22 pertain to the following passage:

During the last 100 years of medical science, the drugs that have been developed have altered the way people live all over the world. Over-the-counter and prescription drugs are now the key for dealing with diseases, bodily harm, and medical issues. Drugs like these are used to add longevity and quality to people's lives. But not all drugs are healthy for every person. A drug does not necessarily have to be illegal to be abused or misused. Some ways that drugs are misused include taking more or less of the drug than is needed, using a drug that is meant for another person, taking a drug for longer than needed, taking two or more drugs at a time, or using a drug for a reason that has nothing to do with being healthy. Thousands of people die from drug misuse or abuse every year in the United States.

21. According to the passage, which of the following is an example of misusing a drug?
 a. Taking more of a prescription drug than the doctor ordered
 b. Taking an antibiotic to kill harmful bacteria
 c. Experiencing a side effect from an over-the-counter drug
 d. Throwing away a medication that has passed the expiration date

22. According to the passage, which of the following is not true?
 a. Over-the-counter drugs are used for medical issues
 b. Every year, thousands of people in the United States die due to using drugs the wrong way
 c. Medical science has come a long way in the last century
 d. All drugs add longevity to a person's life

Writing

Questions 1-6 are based on the following passage:

¹Could the future of crops include planting without soil? ²The concept of hydroponics, or growing plants by directly exposing the roots to water and nutrients, both conserving resources such as water and stimulating extra growth and food production.

³While this concept sounds new and innovative—and in fact has being extensively studied by NASA in recent years—the idea is not original to the past decade, or even the past century. ⁴Books were published, as early as the 17th century, discussing the idea of growing plants without the traditional concept of planting them in the earth. ⁵The term "hydroponics" was first introduced in 1937 by William Gericke, who grew tomatoes in his back yard in a solution of minerals. ⁶Since this time, numerous experiments have been conducted and some large hydroponics farms have even been constructed.

⁷Rather than soil, plants are grown in a variety of substitutes; such as rockwool, clay pellets, pumice, wood fiber, or even packing peanuts. ⁸These allow the roots easy access to both the nutrient-rich water and to oxygen.

⁹There are many advantages to hydroponic farming. ¹⁰Due to the controlled greenhouse environment, crops can be grown and no pesticides. ¹¹There is also less waste of water because of no run-off. ¹²Furthermore, proponents of hydroponics claim that this method can lead to much greater yields. ¹³This is due not only to the better nutrition but additionally to the protection from harsh weather conditions and pests. ¹⁴Additionally, hydroponics farmers are not limited to a single crop during the normal growing season, they can produce year-round.

¹⁵In addition, hydroponics does have disadvantages. ¹⁶Before beginning, a farmer must have a greenhouse with proper growing stations and temperature control. ¹⁷Soil replacement, nutrients, and specialized lighting must also be purchased. ¹⁸Finally, removing exposure to the outdoor environment means that the farmer must eliminate needs such as pollination. ¹⁹The setup for growing without soil is costly.

²⁰Despite the disadvantages, hydroponics is likely to become more popular in coming years. ²¹Not only can crops be grown year-round, but plants can also be much closer together, or even grown vertically, allowing for a much greater yield per acre. ²²Additionally, hydroponics may have implications in other areas. ²³For example, NASA has done research with hydroponics to mimic a Martian environment. ²⁴So, while the work and expense of soil-less gardening is significant, this market, which is already in the hundreds of millions of dollars worldwide, may be a glimpse of the future of farming.

1. Which option describes the BEST change to make in sentence 2?
   a. Change the word *both* to *and*.
   b. Change the word *by* to *through*.
   c. Change the word *directly* to *direct*.
   d. Change the word *conserving* to *conserves*.

2. **Which option describes how to correct a punctuation error in passage 1?**
   a. Change the question mark after the word *soil* in sentence 1 to a colon.
   b. Add a comma after the word *conducted* in sentence 6.
   c. Change the semicolon after the word *substitutes* in sentence 7 to a period.
   d. Remove the comma after the word *nutrients* in sentence 17.

3. **Which sentence in the passage should be moved?**
   a. Sentence 2 should be moved before sentence 1.
   b. Sentence 5 should be moved before sentence 4.
   c. Sentence 19 should be moved before sentence 18.
   d. Sentence 22 should be moved before sentence 21.

4. **Which word or phrase is used incorrectly?**
   a. In sentence 5, the phrase *back yard* should be *backyard*.
   b. In sentence 8, the word *nutrient-rich* should be *nutrient rich*.
   c. In sentence 19, the word *setup* should be *set up*.
   d. In sentence 21, the word *year-round* should be *yearround*.

5. **Which of the following sentences contains an error?**
   a. Sentence 3
   b. Sentence 9
   c. Sentence 12
   d. Sentence 17

6. **Which answer choice shows the correct punctuation for sentence 14?**
   a. Additionally, hydroponics farmers are not limited to a single crop during the normal growing season, they can produce year-round.
   b. Additionally hydroponics farmers are not limited to a single crop during the normal growing season they can produce year-round.
   c. Additionally, hydroponics farmers are not limited to a single crop during the normal growing season; they can produce year-round.
   d. Additionally, hydroponics farmers are not limited to a single crop during the normal growing season: they can produce year-round.

Questions 7-10 are based on the following passage:

¹Throughout human history, mankind sought to track the days and seasons. ²Tracing back millennia, archaeologists have discovered calendars, showing the ancient views of the earth's movement and time's passage. ³Though most calendars are very similar in length, a few changes have been made as measurements have become more precise.

⁴Some calendars have been used for much of recorded human history. ⁵For instance, the Assyrian calendar has been in use for over 6,750 years. ⁶Many communities still celebrate the Assyrian New Year every spring.

⁷The earliest known calendar was discovered in Scotland—twelve pits with a corresponding arc. ⁸Researchers have categorized it as a lunar calendar, the phases of the moon are the basis for this.

⁹Although Scotland is home to the oldest calendar, most current ones are termed solar calendars. ¹⁰That is, they are based on the fact that the earth travels around the sun in a certain

197

number of days. [11]However, several cultures created lunisolar calendars, using both solar and lunar measurements to determine the year and months. [12]The Chinese calendar (that is no longer the country's official calendar but is still used in many places) was originally a lunisolar calendar, with the length of the year based on the sun, however the new year beginning on the new moon before the winter solstice. [13]Lunisolar calendars use intercalary months (a technique similar to a leap day) to add sufficient days to make the lunar months add up to the solar year. [14]Some years have 12 months, but every second or third year, an intercalary month is added to keep the months aligned with the seasons.

[15]In 46 BC, Julius Caesar instituted the Julian calendar, a solar calendar that became the predominant method of measurement in the Western world for over 1600 years. [16]Before this, the Roman calendar was often stabilized by political goals: years were lengthened or shortened to adjust terms of office (since many offices were held for a year), depending on who was in power. [17]To fix this political issue, Caesar consulted with an Egyptian astronomer, who advised him to adopt a solar calendar. [18]This calendar brought stability, but after Caesar's assassination, the Roman priests mistakenly added too many leap days.

[18]Because of this, Easter moved farther from the vernal equinox, so in 1582 AD Pope Gregory XIII introduced a revised calendar, shifted the date forward ten days. [19]Rather than adding an intercalary month every few years, this Gregorian calendar adds a leap day every four years (with a few exceptions), measuring the solar year as 365.2425 days. [20]Though still imprecise, this number is widely accepted worldwide and allows mankind to do what he has attempted throughout history: to keep the year in sync with the seasons.

7. Which sentence would be the most correct replacement for sentence 9?
   a. Although Scotland is home to the oldest calendar, newer ones are termed solar calendars.
   b. Scotland is home to the oldest calendar, newer ones are termed lunar calendars.
   c. Scotland is home to the lunar calendar but newer ones are termed solar calendars.
   d. Although Scotland is home to the lunar calendar, newer ones are termed solar calendars.

8. Which option shows sentence 12 separated into two grammatically correct sentences?
   a. The Chinese lunisolar calendar is no longer the country's official calendar but is still used in many places. The length of the year based on the sun however, the new year begins on the new moon before the winter solstice.
   b. The Chinese lunisolar calendar is no longer the country's official calendar, but is still used in many places. The length of the year is based on the sun, however the new year begins on the new moon before the winter solstice.
   c. The Chinese lunisolar calendar is no longer the country's official calendar but is still used in many places. The length of the year is based on the sun; however, the new year begins on the new moon before the winter solstice.
   d. The Chinese lunisolar calendar is no longer the country's official calendar, but is still used in many places. The length of the year based on the sun; however, the new year begins on the new moon before the winter solstice.

9. Which of the following shows the correct punctuation for sentence 7?

a. The earliest known calendar was discovered in Scotland; twelve pits with a corresponding arc.
b. The earliest known calendar was discovered in Scotland: twelve pits with a corresponding arc.
c. The earliest known calendar was discovered in Scotland, twelve pits with a corresponding arc.
d. The earliest known calendar was discovered in Scotland. Twelve pits with a corresponding arc.

10. Which sentences should be deleted to BEST improve the flow of the passage?

a. Sentences 2 and 3
b. Sentences 5 and 6
c. Sentences 7 and 8
d. Sentences 9 and 10

Questions 11-16 are based on the following passage:

¹The ever-changing technological world in which we live constantly offers new opportunities and perspectives on age-old traditions. ²Communication in particular has changed rapidly, with new ways of connectedness constantly appearing. ³As we are increasingly able to communicate from any place and at any time, this has led to questions of how this ability could help in other areas.

⁴Even if technological advances in communication are often considered from a social standpoint, as people can connect more and more easily, one sector that has been immensely affected is the career sector. ⁵Many companies can now submit deliverables without appearing in person. ⁶Online meetings can conduct from the comfort of each person's office. ⁷Instant communication allows for quick answers and increased productivity.

⁸Not only are employees able to more work from the corporate office, with less need to travel for meetings and site visits, but there is an increasing trend toward employees who work from a home office, although checking in virtually throughout the day or even logging in remotely to a work computer. ⁹Telecommuting has many advantages both to the employee and the employer. ¹⁰The employee, obviously, can save time and money by staying home (studies estimate telecommuters save an average of $4,000 per year in travel and office-related costs), and may be able to have a more flexible schedule to work around children's school days or other responsibilities. ¹¹Companies can also save money with fewer overhead: with off-site employees, they can avoid the cost of office space, lighting, heating/cooling, and other expenses, as well as improving employee retention, saving an estimated $11,000 per telecommuting employee each year. ¹²Ideally, telecommuting can lead to greater profit and efficiency, as employees are able to concentrate on work in their most comfortable environment.

¹³However, telecommuting comes with its drawbacks. ¹⁴Technological glitches (internet connection problems, faulty microphones, etc.) can make virtual meetings an advantage. ¹⁵Security can be a concern when employees are working with sensitive information from their homes. ¹⁶Accountability is also more challenging when one is working from home with minimal supervision. ¹⁷And in an increasingly isolated world, telecommuting keeps people farther apart, removing the social interaction that a job normally provides.

[18]In response, some companies have reached a compromise. [19]Employees may have a mixed schedule, telecommuting one or two days a week and coming in to the office on the others. [20]A 2013 worldwide study shows that nearly half of business managers telecommute for much of the workweek, and over half are willing to manage remote workers. [21]While telecommunication obviously is impractical for certain sectors, it appears to be a promising way for many companies to meet both individual needs and corporate goals.

11. Which of the following would be the most correct replacement for sentence 3?
    a. Because we are increasingly able to communicate from any place and at any time, we question how this ability could help in other areas.
    b. Our increasing ability to communicate from any place and at any time has led to questions of how this ability could help in other areas.
    c. As we are increasingly able to communicate from any place and at any time, this has led us to questions of how this ability could help in other areas.
    d. We are increasingly able to communicate from any place and at any time. How could this ability help in other areas?

12. Which word is used incorrectly in the passage?
    a. The word *perspectives* in sentence 1
    b. The word *deliverables* in sentence 5
    c. The word *increased* in sentence 7
    d. The word *to* in sentence 9

13. Which option BEST describes how to correct the use of an apostrophe in the passage?
    a. In sentence 10, the word *children's* should be *childrens'*.
    b. In sentence 11, the word *Companies* should be *Company's*.
    c. In sentence 15, the word *employees* should be *employees'*.
    d. In sentence 20, the word *managers'* should be *managers*.

14. Where would sentence 9 be placed more appropriately?
    a. Before sentence 1
    b. Before sentence 4
    c. Before sentence 6
    d. Before sentence 12

15. Which option would BEST replace the word *fewer* in sentence 11?
    a. lower
    b. higher
    c. less
    d. more

16. Which change would correct a grammatical error in sentence 21?
    a. Place a comma after the word *telecommunication*.
    b. Switch the order of the phrase *obviously is* to *is obviously*.
    c. Remove the comma after the word *sectors*.
    d. Switch the order of the phrase *meet both* to *both meet*.

Questions 17-21 are based on the following passage:

¹Anyone who has participated in a humanities class or museum visit, has doubtless seen classical paintings depicting bowls of fruit. ²Why is it that clusters of grapes and piles of apples were so intriguing to artists?

³A glance through ancient history shows that this was not merely a Renaissance theme. ⁴Ancient Egyptian paintings of fruit have been discovered in most of the tombs, eliciting a belief that they would become real food for the dead to eat in the afterlife. ⁵They could also symbolize rebirth, fertility, and abundance.

⁶Fruit is meaningful in many other religions and cultures as well, from Greek mythology to Islam to Christianity. ⁷Pomegranates, figs, and apples figure into ancient Greek and Roman myths, symbolic of fertility, temptation, and prosperity. ⁸Both Islam and Christianity link fruit with temptation and sin, even with joy and abundance. ⁹Ancient Chinese beliefs hold pears as signs of immortality.

¹⁰So why did each of these separate cultures find significance in fruit? ¹¹Many scholars believe this is because fruit is a natural allegory for human life. ¹²At its peak, fruit is rich, sweet, and desirable. ¹³Inevitably, though, it withers and decays, a reminder of the transiency of life.

¹⁴Some ancient cultures such as the Romans found particular meaning in life's brevity. ¹⁵Roman mosaics in dining areas often depicted food, symbolizing abundance and pleasure in feasting. ¹⁶Along with skulls to remind viewers that death was imminent and inescapable, even as they ate and drank.

¹⁷In the 1600s, artists reflected from these ancient cultures for inspiration. ¹⁸At the same time, there was an emphasis on the natural world. ¹⁹Since fruit played an important role in both of these, it became a popular subject for the paintbrush. ²⁰Both secular and religious art found beauty and symbolism in various fruits, so a painted cluster of grapes was a common site in many homes.

²¹Even in more modern work, fruit remains a common theme. ²²Picasso painted numerous pieces that included fruit (though it was certainly a departure from the classical style). ²³For his representations of repeating fruits, Andy Warhol is also well known. ²⁴While it may not hold the same symbolism today, fruit is still a visual representation of one of humanity's most basic needs—nourishment. ²⁵It also evokes imagery of fragility and both perfection and flaw, all of which are common themes explored in today's culture.

²⁶From ancient tomb paintings to Renaissance masterpieces to contemporary art, fruit as art has stood the test of time. ²⁷Fruit is thus a reminder of humanity's nature, and though much has changed throughout history, mankind still finds meaning and beauty in the same things...even if for different reasons.

17. Which choice shows correct punctuation in sentence 14?
   a. Some ancient cultures such as the Romans found particular meaning in life's brevity.
   b. Some ancient cultures, such as the Romans found particular meaning in life's brevity.
   c. Some ancient cultures, such as the Romans, found particular meaning in life's brevity.
   d. Some ancient cultures such as the Romans, found particular meaning in life's brevity.

18. Which of the following sentences contains an error?
    a. Sentence 3
    b. Sentence 10
    c. Sentence 13
    d. Sentence 17

19. Which sentence would be the most correct replacement for sentence 22?
    a. Picasso painted numerous pieces that included fruit, though it was certainly a departure from the classical style.
    b. Picasso painted numerous pieces that included fruit, though they were certainly a departure from the classical style.
    c. Picasso painted numerous pieces that included fruit. Though it was certainly a departure from the classical style.
    d. Picasso painted numerous pieces that included fruit. Though they were certainly a departure from the classical style.

20. Which sentence is incomplete?
    a. Sentence 9
    b. Sentence 13
    c. Sentence 16
    d. Sentence 21

21. Which sentence includes an unnecessary comma?
    a. Sentence 1
    b. Sentence 5
    c. Sentence 12
    d. Sentence 26

Mathematics

1. What number is 25% of 400?
   a. 100
   b. 200
   c. 800
   d. 10,000

2. What is the reciprocal of 6?
   a. $\frac{1}{2}$
   b. $\frac{1}{3}$
   c. $\frac{1}{6}$
   d. $\frac{1}{12}$

3. A roast was cooked at 325 °F in the oven for 4 hours. The internal temperature of the roast rose from 32 °F to 145 °F. What was the average rise in temperature per hour?
   a. 20.2 °F/hr
   b. 28.25 °F/hr
   c. 32.03 °F/hr
   d. 37 °F/hr

4. Your supervisor instructs you to purchase 240 pens and 6 staplers for the nurse's station. Pens are purchase in sets of 6 for $2.35 per pack. Staplers are sold in sets of 2 for $12.95 per set. How much will purchasing these products cost?
   a. $132.85
   b. $145.75
   c. $162.90
   d. $225.05

5. Which of the following percentages is equivalent to the decimal 0.45?
   a. 0.045%
   b. 0.45%
   c. 4.5%
   d. 45%

6. A vitamin's expiration date has passed. It was supposed to contain 500 mg of calcium, but it has lost 325 mg of calcium. How many mg of calcium remain?
   a. 135 mg
   b. 175 mg
   c. 185 mg
   d. 200 mg

7. You have orders to give a patient 20 mg of a certain substance. The concentration of the substance within the medication is 4 mg per 5-mL dose. How much medication should be given?
   a. 15 mL
   b. 20 mL
   c. 25 mL
   d. 30 mL

8. In the number 743.25 which digit represents the tenths space?
   a. 2
   b. 3
   c. 4
   d. 5

9. Which of these percentages is equivalent to the decimal 1.25?
   a. 0.125%
   b. 12.5%
   c. 125%
   d. 1250%

10. If the average person drinks eight 8-oz glasses of water per day, a person who drinks 12.8 oz of water after a morning exercise session has consumed what fraction of the daily average?
    a. 1/3
    b. 1/5
    c. 1/7
    d. 1/9

11. What number is 33% of 300?
    a. 3
    b. 9
    c. 33
    d. 99

12. You need $\frac{4}{5}$ cup of water for a recipe. You accidentally put $\frac{1}{3}$ cup into the mixing bowl with the dry ingredients. How much more water do you need to add?
    a. $\frac{1}{3}$ cups
    b. $\frac{2}{3}$ cups
    c. $\frac{1}{15}$ cups
    d. $\frac{7}{15}$ cups

13. $\frac{3}{4} - \frac{1}{2} = ?$
    a. $\frac{1}{4}$
    b. $\frac{1}{3}$
    c. $\frac{1}{2}$
    d. $\frac{2}{3}$

14. In your class there are 48 students, 32 of whom are female. Approximately what percentage of the class is male?
    a. 25%
    b. 33%
    c. 45%
    d. 66%

15. Fried's rule for computing an infant's dose of medication is:
$$\text{infant's dose} = \frac{[\text{child's age in months}] \times [\text{adult dose}]}{150}$$
If the adult dose of medication is 15 mg, how much should be given to a 2-year-old child?
    a. 1.2 mg
    b. 2.4 mg
    c. 3.6 mg
    d. 4.8 mg

16. $7\frac{1}{2} - 5\frac{3}{8} = ?$
    a. $1\frac{1}{2}$
    b. $1\frac{2}{3}$
    c. $2\frac{1}{8}$
    d. $3\frac{1}{4}$

17. 35 is 20% of what number?
    a. 175
    b. 186
    c. 190
    d. 220

18. $6 \times 0 \times 5 = ?$
    a. 30
    b. 11
    c. 25
    d. 0

19. $7.95 \div 1.5 = ?$
   a. 2.4
   b. 5.3
   c. 6.2
   d. 7.3

20. The fraction $\frac{7}{10}$ is equivalent to which decimal?
   a. 0.007
   b. 0.07
   c. 0.7
   d. 7.10

21. The fraction $\frac{4}{8}$ is equivalent to which decimal?
   a. 0.05
   b. 0.48
   c. 0.5
   d. 4.8

22. $-32 + 7 = ?$
   a. −25
   b. 25
   c. −26
   d. 26

23. The percentage 41% is equivalent to which decimal?
   a. 4.1
   b. 0.41
   c. 0.041
   d. 0.0041

24. $248 + 311 = ?$
   a. 557
   b. 559
   c. 659
   d. 667

25. $13,980 + 7,031 = ?$
   a. 20,010
   b. 20,911
   c. 21,011
   d. 21,911

26. $8,537 - 6,316 = ?$
   a. 1,221
   b. 2,221
   c. 2,243
   d. 2,841

27. $643 \times 72 = ?$
   a. 44,096
   b. 44,186
   c. 46,296
   d. 45,576

28. $18,144 \div 63 = ?$
   a. 256
   b. 258
   c. 286
   d. 288

Science

1. Which of the following sentences is true?
   a. All organisms begin life as a single cell
   b. All organisms begin life as multi-cellular
   c. Some organisms begin life as a single cell and others as multi-cellular
   d. None of the above

2. Which of the following is the best definition for metabolism?
   a. The process by which organisms lose weight
   b. The process by which organisms use energy
   c. The process by which organisms return to homeostasis
   d. The process by which organisms leave homeostasis

3. Which of the following is not true for all cells?
   a. Cells are the basic structures of any organism
   b. Cells can only reproduce from existing cells
   c. Cells are the smallest unit of any life form that carries the information needed for all life processes
   d. All cells are also called eukaryotes

4. What are the two types of cellular transport?
   a. Passive and diffusion
   b. Diffusion and active
   c. Active and passive
   d. Kinetic and active

5. What does aerobic mean?
   a. In the presence of oxygen
   b. Calorie-burning
   c. Heated
   d. Anabolic

6. When both parents give offspring the same allele, the offspring is _____ for that trait.
   a. Heterozygous
   b. Homozygous
   c. Recessive
   d. Dominant

7. Genetics is the study of:
   a. Anatomy
   b. Physiology
   c. Heredity
   d. Science

8. Scientists suggest that _____ has occurred through a process called _____.
   a. evolution... differentiation
   b. evolution... natural selection
   c. natural selection... homeostasis
   d. homeostasis... reproduction

9. Which of the following correctly lists the cellular hierarchy from the simplest to the most complex structure?
   a. tissue, cell, organ, organ system, organism
   b. organism, organ system, organ, tissue, cell
   c. organ system, organism, organ, tissue, cell
   d. cell, tissue, organ, organ system, organism

10. If a cell is placed in a hypertonic solution, what will happen to the cell?
    a. It will swell
    b. It will shrink
    c. It will stay the same
    d. It does not affect the cell

11. Which hormone is *not* secreted by a gland in the brain?
    a. Human chorionic gonadotropin (HCG)
    b. Gonadotropin releasing hormone (GnRH)
    c. Luteinizing hormone (LH)
    d. Follicle stimulating hormone (FSH)

12. Select the most accurate statement among the following regarding the human circulatory system:
    a. All arteries carry oxygenated blood away from the heart
    b. Blood flows faster through capillaries than through veins
    c. The walls of both arteries and veins are made of three main layers
    d. An increase in heart rate correlates with an increase in blood pressure

13. Which of the following is not a type of muscle tissue?
    a. Skeletal
    b. Smooth
    c. Cardiac
    d. Adipose

14. Which of the following organ systems has the purpose of producing movement through contraction?
    a. Skeletal
    b. Muscular
    c. Cardiovascular
    d. Respiratory

15. Which of the following terms means toward the front of the body?
    a. Superior
    b. Anterior
    c. Inferior
    d. Posterior

16. The brain is part of the:
    a. Integumentary system
    b. Nervous system ✓
    c. Endocrine system
    d. Respiratory system

17. Which of the following is the name for the study of the structure and shape of the human body?
    a. Physiology
    b. Anatomy ✓
    c. Biology
    d. Genetics

18. Which of the following is the name for the study of how parts of the body function?
    a. Physiology ✓
    b. Anatomy
    c. Biology
    d. Genetics

19. Which of the below is the best definition for the term <u>circulation</u>?
    a. The transport of oxygen and other nutrients to the tissues via the cardiovascular system ✓
    b. The force exerted by blood against a unit area of the blood vessel walls
    c. The branching air passageways inside the lungs
    d. The process of breathing in

20. Which of the following is not a type of connective tissue?
    a. smooth ✓
    b. cartilage
    c. adipose tissue
    d. blood tissue

Answer Key and Explanations for Test #2

Reading Comprehension

1. C: The passage uses this word to discuss how your brain ignores the presence of your nose unless you specifically look at it. Thus, the best answer is choice C, *ignores*.

2. B: The retina is the part of the eye that processes the light that comes in through the lens and converts the visual signals into a form that the brain can more easily interpret. Thus, the best answer is choice B, *part of the eye*.

3. B: The final sentence reads, "Your brain works hard to make the world look continuous." This is another way of saying that visual perception is an active and *not a passive process*, making choice B the best answer.

4. A: If the reader follows the instructions given in the paragraph, the O and X in the middle of the passage can be used to demonstrate the blind spot in the visual field. Choice A is the best answer.

5. B: The passage spends most of its time explaining the way that visual perception works. Choice B is the best answer.

6. D: Much of the information in the passage is provided to show examples of how the brain fills in gaps in the visual field. Choice D is the best answer.

7. A: The author of the passage mentions the nose to demonstrate how the brain filters information out of the visual field. Choice A is the best answer.

8. B: The second paragraph states that the brain filters out information, which means that the brain does not perceive all activity in the visual field. In fact, it intentionally ignores some things in order to simplify the process of perception. Choice B is the best answer.

9. D: Of the given options, only choice D can be inferred from the passage. The passage states that parents should "try not to *feed into* oppositional behavior by reacting emotionally," which implies that reacting emotionally to defiant behavior can worsen it.

10. B: Choice B, "ODD is a complex condition" is the best answer out of the four that are given. It is the only choice that can be inferred from the passage as a whole.

11. A: Choice A is the best choice. *Oppositional* means uncooperative.

12. B: Choice B is the best interpretation of paragraph one. The passage states that many people exhibit ODD symptoms from time to time.

13. C: Choice C is the best choice. *Feed into* in this sentence means to encourage oppositional behavior.

14. C: Someone with a *low frustration tolerance* has a difficult time tolerating or dealing with frustration. Choice C is the best answer.

15. C: This passage is meant to inform the reader about ODD. Choice C is the best choice.

16. C: While some of these answer choices may contribute to ODD, the passage mentions only choice C, severe or unpredictable punishment.

17. A: The only statement directly supported by the passage is choice A.

18. D: Since the passage describes superstitions from days gone by about treating asthma, answer choice D is the correct one.

19. A: The reader can infer from the opening sentence that, if so many people have asthma today, many would probably have had asthma long ago as well. Even though the environment today is different than it was long ago, people would still have suffered from the condition. The sentence explains why people long ago may have needed to try homemade methods of treating the condition.

20. B: The purpose of the passage is to describe different measures that people took for asthma long ago, before the advent of modern medicine.

21. A: Of all the choices listed, only answer choice A is an example of misusing a drug. It is listed as one of the ways that drugs are misused in the middle of the passage. Taking more or less of a prescription drug than the amount that the doctor ordered can be harmful to one's health.

22. D: The passage does not say that ALL drugs add longevity. It says that drugs that are healthy and used properly add longevity. The word *all* makes the statement untrue.

Writing

1. D: The verb *conserves* agrees with the subject of the sentence, *concept of hydroponics*. Similarly, the word *stimulating* should be changed to *stimulates*. In choices A, B, and C, the words are already used correctly.

2. B: The conjunction *and* in sentence 6 connects two independent clauses, so it should be preceded by a comma. In choice A, sentence 1 is a question, so the question mark is appropriate. In choice C, changing the semicolon in sentence 7 to a period would make the phrase that follows an incomplete sentence. In choice D, the comma is a necessary serial comma before the conjunction *and* in the list.

3. C: Because sentence 18 starts with the word *finally*, it should be the last point made in the series of disadvantages listed. Choices A, B, and D are all positioned appropriately in the passage.

4. A: *Backyard* is one word. In choice B, *nutrient-rich* is a compound adjective that comes before the noun it modifies, so it should be hyphenated. In choice C, *setup* is a single word when used as a noun. In choice D, *year-round* is a compound adverb, so it should be hyphenated; *year-round* is not a proper word.

5. A: In sentence 3, the word *being* should be *been*. Further, there should be no comma after the word *decade*, because the clause that follows the word *or* is dependent. Choices B, C, and D refer to error-free sentences.

6. C: A comma is necessary after the introductory word *Additionally*, and the semicolon connects the two independent clauses of the sentence without a coordinating conjunction. Choices A and B contain a comma splice—the comma after *season* incorrectly joins two independent clauses without a coordinating conjunction. Choice B also lacks a comma after the introductory word *Additionally*. In choice D, the colon is incorrect because the second independent clause does not explain or expand the first.

7. D: The first and second clauses of choice D are consistent in discussing calendar type as parallel ideas. In choice A, the clauses lack parallelism: the first discusses calendar age, while the second discusses calendar type. Choice B also lacks parallelism, erroneously uses *lunar* in place of *solar*, and contains a comma splice. Choice C lacks a comma before the coordinating conjunction *but*, which joins two independent clauses.

8. C: This choice contains two grammatically correct sentences. Choice A lacks a necessary semicolon before the word *however*. In choice B, the comma before *but* is not correct because the second clause is dependent. Additionally, the comma before *however* should be a semicolon. In choice D, the comma before *but* is not correct because the second clause is dependent.

9. B: A colon is used to restate and add information to the clause that precedes it. Choices A, C, and D are incorrect because the clause starting with *twelve* is dependent. These sentences use a semicolon, comma, and period, respectively, to incorrectly separate the dependent clause from the preceding independent clause.

10. B: While most of the passage is organized chronologically, sentences 5 and 6 include information about calendars that are not as old as the one presented in sentence 7, the "earliest known calendar." The sentences in choices A, C, and D all follow a logical flow.

11. A: The main clause starts with *we*, which connects the content of the two parts and makes the sentence flow better. Additionally, some readers will find that starting the introductory clause with *Because* is clearer than using *As* to do the same thing. Choices B, C, and D could all be more concise.

12. D: The word *to* should be replaced with the word *for* in sentence 9. The words listed in choices A, B, and C are used correctly.

13. D: The word *managers* in sentence 20 is plural but not possessive. *Telecommute* is the verb in the sentence, so the word *managers* does not need an apostrophe. In choice A, the word *children* is already plural and possessive of the object *school days*, so it requires an apostrophe followed by an "s." In choices B and C, the words are plural but not possessive; they are correct in the passage.

14. C: Sentence 9 is a about the overall advantages of telecommuting, so it serves as a good transition to the more specific discussion of advantages in sentences 5 through 12. Choices A and B are both general sentences that serve best as an introduction before the discussion of specific advantages and disadvantages. In choice D, sentence 13 begins the discussion of disadvantages, and sentence 9 would be off topic there.

15. A: *Lower* and *fewer* are distinguished in this way: *lower* refers to an amount or an uncountable noun, while *fewer* refers to a number or to separate, countable items. If sentence 11 were about a smaller number of discrete line items in a budget, *fewer* would correct. But sentence 11 uses the uncountable noun *overhead* in general, so choice A, *lower*, is correct. Choices B and D are incorrect because saving money results from decreased overhead, not increased. Choice C is incorrect because decreased overhead is a relative term; it may not necessarily mean there is a small amount of overhead.

16. B: The word *obviously* is an adverb of certainty, and so it should follow the verb *is*, not precede it. Choice A is incorrect because, in sentence 21 as written, no comma is necessary after the word *telecommunication*. Choice C is incorrect because, in sentence 21 as written, the comma is correctly placed after the introductory phrase. In choice D is incorrect because, in sentence 21 as written, the verb *meet* refers to *individual needs and corporate goals*, so the word *both* is correctly placed after the verb.

17. C: In this sentence, the Romans are just one example among many possible ones; the sentence would also be correct without any examples. Therefore, the phrase *such as the Romans* is not essential to the meaning of the sentence; it is also called a nonrestrictive phrase. A nonrestrictive phrase in this position should have a comma before and after it. Therefore, choices A, B, and D are incorrect.

18. D: Sentence 17 should read *artists reflected on*, not *artists reflected from*. The sentences in choices A, B, and C are grammatically correct.

19. B: The second clause in the sentence refers to the *pieces* Picasso painted, so the subject should be *they*, not *it*. Additionally, the comma before *though* has correctly been removed. Choice A is incorrect because the second clause in the sentence refers to the *pieces* Picasso painted; therefore, the subject should be *they*, not *it*. Choices C and D are incorrect because the clause beginning with *Though* is not a complete sentence.

20. C: Sentence 16 lacks a subject and a verb, so it is an incomplete sentence. Choices A, B, and D are all complete sentences with a subject and a verb.

21. A: The comma in sentence 1 incorrectly separates the subject and verb of the sentence. In choice B, the commas are necessary after the items in the serial list. In choice C, the comma after *peak* is correctly placed at the end of the introductory phrase; the other commas are necessary after items in the serial list. In choice D, the comma is correctly placed after the introductory phrase.

Mathematics

1. A: The word "percent" literally means per hundred; a percentage is a fraction over 100. 25% is therefore equal to $\frac{25}{100}$. To find a percentage of a number, you can multiply the number by the percentage and then divide by 100. 25% of 400 is therefore $400 \times 25 \div 100 = 100$.

Alternatively, you can remember that 25% is equal to one quarter—this is one of a few percentages that is simple enough to be worth committing to memory. Thus 25% of 400 is one quarter of 400; $400 \div 4 = 100$.

2. C: The **reciprocal** of a number is the number which, when multiplied by the first number, makes a product of 1. In other words, it's one divided by the first number. (Zero has no reciprocal.) For a fraction, you can find the reciprocal easily by just switching the numerator and denominator—turning the fraction "upside-down". For instance, the reciprocal of $\frac{2}{3}$ is $\frac{3}{2}$: $\frac{2}{3} \times \frac{3}{2} = 1$. An integer can be written as a fraction with a denominator of 1: $6 = \frac{6}{1}$. Therefore, we can find the reciprocal of 6 by swapping the numerator and denominator of $\frac{6}{1}$ to get $\frac{1}{6}$.

3. B: The average rate of change of a quantity over a period of time is equal to the change in the quantity divided by the time. In this case, the change in temperature is $145\ °F - 32\ °F = 113\ °F$. This occurs over four hours, so the average rate of change is $113° \div 4\ \text{hr} = 28.25\ °F/\text{hr}$.

4. A: We can find the cost of the pens and staplers separately and then add the two together. We are purchasing 240 pens, and they cost $2.35 per pack. Since there are six pens per pack, we can find the number of packs needed by dividing the number of pens by six: $240/6 = 40$. (If we had come up with a fraction, we would have rounded up, since we presumably can't purchase a partial pack, but in this case 240 is evenly divisible by 6 anyway.) So the cost of the pens is equal to 40 packs × $2.35/pack = $94. Similarly, we need $6/2 = 3$ sets of staplers, which will cost 3 sets × $12.95/set = $38.85. $94 + $38.85 = $132.85.

5. D: A percentage is equal to a fraction over 100: $p\% = \frac{p}{100}$. That means to find a number x that corresponds to $p\%$, we need to solve $x = \frac{p}{100}$, which just comes out to $p = 100x$. In other words, to convert a decimal to a percentage, we just multiply by 100. So to find the percentage that corresponds to 0.45, we just multiply $0.45 \times 100 = 45$: $0.45 = 45\%$. (Note that $45\% = \frac{45}{100} = 0.45$, as desired.)

6. B: If the vitamin lost a certain quantity of calcium, it means the amount of calcium was reduced by that amount. So we can subtract that amount from the original amount of calcium to find the amount that remains. 500 mg – 325 mg = 175 mg.

7. C: Each dose contains 4 mg, and you have to give the patient a total of 20 mg. So we can find out how many doses you need to give the patient by finding out how many times 4 mg goes into 20 mg: $20\ \text{mg} \div 4\ \text{mg} = 5$. So the patient needs 5 doses. Now, to find the total volume of the doses, you can multiply the volume of each dose by the number of doses. Each dose has a volume of 5 mL, so the total volume is $5\ \text{mL} \times 5 = 25\ \text{mL}$.

8. A: In a decimal number, the digit just before the decimal point represents the unit space, or the ones space. (For a number without a decimal, the last digit is in the ones space.) Each space to the left represents a larger space by a factor of ten: so the digit left of the ones place is the tens place, the digit left of that is the hundreds space, and so on. Each space right represents a *smaller* space by a factor of ten: so the digit to the right of the ones place (the digit just right of the decimal point) is the tenths place, the digit to the right of that is the hundredths space, and so on.

In this case, we're asked for the tenths place, which as we've just seen is the digit just right of the decimal point: 2. The 3 represents the ones space, the 4 represents the tens space, and the 5 represents the hundredths space.

9. C: A percentage represents a number of hundredths, so to convert a decimal to a percentage, we multiply by 100. (This is equivalent to moving the decimal point two spaces to the right, adding zeroes as necessary.) In this case, then, the percentage we need is $1.25 \times 100 = 125$; 1.25 is equal to 125%. That's greater than 100%, but that makes sense, because 100% = 1 and 1.25 is greater than one.

10. B: The fraction is simply equal to the part over the whole. In this case, if the average person drinks eight 8-oz glasses of water during a day, then the total amount of water the person drinks is 8×8 oz = 64 oz. If we now want to know what fraction 12.8 oz is of this number, we write 12.8 oz / 64 oz, or just $\frac{12.8}{64}$.

This, however, is a messy fraction; we'd like to simplify and get rid of the decimals. We can rewrite a fraction in equivalent form by multiplying or dividing both the numerator and denominator by the same number. Multiplying by 10 gets rid of the decimal, leaving $\frac{128}{640}$. Now, both the numerator and denominator are even, so we can divide them both by 2, leaving $\frac{128 \div 2}{640 \div 2} = \frac{64}{320}$. They're still even, so we can repeat the process, and keep repeating until they no longer have a common factor, yielding $\frac{32}{160}$, then $\frac{16}{80}$, then $\frac{8}{40}$, then $\frac{4}{20}$, then $\frac{2}{10}$, and finally $\frac{1}{5}$. (We could have done this in fewer steps by dividing by larger factors, but those larger common factors are less obvious.)

For this problem, though, there's a significant shortcut: all of the answer choices have a 1 in the numerator, which we know we can get by dividing the numerator by itself. So we can just divide the numerator and denominator by 12.8: $\frac{12.8 \div 12.8}{64 \div 12.8} = \frac{1}{5}$.

11. D: A percentage is a number of hundredths, thus $33\% = \frac{33}{100}$. So to find a given percentage of a number, we can just multiply the number by the corresponding fraction: 33% of 300 = $\frac{33}{100} \times 300 = \frac{9900}{100} = 99$.

12. D: To find the amount of water you need to add, you can subtract the amount you've already added from the total required. In this case, that means $\frac{4}{5} - \frac{1}{3}$. To add or subtract fractions, it's necessary to rewrite them so that their denominators match; we then subtract the numerators, keeping the same denominator. We can rewrite a fraction in an equivalent form by multiplying the numerator and denominator of the fraction by the same number.

For us to subtract the fractions, their new denominator should be the lowest common multiple of the original denominators: that is, the smallest number that is divisible by the denominators of both fractions. In this case, the lowest common multiple of 3 and 5 is 15. We therefore rewrite $\frac{4}{5}$ as $\frac{4 \times 3}{5 \times 3} = \frac{12}{15}$, and $\frac{1}{3}$ as $\frac{1 \times 5}{3 \times 5} = \frac{5}{15}$. The difference is then $\frac{12}{15} - \frac{5}{15} = \frac{7}{15}$.

13. A: To add or subtract fractions, we have to rewrite them so that they have the same denominator. We then subtract the numerators, keeping the same denominator (and simplifying if possible). This new denominator is the lowest common multiple of the original fractions: the smallest number that is divisible by both the original denominators. The lowest common multiple of 2 and 4 is 4, so we need to rewrite both fractions with this denominator. $\frac{3}{4}$ already has the correct denominator; to rewrite $\frac{1}{2}$ we multiply both sides of the fraction by 2: $\frac{1}{2} = \frac{1 \times 2}{2 \times 2} = \frac{2}{4}$. Our subtraction problem then becomes $\frac{3}{4} - \frac{2}{4} = \frac{1}{4}$.

14. B: The total number of students in the class is 48, and 32 are female, which means the number of male students is $48 - 32 = 16$. The fraction of students that are male is therefore $\frac{16}{48}$.

There are two ways to proceed from here. We can convert the fraction into a decimal by dividing, using a calculator if necessary: $16 \div 48 = 0.3333 \ldots$; multiplying by 100 gives approximately 33.

In this case, however, there's another way to solve the problem. We can reduce the fraction by dividing both sides of the fraction by 16: $\frac{16}{48} = \frac{16 \div 16}{48 \div 16} = \frac{1}{3}$. This is a common enough fraction that the equivalent percentage may be worth committing to memory: $\frac{1}{3}$ is approximately equal to 33%.

15. B: The necessary formula is given in this problem, so all we have to do is put the given numbers into the given formula. It is, however, important to note that the formula requires the child's age in months, whereas the given age is in years. That's easy to convert, however: 2 years × 12 months/year = 24 months. Putting this into the formula, we get $\frac{24 \times 15 \text{ mg}}{150} = \frac{360 \text{ mg}}{150} = 2.4$ mg.

16. C: One way to subtract mixed numbers is to subtract the integer and fractional parts separately. To subtract the fractions, we first have to convert both fractions to the lowest common denominator: in this case, 8. So we can rewrite $\frac{1}{2}$ as $\frac{1 \times 4}{2 \times 4} = \frac{4}{8}$. Subtracting the fractional parts yields $\frac{4}{8} - \frac{3}{8} = \frac{1}{8}$. (If the right fraction had been larger, we would have had to borrow one from the left integer, but in this case that isn't necessary.) Subtracting the integer parts gives $7 - 5 = 2$. So the solution to the problem is $2\frac{1}{8}$.

Alternatively, we can first convert the mixed numbers to improper fractions: $7\frac{1}{2} = \frac{7 \times 2 + 1}{2} = \frac{15}{2}$, and $5\frac{3}{8} = \frac{5 \times 8 + 3}{8} = \frac{43}{8}$. As above, we rewrite the fractions with the same denominator: $\frac{15}{2} = \frac{15 \times 4}{2 \times 4} = \frac{60}{8}$. Now, $\frac{60}{8} - \frac{43}{8} = \frac{17}{8}$. Finally, we convert this improper fraction back into a mixed number: 8 goes into 17 2 times with a remainder of 1, so $\frac{17}{8} = 2\frac{1}{8}$.

17. A: Recall that a percentage is a number of hundredths, thus $20\% = \frac{20}{100} = 0.2$. To find 20% of a number, we multiply the number by 0.2. In that case, therefore, we're looking for the number that, when multiplied by 0.2, yields 35. That would be $35 \div 0.2 = 175$.

18. D: We could multiply this out with a calculator, but there is an even simpler way to solve this problem. Note that one of the numbers in the product is zero. Zero multiplied by anything is zero; no matter how many other numbers are multiplied together, if one of the factors is zero, the product is zero. Therefore, we know immediately that the product of this series of numbers is zero without having to use a calculator or do any lengthy calculations.

19. B: We could easily solve this problem with a calculator, but it's also possible to solve it without one. We could solve it as a regular long division problem, but we have to first get rid of the decimal point in the divisor. We can do that by moving the decimal point the same number of spaces in both the divisor and the dividend. Moving the decimal point one space to the right gives 79.5 ÷ 15. Now, we can proceed with a regular long division, putting the decimal point in the quotient directly above the decimal point in the dividend:

$$\begin{array}{r} 5.3 \\ 15{\overline{\smash{\big)}\,79.5}} \\ \underline{75} \\ 4\,5 \\ \underline{4\,5} \\ 0 \end{array}$$

20. C: To convert a fraction to a decimal, just divide the numerator by the denominator: $\frac{7}{10} = 7 \div 10 = 0.7$ (as can be verified either by using a calculator or by performing the division by hand). Alternatively, we can remember that the first digit after the decimal point is the tenths place, so any proper fraction with a 10 in the denominator is just the digit in the numerator after a decimal point: $\frac{1}{10}$ is 0.1, $\frac{3}{10}$ is 0.3, etc., and so $\frac{7}{10}$ is 0.7.

21. C: To convert a fraction to a decimal, just divide the numerator by the denominator: $\frac{4}{8} = 4 \div 8 = 0.5$ (as can be verified either by using a calculator or by performing the division by hand). Alternatively, we can observe that the fraction $\frac{4}{8}$ can be reduced, since both the numerator and denominator are divisible by 4: $\frac{4}{8} = \frac{4 \div 4}{8 \div 4} = \frac{1}{2}$, and $\frac{1}{2}$ is a common enough fraction that it's worth remembering its decimal and percentage equivalents: $\frac{1}{2} = 50\% = 0.5$.

22. A: When adding a positive and negative number, the absolute value of the result is equal to the *difference* of the absolute values of the individual numbers: 32 − 7 = 25. The sign of the result is the same as the sign of the number with the *larger* absolute value. In this case, |32| > |7|, so since the 32 is negative so is the result: −25.

We can also visualize this with a number line. Negative numbers are to the left of zero on the number line; positive numbers are to the right. Adding a positive number moves us right on the number line; adding a negative number moves us left. We start at −32, to the left of zero, and move seven places to the right, bringing us closer to zero, and specifically to −25.

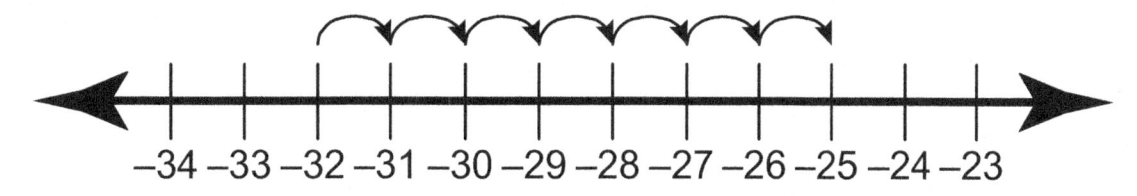

23. B: A percentage is equal to a number of hundredths: thus 41% is equal to $\frac{41}{100}$. To convert a percentage to a decimal, therefore, you just have to divide the percentage by 100—which is equivalent to moving the decimal point two places to the left. (If the number has no decimal point, you can consider the decimal point to be just to the right of the final digit.) In this case, $\frac{41}{100} = 0.41$.

24. B: This is a simple addition problem. Start with the ones column (on the right). Add the figures 8+1, 4+1, 2+3 to get the answer 559.

25. C: This is a simple addition problem with carrying. Start with the ones column and add 0+1. Write down the 1 and add the digits in the tens column: 8+3. Write down the 1 and add the 1 to the digits in the hundreds column. Add 9+1+1 and write down 1. Add the 1 to the digits in the thousands column. Add 3+7+1 and write down the 1. Add the 1 to the digits in the ten-thousands column. Add 1+1 and write down 2 to get the answer 21,011.

26. B: This is a simple subtraction problem. Start with the ones column and subtract 7-6, then 3-1, then 5-3, then 8-6 to get 2,221.

27. C: This is a multiplication problem with carrying. Start with the ones column. Multiply 2 by each digit above it beginning with the ones column. Write down each product: going across-- it will read 1268. Now multiply 7 by each of the digits above it. Write down each product: going across, the figure will read 4501. Ensure that the 1 is in the tens column and the other numbers fall evenly to the right. Now add the numbers like a regular addition problem to get 46,296.

28. D: This is a simple division problem. Divide 63 into 181. It goes in 2 times. Write 2 above the 1 and subtract 136 from 181. The result is 55. Bring down the 4. Divide 63 in 554. It goes in 8 times. Write 8 above the first 4 and subtract 504 from 554 to get 50. Bring down the 4. Divide 63 into 504. It goes in 8 times.

Science

1. A: All organisms begin life as a single cell.

2. B: The process by which organisms use energy is called metabolism.

3. D: Only cells with a membrane around the nucleus are called eukaryotes.

4. C: The two types of cellular transport are active (which requires the cell to invest energy) and passive (which does not require the cell to expend energy).

5. A: Aerobic means in the presence of oxygen.

6. B: When both parents give offspring the same allele, the offspring is homozygous for that particular trait.

7. C: Genetics is the study of heredity.

8. B: Scientists suggest that evolution has occurred through a process called natural selection.

9. D: The cellular hierarchy starts with the cell, the simplest structure, and progresses to organisms, the most complex structures.

10. B: A hypertonic solution is a solution with a higher particle concentration than in the cell, and consequently lower water content than in the cell. Water moves from the cell to the solution, causing the cell to experience water loss and shrink.

11. A: HCG is secreted by the trophoblast, part of the early embryo, following implantation in the uterus. GnRH is secreted by the hypothalamus, while LH and FSH are secreted by the pituitary gland.

12. C: The layers are the tunica externa, tunica media, and tunica interna. Unlike most arteries, the pulmonary artery carries deoxygenated blood to the lungs for oxygenation. Blood flow in capillaries is significantly slower than in veins. Blood pressure is not always directly impacted by heart rate.

13. D: Skeletal, smooth, and cardiac are all types of muscle tissue. Adipose is not.

14. B: The only purpose of muscles is to produce movement through contraction

15. B: Anterior means toward the front of the body.

16. B: The brain is part of the nervous system.

17. B: Anatomy is the study of the structure and shape of the body.

18. A: Physiology is the study of how parts of the body function.

19. A: Circulation is transporting oxygen and other nutrients to the tissues via the cardiovascular system.

20. A: Smooth is not a type of connective tissue. Cartilage, adipose tissue, and blood tissue all are.

KNAT Practice Test #3

Reading Comprehension

Questions 1-10 pertain to the following passage:

The disease known as rickets causes the bones to soften and creates a risk of bone fractures and even permanent bone deformation. It is most common in children, since their bones are already soft and are still growing. Rickets is believed to result from a lack of vitamin D and calcium, although some researchers will add a lack of phosphorus to this list. The disease is usually seen in parts of the world where children are suffering from poor nutrition. In the United States, doctors believed that the disease has been all but obsolete since the end of the Great Depression.

In fact, they were mistaken. Doctors are seeing a return of rickets, not just in the United States but also in other places where it was long since written off as no longer something to worry about. Cases of rickets are on the rise in states such as Georgia and North Carolina, and doctors are not entirely sure of the cause. They attribute the likely cause of the condition to poor nutrition and a lack of necessary vitamins and minerals. Many doctors believe that there is a twofold problem: low levels of calcium in young children who do not consume enough dairy products and low levels of vitamin D in breastfed babies. While breastfeeding is recommended, doctors point out that breast milk does not naturally contain high levels of vitamin D. This can be fine if the mother herself has adequate levels, but mothers with low levels of vitamin D will not provide enough for the baby as it nurses.

Among other developed nations, rickets is also making a reappearance in Great Britain. Doctors across England are seeing unexpected cases of rickets in children, and they believe that this is connected largely to low vitamin D levels. Some blame is placed on weather conditions, since Great Britain is not known for having copious amounts of sunshine, but also on lifestyle. Children are spending more time indoors watching television and playing video games, and in doing so they miss the sunshine when it is available. Additionally, parents are having their children wear sunscreen, which appears to be blocking what vitamin D would be absorbed while the children are outdoors.

Rickets is not yet considered an epidemic in developed nations, but there is enough concern among doctors and researchers to encourage awareness among parents. Children are encouraged to spend some time outdoors and to allow their skin to receive a little sun—just a few minutes a day is enough. Vitamin D and calcium supplements are also recommended, and nursing mothers are advised to have their levels checked. With any luck, rickets will once again become a disease of the past.

1. What is the author's primary purpose in writing the essay?
   a. to persuade
   b. to inform
   c. to analyze
   d. to entertain

2. What is the main idea of the passage?
   a. Rickets should once again be a disease of the past
   b. Rickets has once again become a problem in some developed nations
   c. Children need vitamin D and calcium to avoid rickets, and nursing mothers need to have their levels checked
   d. Rickets has reappeared only in the United States and Great Britain

3. Which of the following is *not* a detail from the passage?
   a. A lack of phosphorus is a possible contributor to rickets
   b. Sunscreen can block the skin's absorption of necessary vitamin D
   c. Adults in Great Britain also have low vitamin D levels
   d. Rickets has not been a problem in the United States since the time after the Great Depression

4. Based on the information provided in the passage, what can the reader infer about why the return of rickets is such a surprise in the United States?
   a. The diet in the United States has improved since the Great Depression
   b. People are already taking vitamin D and calcium supplements
   c. Unlike in Great Britain, there is plenty of sunshine in many parts of the United States
   d. Children in the United States spend enough time playing outdoors without wearing sunscreen

5. Which of the following *cannot* be inferred from the information in the passage?
   a. Rickets has always been most common in third world nations among people who have a poor diet
   b. Nursing mothers with low vitamin D levels should consider adding a supplement to their diet
   c. The number of rickets cases in developed nations is not necessarily high, but the rise in expected cases is enough to concern doctors about the cause
   d. Doctors are advising mothers with nursing babies to use formula that supplements vitamin D

6. Which of the following *can* be inferred from the information in the passage?
   a. Doctors believe that the cases of rickets in Great Britain are linked more to lack of vitamin D than to low levels of calcium
   b. Doctors now believe that children should not wear sunscreen while playing outside
   c. Nursing mothers in Great Britain typically have higher levels of vitamin D in their breast milk
   d. The majority of researchers believe that rickets is caused by lack of vitamin D and calcium only

7. The author uses the term *developed nations* to indicate which of the following in the passage?
   a. nations that are constantly improving the status quo for citizens
   b. nations that are world leaders in politics and economics
   c. nations in which citizens receive plenty of sunshine for vitamin D absorption
   d. nations in which most citizens have access to adequate nutritional options

8. What is the meaning of the word *copious* as it is used in the third paragraph?
   a. abundant
   b. small
   c. expected
   d. appropriate

9. What is the purpose of the final paragraph of the passage?
   a. to offer solutions for preventing and eliminating rickets
   b. to advise developing nations on how to avoid rickets
   c. to warn nursing mothers about the importance of vitamin D
   d. to provide hope for the future of a world without rickets

10. Which of the following is *not* a recommendation for ridding developed nations of rickets, as presented by the author?
   a. People should consider taking vitamin D and calcium supplements
   b. Children should get a little sun each day
   c. Television and video games should be limited among children
   d. Nursing mothers should have their vitamin D and calcium levels checked

Questions 11–20 pertain to the following passage:

So, your children got the chicken pox vaccine, and you think they will be all right. Not so fast. As it turns out, the chicken pox vaccine may only increase the risk of problems over time. Make no mistake: vaccination is not necessarily a bad thing, and vaccines have gone a long way toward eliminating illnesses that were once feared as life threatening or permanently disabling. But vaccines for some diseases, chicken pox in particular, come with side effects that create long-term uneasiness for doctors and researchers.

In fact, many scientists are increasingly concerned that *not* getting chicken pox might be more dangerous. Many people remember chicken pox as a standard childhood disease. Everyone seemed to get it, and everyone who had it probably knows that it is supposed to be a one-time deal. In others words, you catch chicken pox, scratch for about a week, and you never see it again—at least in theory. What happens in reality is that once a person catches chicken pox, the virus stays in the body. It typically remains dormant for the life of the individual, however, and the reason for this is only now being appreciated.

Researchers believe that those who have had chicken pox, those with the dormant virus in their bodies, should be around others who have had the disease. Doing so actually appears to boost the body's ongoing immunity against the virus. This means that spending time around children who have or have had chicken pox can help ensure that it never comes back. It can also help prevent the disease known as shingles later in life. Shingles, which is a more severe version of chicken pox, usually strikes adults after the age of sixty and can come with far more severe side effects than one week of scratching and sitting in an oatmeal bath. In some cases, shingles can cause problems that affect the sufferer for the rest of his or her life. But there appears to be a natural immunity that is built into getting chicken pox and then being around others with chicken pox, and researchers now believe that this explains the low rate of shingles that has traditionally been seen in the United States.

But what happens if very few people get chicken pox and most people are vaccinated? Children who are vaccinated do not contract the disease, and the amount of virus in the vaccine is not enough to boost immunity and thus prevent the contraction of shingles in many adults.

And shingles is particularly dangerous because many of the elderly who contract it are already in poor health and struggle to recover from it. Some epidemiologists suggest that the use of the chicken pox vaccine in the United States alone could lead to more than 20 million cases of shingles and at least 5,000 deaths from the disease. The potential concerns scientists enough that there remains ongoing debate about the value of the chicken pox vaccine.

11. What is the main idea of the passage?
   a. Getting the chicken pox vaccine can lead to shingles later in life
   b. Many children are getting the chicken pox vaccine throughout the United States
   c. The chicken pox vaccine has the potential to create long-term problems
   d. Chickenpox is no longer a childhood disease, as many adults now contract it

12. What is the author's primary purpose in writing the essay?
   a. to entertain
   b. to persuade
   c. to analyze
   d. to inform

13. Based on the information in the passage, what does an *epidemiologist* do?
   a. study diseases among a population
   b. study the internal organs of the human body
   c. study viruses that are contracted among children
   d. study adult problems that develop from childhood diseases

14. Which of the following is *not* a detail from the passage?
   a. There are deaths from chicken pox each year in the United States
   b. Shingles is a disease that develops from the same virus as chicken pox
   c. Some researchers believe that not getting chicken pox can cause problems
   d. Adults who contract shingles face a more dangerous disease than chicken pox

15. Based on the information in the passage, what is the value in contracting chicken pox during childhood?
   a. to get it over with as early as possible
   b. to avoid contracting shingles later in life
   c. to have the dormant virus in the body throughout life
   d. to demonstrate the body's natural immunity to some viruses

16. Based on the information in the passage, why is it important for people who have had chicken pox to be around others who have or have had the disease?
   a. to help keep the disease in circulation and avoid shingles
   b. to keep from catching chicken pox again
   c. to boost the body's immunity to the virus
   d. to maintain a low level of adult-contracted shingles

17. Which of the following *cannot* be inferred from the information in the passage?
   a. People typically have contracted chicken pox in childhood
   b. The age of shingles sufferers contributes to its serious effects on health
   c. Many vaccines have helped rid society of dangerous diseases
   d. Researchers believe that no one should get the chicken pox vaccine

18. Based on the information in the passage, why are some scientists concerned about extensive vaccination against chicken pox?
   a. There is very little disease in the vaccine, but it is just enough for adults who have not had chicken pox to contract shingles
   b. Researchers will be unable to locate enough subjects for ongoing study of health patterns among those who contract the disease
   c. The contraction of chicken pox among adults is far more inconvenient than it is for children, so it is easier to contract the disease in childhood
   d. Without frequent outbreaks of the disease, those who have already had it cannot build up their immunity to it

19. Which of the following pieces of information would make the author's point about the projected cases of shingles and deaths from shingles stronger in the final paragraph?
   a. the names of researchers who are active in educating people about the chicken pox vaccine
   b. the time period for the projected cases of shingles and the deaths from shingles
   c. the countries where the chicken pox vaccine is currently in wide use
   d. the number of people who are vaccinated against chicken pox each year

20. Which of the following *can* be inferred from the information in the final sentence?
   a. More and more researchers are advising against widespread vaccination against chicken pox
   b. The numbers are enough to concern researchers that the chicken pox vaccine might prove to do more harm than good
   c. Researchers continue to evaluate and consider the long-term effects of the chicken pox vaccine
   d. The concern about the effects of the chicken pox vaccine has led to a decrease in vaccinations

Questions 21–22 pertain to the following passage:

It seems like an obvious choice: do we destroy the final remaining samples of the smallpox virus or not? Smallpox, the terror that ravaged nations for centuries, was virtually destroyed in the latter part of the twentieth century—but not before it took about 500,000,000 people with it. Smallpox is one of the most dangerous viruses, attacking only humans (but not animals) and leaving only 70 percent of those infected with it alive. In some cases, survival brought its own challenges. The virus has been known to leave severe scarring, and many victims also lost their eyesight. Smallpox is so virulent that the small amount in the vaccine has been known to cause minor side effects.

So why would anyone want to keep samples around? Why not destroy what is left of the disease and eradicate it for good? After its successful inoculation program, the World Health Organization (WHO) has continued to maintain a selection of smallpox virus samples; more than 400 samples sit in laboratories in the United States and in Russia. The WHO has agreed that the samples should be consigned to the dustbin of history. They just cannot agree on whether all samples should be destroyed, and when the destruction should occur. The Soviet Union collapsed in 1991, but there were suggestions that the Soviet government, among others, had hidden samples of the smallpox virus separate from the official samples that were acknowledged. Should the WHO destroy all official samples, any remaining unofficial samples (never confirmed to be real) could be used to attack a population in an act of bioterrorism.

Without its own samples, the WHO and its researchers might be unable to create an effective treatment or vaccine.

Bioterrorism remains a real threat, and smallpox continues to be a concern for those looking at potential diseases that terrorists might use. What is more, the WHO points out that the majority of people today have no defense against outbreaks of the disease. Inoculation against smallpox ended in the early 1980s, and smallpox was declared to be officially defeated. Should a terrorist choose to attack people with smallpox, most would be completely susceptible to its dangers. As a result, many scientists—and particularly those who study infectious diseases—believe that the WHO should continue to delay destruction of the smallpox virus samples. Others claim that there are currently effective vaccines that could be used to protect a population. Even the two nations that hold these final samples are at loggerheads about the issue. One thing seems to be certain: the WHO still agrees that the smallpox samples should be destroyed. They just do not seem to know how *many* of the samples to destroy and *how soon*.

21. Which of the following words describes the author's primary purpose in writing the essay?
   a. persuasive
   b. Investigative
   c. Expository
   d. Advisory

22. What is the main idea of the passage?
   a. The smallpox vaccine should be destroyed to eradicate the disease and prevent future outbreaks
   b. The smallpox vaccine should not be destroyed to maintain samples that can be used in the event of a bioterrorism attack
   c. The United States and Russia cannot agree on how many of the remaining smallpox samples to destroy, so the World Health Organization has stepped in to assist
   d. The World Health Organization would prefer to destroy remaining samples of the smallpox vaccine but cannot decide when to do so

Writing

Questions 1-4 are based on the following passage:

¹While best known for pulling Santa's sleigh every Christmas on his mythical trip to every child's home, reindeer (or caribou as they are typically called in North America) have played an important role in human history. ²For many people groups in Arctic or subarctic regions, their way of life has depended on reindeer. ³In Finland, Norway, and other Scandinavian countries, the reindeer serve multiple purposes. ⁴They are milked, their meat is a staple part of the diet, their fur is sold or used for clothing, and even its antlers can be powdered for a nutritional supplement. ⁵Reindeer were also traditionally used for transportation (and in some regions are still used to pull sleds). ⁶Some people groups travel with herds of wild caribou, following their grazing route and depending on the herds of reindeers' for food and shelter. ⁷Caribou are so integral to their life that not only the people's physical needs and also their entertainment is centered around the animals, such as games, toys, and songs.

⁸Life dependent on caribou is a nomadic life. ⁹Caribou can travel for hundred's or even thousand's of miles each year as they seek new pasture, as well as traveling to give birth. ¹⁰Through the winter, animals roam to find food. ¹¹In the spring, females travel to remote areas to calve, having then chosen locations such as islands for the safety of their newborn calves. ¹²Although newborn caribou weigh less than fifteen pounds, on average, they begin to walk immediately, and within 24 hours of birth, they are faster than an adult human. ¹³Thus, they can keep up with the herd immediately, which increases safety.

¹⁴As beforely mentioned, caribou weigh less than fifteen pounds at birth, but may be up to 400 pounds at maturity. ¹⁵Despite their bulk they can run at 50 mph for short distances and can maintain a pace of 20 mph for long periods of time. ¹⁶They can also swim quickly across lakes and rushing rivers. ¹⁷Their thick coats protect them against the brutally cold temperatures.

¹⁸In the cold climate where they live, very little vegetation grows. ¹⁹During the coldest months little can be found: grasslike plants, small shrubs, and lichen. ²⁰This lichen is called "reindeer moss" since they are the only animals in the world that can ingest it due to a particular stomach enzyme that only reindeer have. ²¹They roam the frozen tundra, which using their powerful sense of smell to locate anything edible beneath the snow and digging to uncover it.

²²Through the harsh conditions, caribou continue to thrive, migrating annually. ²³Some subspecies have become endangered, but as a whole, the species is still populous. ²⁴Despite wolves and bears, and the constant threat of starvation, they remain. ²⁵However, their role has changed over the years.

1. Which sentence includes an unnecessary word or phrase?
 a. Sentence 3 includes the unnecessary word *the*.
 b. Sentence 5 includes the unnecessary word *pull*.
 c. Sentence 14 includes the unnecessary phrase *at birth*.
 d. Sentence 21 includes the unnecessary word *edible*.

2. Which option BEST describes how to correct the use of an apostrophe in the passage?
 a. In sentence 1, the word *child's* should be *childs*.
 b. In sentence 4, the word *its* should be *it's*.
 c. In sentence 6, the word *reindeers'* should be *reindeer's*.
 d. In sentence 9, the word *hundred's* should be *hundreds*.

3. **Which sentence would be the most correct way to rewrite sentence 20?**
   a. This lichen is called "reindeer moss," since reindeer are the only animals in the world with the stomach enzyme to digest it.
   b. This lichen is called "reindeer moss" because reindeer are the only animals in the world with the stomach enzyme necessary to digest it.
   c. Reindeer are the only animals in the world with the stomach enzyme necessary to digest it, so this lichen is called "reindeer moss".
   d. Reindeer are the only animals in the world with the stomach enzyme necessary to digest this lichen called "reindeer moss".

4. **Which sentence could be removed because it is unnecessary?**
   a. Sentence 4
   b. Sentence 8
   c. Sentence 10
   d. Sentence 16

Questions 5-9 are based on the following passage:

¹In lists of familiar instruments, oboes rarely appear near the top. ²While most people would easily recognize a piano or violin, many would not be able to identify an oboe, much less to identify it by sound. ³Yet it is an instrument that has been used for millennium. ⁴The predecessors of today's oboes were popular among shepherds. ⁵And in ancient Greece, the famous aulos was a version of the oboe as well.

⁶The oboe is a woodwind instrument, along with instruments such as: the flute, clarinet, and saxophone. ⁷Many of these instruments are reed pipes, meaning that a reed is fixed in the mouthpiece. ⁸When air is blown into the mouthpiece, the reed causes vibration, which produces a distinctive musical note. ⁹The oboe differs from many other reed pipes because of its double reed. ¹⁰This double reed is exposed, meaning it is placed directly in the player's lips rather than being covered by a mouthpiece.

¹¹In concert performances, the oboe is used to tune the rest of the instruments. ¹²Its unique, penetrating sound is easily distinguished from the other instruments, making it easy to follow. ¹³And it has a steady pitch, more so than most instruments, making it more undependable for tuning.

¹⁴An oboe's pitch depends on many factors such as humidity and temperature, but also on how the reed is made. ¹⁵Experienced oboists often make their own reeds. ¹⁶Customizing them to their specific needs and preferences, the reeds are carefully suited for each individual musician. ¹⁷Reeds are often made from a cane called *Arundo donax*, also known as giant reed or elephant grass. ¹⁸For centuries, this cane has been used by artisans to create not only oboes but also other woodwind instruments. ¹⁹Professional oboists often have special tools; making and then adjusting their reeds as needed.

²⁰There are several members of the oboe family, some with lower pitches such as the bass oboe and some with higher pitches like the piccolo oboe. ²¹However, the treble and soprano oboes are the most commonly played. ²²The player controls the notes by pressing keys to cover the tone holes. ²³An oboe usually has 23 or 24 tone holes, which are smaller than in many other woodwind instruments. ²⁴This small size causes the distinctive tone oboes are known for.

²⁵Oboes are used in a variety of musical styles, from classical to folk to jazz. ²⁶Composers such as Bach, Handel, and Haydn composed pieces specifically designed for the oboe. ²⁷Oboes are often used in film scores, adding to a somber or meaningful scene.

²⁸The oboe is unlikely to ever become one of the world's most popular instruments, so it has endured and continues to contribute to the musical scene. ²⁹From its first orchestral appearance nearly 400 years ago in the 1600's to its varied uses today, it has made its mark. ³⁰From its haunting notes with only sheep as an audience to its performance in today's largest concert, the oboe creates a unique listening experience.

5. Which word should be made plural?
- a. The word *millennium* in sentence 3.
- b. The word *vibration* in sentence 8.
- c. The word *reed* in sentence 17.
- d. The word *sheep* in sentence 30.

6. What is the BEST way to correct an error in sentence 18?
- a. Remove the comma after *centuries*.
- b. Add a comma after *create*.
- c. Add the word *reeds* after *create*.
- d. Add the word *many* after *For*.

7. Which sentence contains a grammatical error?
- a. Sentence 4
- b. Sentence 12
- c. Sentence 16
- d. Sentence 26

8. Which word would be the BEST replacement for the word *so* in sentence 28?
- a. because
- b. and
- c. while
- d. but

9. Which option BEST describes how to correct a punctuation error in the passage?
- a. In sentence 4, insert a comma after *popular*.
- b. In sentence 14, remove the comma after *temperature*.
- c. In sentence 17, insert a comma after *called*.
- d. In sentence 29, remove the comma after *today*.

Questions 10-16 are based on the following passage:

¹While portrayals of ancient humans typically depict them in coverings made of animal skin, woven fabric was actually a very early invention. ²Although "The Flintstones" popularized the caveman look of skins, woven flax fibers have been discovered that date back thousands of years. ³The ancient art of weaving is less unknown today, as machines have largely replaced the handwork of past millennia.

⁴In today's textile industry, materials are sourced from four main types: three natural and one artificial. ⁵Natural sources include animals, plants, and minerals. ⁶Artificial, or synthetic, sources,

such as polyester, are unique to the last two centuries and have slowly been reducing their portion of the textile market, offering new options to the traditional fabrics.

⁷There is an increasingly demand for inexpensive fabrics for mass production. ⁸Traditionally, most people had a small wardrobe and did not replace their clothing often. ⁹Today's production is highly wasteful and destructive to the environment, and changes need to be made. ¹⁰Today the average person purchases multiple pieces of clothing every year and landfills are full of discarded items that have went out of style or are too poor in quality to last more than a few months. ¹¹Fashion trends tend to be fleeting, so new clothing is often worn for a short time before replacing. ¹²Thus, there is demand for cheaper materials, and less overall concern with durability.

¹³Despite this trend, many high-quality fabrics are still produced today. ¹⁴Many of these come from natural sources, such as animal fibers and cotton. ¹⁵One of the most prized materials throughout history has been wool. ¹⁶Wool comes primarily from sheep but can also include the hair of alpacas, camels, and goats, among other animals. ¹⁷Wool was a plausible export for many countries in medieval times, but since the 1960s, the value of and demand for wool has dropped significantly due to the development of synthetic fibers.

¹⁸Another natural material that has stood the test of time is silk. ¹⁹Despite wool, it has an animal source, but instead of being made from animal hair, it is made from a protein fiber spun by silkworms. ²⁰The process of harvesting silkworm cocoons, unwinding the thread, and weaving it into fabric has been used for thousands of years. ²¹The earliest known example was in China, and China is still the world's top producer by far.

²²As production of wool and silk continue to grow, they are still in demand throughout the world. ²³Although made more efficient by technological advances, much of the original knowledge from past civilizations is still used. ²⁴Along with other natural fibers, as well as the more modern synthetic materials, textiles continue to be an important part of human culture, not only to keep people clothed and warm but also to express personality, belief, and values.

10. Which sentence is redundant and could be removed?
    a. Sentence 2
    b. Sentence 7
    c. Sentence 13
    d. Sentence 17

11. Which word is the BEST replacement for *went* in sentence 10?
    a. been
    b. going
    c. gone
    d. fell

12. Which sentence below shows correct punctuation for sentence 12?
    a. Thus, there is demand for cheaper materials, and less overall concern with durability.
    b. Thus there is demand for cheaper materials, and less overall concern with durability.
    c. Thus, there is demand for cheaper materials and less overall concern with durability.
    d. Thus there is demand for cheaper materials; and less overall concern with durability.

13. Which word or phrase is used incorrectly?
   a. In sentence 3, the word *unknown* should be *known*.
   b. In sentence 7, the word *inexpensive* should be *expensive*.
   c. In sentence 14, the word *natural* should be *synthetic*.
   d. In sentence 23, the word *more* should be *less*.

14. Which sentence could be removed because it is irrelevant?
   a. Sentence 6
   b. Sentence 9
   c. Sentence 12
   d. Sentence 18

15. Which sentence is the most correct way to rewrite sentence 21?
   a. The earliest known example was in China and China is still the world's top producer by far.
   b. The earliest known example was in China, which is still the world's top producer by far.
   c. The earliest known example was in China, because it is still the world's top producer by far.
   d. The earliest known example was in China the world's top producer by far.

16. Which sentence contains a word that is used incorrectly?
   a. Sentence 8
   b. Sentence 12
   c. Sentence 19
   d. Sentence 23

Questions 17-21 are based on the following passage:

[1]Scientific Classification, also known as taxonomy, is a methodology of classifying every living being. [2]This provides a way, to organize all animals, plants, and other living things into a database that can be used for comparing and understanding how various parts of the ecosystem fit together.

[3]There are seven levels of classification, beginning with Kingdom, which separates beings into basic categories like plants or animals, and ending with Species, the most specific category, such as a human being or a particular type of mushroom. [4]The animal kingdom, including over one million species, is the largest of the kingdoms. [5]Classification of these animals were determined by their eating and reproductive habits, their breathing and moving, and their embryonic development. [6]Animals range from organisms so small they are invisible to the naked eye to the blue whale, but the one thing all have in common is that they have multiple cells.

[7]The second most populous kingdom is Kingdom Plantae, or plants, with over 250,000 species. [8]These include the familiar trees, bushes, and flowers, but also certain types of algae and moss. [9]Like animals, plants are multicellular. [10]They have cell walls made of cellulose. [11]Plants utilize photosynthesis for food. [12]By depending on the sun. [13]This is called being autotrophic. [14]A side effect of photosynthesis is the production of oxygen, benefiting the earth's ecosystems.

[15]The other kingdoms are Fungi, Protista, and Monera (which is often divided into separate kingdoms of Eubacteria and Archaebacteria). [16]Within each of the kingdoms, the classification can be further broken into the following levels: Phylum, Class, Order, Family, Genus, Species. [17]Each different classification level is a taxon. [18]An organism is known by it's last two divisions, genus and species. [19]This is called its binomial nomenclature. [20]Each taxon creates more and more distinctions, from the broadest distinction of Kingdom, such as all animals, to the narrowest distinction of Species, such as *Harmonia axyridis*, or a ladybug.

21This binomial nomenclature gives a universal identification for each species, aiding scientists and anyone studying or researching a particular organism. 22This name not only identifies the exact species of an organism in the second word, but also its biological relatives in the first word, this is similar to a person's last name.

23The scientific classification system has been developed and adapted over the past few centuries, with contributions from many major scientists such as Carl Linnaeus and Charles Darwin. 24In fact, long before today's system was in place, Aristotle created a system, first dividing organisms into plants and animals and then further classifying by attributes such as whether an animal was a vertebrate, laid eggs, etc. 25Some animals, like the platypus, are more challenging to classify. 26Humans have long sought to understand their world better, organizing and comparing the various beings in our ecosystem. 27While we still have much to discover, and not everyone agrees on how organisms fit together, taxonomy has greatly helped us to know and care for the ecosystems.

17. Where is the BEST place to add this introductory phrase?

    However, unlike animals,

    a. At the beginning of sentence 8
    b. At the beginning of sentence 10
    c. At the beginning of sentence 11
    d. At the beginning of sentence 18

18. Which word or phrase is the BEST replacement for *it's* in sentence 18?

    a. its
    b. its'
    c. their
    d. they're

19. Which option BEST describes how to correct a word used in sentence 5?

    a. Change the word *animals* to *kingdoms*.
    b. Change the word *were* to *was*.
    c. Change the word *habits* to *habitats*.
    d. Change the word *development* to *developing*.

20. Which option BEST describes how to correct a punctuation error in the passage?

    a. In sentence 5, add a semicolon after *by*.
    b. In sentence 16, replace the colon after *levels* with a semicolon.
    c. In sentence 20, remove the comma after *Species*.
    d. In sentence 23, remove the comma after *centuries*.

21. Which sentence could be removed because it is irrelevant?

    a. Sentence 1
    b. Sentence 7
    c. Sentence 18
    d. Sentence 25

Mathematics

1. What number is 75% of 500?

    a. 365
    b. 375
    c. 387
    d. 390

2. $(7 \times 5) + (8 \times 2) = ?$

    a. 51
    b. 57
    c. 85
    d. 560

3. $(8 \div 2) \times (12 \div 3) = ?$

    a. 1
    b. 8
    c. 12
    d. 16

4. Which of the following numbers is a factor of 36?

    a. 5
    b. 7
    c. 8
    d. 9

5. $75 \times 34 = ?$

    a. 1200
    b. 2050
    c. 2550
    d. 3100

6. Solve for x:

$$x + 372 = 853$$

    a. 455
    b. 481
    c. 520
    d. 635

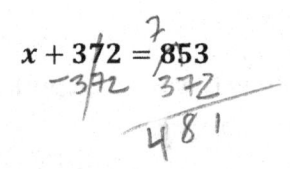

7. Which fraction is equivalent to the decimal 0.25?

    a. $\frac{1}{4}$
    b. $\frac{1}{2}$
    c. $\frac{1}{8}$
    d. $\frac{2}{3}$

8. The decimal 0.85 is equivalent to which fraction?
    a. $\frac{13}{15}$
    b. $\frac{17}{20}$
    c. $\frac{18}{19}$
    d. $\frac{19}{22}$

9. Which of the following fractions is closest to $\frac{2}{3}$ without going over?
    a. $\frac{6}{13}$
    b. $\frac{7}{12}$
    c. $\frac{11}{16}$
    d. $\frac{9}{12}$

10. A circle graph is used to show the percentage of each patient class that a hospital sees. If $\frac{1}{3}$ of the patients seen are pediatric patients, how much of the circle should indicate pediatric?
    a. 90 degrees
    b. 120 degrees
    c. 180 degrees
    d. 210 degrees

11. A traveler spent $25 on food during his first week of vacation. He then spent $52 on food each of the next two weeks. The fourth week he spent $34 on food. What was his average weekly food expenditure over his four-week vacation?
    a. $ 37.00
    b. $ 38.25
    c. $ 40.75
    d. $ 52.00

12. $437.65 - 325.752 = ?$
    a. 111.898
    b. 121.758
    c. 122.348
    d. 133.053

13. $43.3 \times 23.03 = ?$
    a. 997.199
    b. 999.999
    c. 1010.03
    d. 1111.01

14. After two weeks of dieting, a patient lost 6% of their original body weight. If the original weight was 157 pounds, what was the final weight after two weeks (to the nearest pound)?
    a. 139 lbs
    b. 142 lbs
    c. 145 lbs
    d. 148 lbs

15. In order for a school to allow a vending machine to be placed next to the cafeteria, 65% of the student population must request it. If 340 of the school's 650 students have already requested the vending machine, how many more must request it in order for the vending machine to be installed?

   a. 75
   b. 83
   c. 89
   d. 99

16. Round this number to the nearest hundredth: 390.24657

   a. 400
   b. 390.247
   c. 390.25
   d. 390.2

17. What number, when multiplied by $\frac{4}{5}$, gives an answer of 1?

   a. $\frac{5}{4}$
   b. $\frac{1}{2}$
   c. $\frac{1}{4}$
   d. $\frac{4}{3}$

18. During a given week, a patient's sodium intake was 300 mg on Monday, 1240 mg on Tuesday, 900 mg on Wednesday and on Friday, and 1500 mg on Thursday. What was the patient's average sodium intake for those five days?

   a. 476 mg
   b. 754 mg
   c. 968 mg
   d. 998 mg

19. Which of the following numbers is correctly rounded to the nearest tenth?

   a. 3.756 rounds to 3.76
   b. 4.567 rounds to 4.5
   c. 6.982 rounds to 7.0
   d. 54.32 rounds to 54.4

20. Which of the following fractions is equivalent to the decimal 0.625?

   a. 3/4
   b. 5/6
   c. 5/8
   d. 2/3

21. A 6% (by volume) solution of bleach in water is required for cleaning a bathroom. How many mL of the solution can be made from 50 mL of pure bleach?

   a. 833 mL
   b. 952 mL
   c. 1054 mL
   d. 2000 mL

22. $8.7 \times 23.3 = ?$

    a. 202.71
    b. 2027.1
    c. 212.71
    d. 2127.1

23. $134.5 \div 5 = ?$

    a. 26.9
    b. 25.9
    c. 23.9
    d. 22.9

24. $23 \div 3 = ?$

    a. $6\frac{2}{3}$
    b. $7\frac{1}{3}$
    c. $7\frac{2}{3}$
    d. $8\frac{1}{3}$

25. $4500 + 3422 + 3909 = ?$

    a. 12,831
    b. 12,731
    c. 11,831
    d. 11,731

26. $14,634 + 7,377 = ?$

    a. 21,901
    b. 21,911
    c. 22,011
    d. 22,901

27. $9,645 - 6,132 = ?$

    a. 2,513
    b. 2,517
    c. 3,412
    d. 3,513

28. $893 \times 64 = ?$

    a. 54,142
    b. 56,822
    c. 56,920
    d. 57,152

Science

1. Which chemicals are responsible for conveying an impulse along a nerve cell?
    a. Sodium and potassium
    b. Calcium
    c. Actin and myosin
    d. Phosphorus

2. What type of genetic mutation occurs when a piece of DNA breaks off the chromosome and attaches to a different chromosome?
    a. Nondisjunction
    b. Translocation
    c. Deletion
    d. Crossing over

3. What is the first line of defense against invading bacteria?
    a. The skin
    b. Macrophages
    c. T-cells
    d. Lymphocytes

4. What is the purpose of capping the 5' end of mRNA?
    a. To signal the end of the mRNA strand
    b. To prepare it to attach to the complementary DNA strand
    c. To protect the end of the strand from degradation
    d. There is no known reason for capping the end of an mRNA strand

5. During what process does hydrolysis occur to provide electrons to chlorophyll, which subsequently absorb energy?
    a. Light-dependent reactions of photosynthesis
    b. Light-independent reactions of photosynthesis
    c. Calvin cycle
    d. Krebs cycle

6. What is the process called when root hairs capture water and move it upwards into the rest of the plant?
    a. Photosynthesis
    b. Diffusion
    c. Active transport
    d. Transpiration

7. Which plant hormone causes fruit to ripen?
    a. Auxins
    b. Cytokinins
    c. Ethylene
    d. Abscisic Acid

8. What is thigmotropism?
    a. Growth of plant materials toward light
    b. Growth of leaves and stems opposite to the pull of gravity
    c. Growth toward a source of nutrition
    d. Growth of plant structures in response to contact with a physical structure

9. What is the purpose of the stigma?
    a. To gather pollen
    b. To attract pollinators like birds and bees
    c. To nourish the fertilized ovum
    d. To produce pollen

10. Organisms with the same _____ are most closely related.
    a. order
    b. genus
    c. family
    d. class

11. The triceps reflex:
    a. forces contraction of the triceps and extension of the arm
    b. forces contraction of the biceps, relaxation of the biceps, and arm extension
    c. causes the triceps to contract, causing the forearm to supinate and flex
    d. causes the triceps to relax and the upper arm to pronate and extend

12. Which cranial nerve is responsible for hearing and balance?
    a. CN III
    b. CN V
    c. CN VIII
    d. CN XII

13. Which gland is responsible for the regulation of calcium levels?
    a. The parathyroid glands
    b. The pituitary gland
    c. The adrenal glands
    d. The pancreas

14. Which hormone is predominantly produced during the luteal phase of the menstrual cycle?
    a. Estrogen
    b. Luteinizing hormone
    c. Follicle stimulating hormone
    d. Progesterone

15. The pancreas secretes what hormone in response to low blood glucose levels?
    a. Insulin
    b. Glucagon
    c. Somatostatin
    d. Amylase

16. **Which part of the cardiac conduction system is the most distal from the initial impulse generation and actually conducts the charge throughout the heart tissue?**
    a. SA node
    b. AV node
    c. Purkinje fibers
    d. Bundle of His

17. **Which blood vessel carries oxygenated blood back to the heart?**
    a. Pulmonary vein
    b. Pulmonary artery
    c. Aorta
    d. Superior vena cava

18. **Which vitamin is essential for proper formation of clotting factors?**
    a. Vitamin A
    b. Vitamin K
    c. Vitamin B
    d. Vitamin C

19. **Afferent lymph vessels carry lymph:**
    a. toward the spleen
    b. away from the spleen
    c. toward the lymph node
    d. away from the lymph node

20. **Which of the following is not found in the mediastinum?**
    a. Xiphoid process
    b. Thymus
    c. Trachea
    d. Vagus nerve

Answer Key and Explanations for Test #3

Reading Comprehension

1. B: The author's primary purpose is to inform the reader about the apparent increase in cases of rickets in developed nations. There is nothing about the essay that suggests persuasion, as the author is simply providing information rather than attempting to persuade the reader to agree with a certain position or opinion. The author provides information but does not necessarily analyze it too closely, so the author's purpose is not to analyze. Additionally, there is little in the essay that indicates a desire to entertain.

2. B: Based on the information at the end of the first paragraph and at the beginning of the second paragraph, the author's main point is that rickets has once again become a problem in some developed nations. (The author starts by noting that this disease is typically seen in nations where children face malnourishment, but that this has not occurred in developed nations for many decades.) Answer choice A suggests a persuasive argument that is not present within the essay. The author does make a final note at the end about rickets becoming a disease of the past, but this is more of a hopeful comment than a call to action. Answer choice C offers information that the author includes as part of the explanation about rickets, but it is supporting information and not the main point. The author singles out the United States and Great Britain but also refers to "other places" where the disease has surprised doctors with its reappearance. This suggests other countries besides the United States and Great Britain, so answer choice D cannot be correct.

3. C: The author clearly mentions the information that is in answer choices A, B, and D. The possibility of a phosphorus deficiency contributing to rickets is noted in the first paragraph. The fact that sunscreen has been identified as a possible vitamin D blocker is mentioned in the third paragraph. The fact that rickets has not been a problem in the United States since the Great Depression is also included in the first paragraph. The author says that *children* in Great Britain are identified as having low vitamin D levels, but there is no mention of vitamin D levels in adults in Great Britain. (This information is actually true, but it is not included in the essay, so answer choice C is correct.)

4. A: If rickets—at least in the United States—was usually a problem that accompanied poor nutrition, and rickets has not been a problem since the Great Depression, the reader can infer that the diet in the United States has improved since the Great Depression. There is nothing in the passage to suggest that people are already taking calcium and vitamin D supplements; in fact, the author notes that doctors are recommending it because people do not have enough calcium and vitamin D. (If they do not have enough, they cannot already be taking the supplements.) The author mentions that sunshine in Great Britain is often in short supply, but there is no discussion of sunshine in the United States. What is more, the author mentions Georgia and North Carolina, neither of which is known for being excessively overcast. And there is no discussion about children's play patterns in the United States, so it cannot be inferred that children in the United States have a vitamin D deficiency because they spend too much time indoors and/or wear too much sunscreen. This discussion is limited to the third paragraph, about Great Britain.

5. D: The author states the exact opposite of the information in answer choice D: far from discouraging breastfeeding, doctors still recommend it. They just encourage nursing mothers to have their vitamin D levels checked and to add a supplement if the levels are low. The author contrasts the developed nations with those that traditionally have poor nutrition and where children suffer from rickets. Developing nations tend to fall into the category of the "third world," so answer choice A is a safe inference. The author includes the information from answer choice B in the final paragraph, so this cannot be correct. Similarly, the author notes in the first sentence of the final paragraph that rickets is not yet considered an epidemic in developed nations but that doctors are concerned about seeing it at all.

6. A: Given the shift in focus from the second paragraph to the third, it is safe to assume that the cause of rickets in Great Britain is linked more to low vitamin D than to low calcium. In fact, the author states outright that doctors in Great Britain believe the cases of rickets are "connected largely to low vitamin D levels." That sunscreen is connected to blocking vitamin D is mentioned, but nothing is said about whether doctors recommend that children wear (or stop wearing) sunscreen. There is no discussion about nursing mothers in Great Britain, so it is impossible to infer anything about the levels of vitamin D in their breast milk. In the first paragraph, low levels of phosphorus are noted as a possible cause of rickets; it is also mentioned that "some researchers" believe this. The word *some* is too vague to determine in any quantity, so it is impossible to say with any certainty if "most researchers" disagree with this.

7. D: In the first paragraph, the author clearly connects rickets with poor nutrition. The author also mentions a time (the Great Depression) when there was poor nutrition in the United States. This would suggest that the term *developed nations* refers to those nations where the citizens have access to adequate nutritional options. There is no mention of a "status quo" anywhere in the passage, so answer choice A makes no sense. Additionally, there is no discussion of politics and economics, so answer choice B cannot be correct. As Great Britain is included among the developed nations but is also noted for having limited sunshine, answer choice C is also incorrect.

8. A: Among the available answer choices, only the word *abundant* makes real sense in the context of the paragraph: Great Britain is not known for having abundant amounts of sunshine. The word *small* makes no sense in the paragraph, since the author is claiming that there is often limited sunshine. The word *expected* does not work, since there is no mention about the amount of sunshine that would be expected. The word *appropriate* does not work, since it is difficult to say whether a certain amount of sunshine is appropriate.

9. A: In the final paragraph, the author simply provides information for preventing and eliminating rickets. Again, this is not a persuasive essay, but the final paragraph is not persuasive in tone. It is largely informative, and the essay would feel incomplete without it. After all, if the essay ended after the third paragraph, the reader would likely wonder about the solution to the problem of rickets. The author says nothing about developing nations in the final paragraph; in fact, the focus is largely on ridding developed nations of a disease that has returned. The author mentions nursing mothers in the final paragraph, but this is in conjunction with the other possible solutions; so, the final paragraph is clearly not focused only on nursing mothers. And answer choice D is too broad for the information in the final paragraph. The author suggests possible options for getting rid of rickets in developed nations, but there is little to infer a "world without rickets" from the information in the paragraph.

10. C: The author focuses on three primary recommendations in the final paragraph: children getting a little sunshine each day (to ensure some vitamin D absorption), people taking vitamin D and calcium supplements, and nursing mothers having their vitamin D levels checked. Limiting television and video games among children is not included as a recommendation, so answer choice C is correct.

11. C: The last sentence of the first paragraph shapes the main idea of the essay: doctors and researchers are concerned about the long-term problems that might result from the chicken pox vaccine. Additionally, the final sentence in the essay notes that there is "ongoing debate about the value of the chicken pox vaccine." These statements offer a clear sense of focus for the essay. The passage does not say that getting the chicken pox vaccine can cause problems with shingles later in life, but this is a supporting point in the passage and not the main idea. Similarly, the author mentions that an increasing number of people in the United States are getting the chicken pox vaccine, but this is a fact the author uses to shape the main point and not the main point itself. The author notes that many children contract chicken pox, but the only mention of adults is in connection with shingles. In fact, there are adults that catch chicken pox, but this is not mentioned in the essay, nor can it be identified as the main point.

12. D: The author's primary purpose is simply to inform the reader about the concerns that many doctors and researchers have about the chicken pox vaccine. The author does not take a clear stand on the issue, and the author does not attempt to persuade the reader either way. The author includes information that analyzes the problem, but the overall focus is on providing information rather than on analyzing. And while the tone of the essay is occasionally playful, the topic is not, so it cannot be said that the author's purpose is to entertain—particularly on so serious a subject.

13. A: The author refers to epidemiologists in conjunction with the potential outbreak of shingles among the people in the United States. This would suggest that an epidemiologist studies diseases among a population. (Looking more closely at the word, the reader can also see a connection to the word *epidemic*, which is the outbreak of disease among a large number of people in a population.) There is no mention of internal organs anywhere in the essay, and as anyone who has had chicken pox knows it reveals itself at the topical level; answer choice B cannot be correct. Chicken pox is indeed a virus (*varicella*), and it is most common among children, but the word *epidemiologist* is not used anywhere near the specific discussion of children and viruses, so answer choice C is too great a stretch. Similarly, the author mentions the outbreak of shingles, but the word *problems* is itself a problem in answer choice D. Shingles is a *disease* that results from a *virus*. What is more, the author makes it clear that shingles is serious enough to go beyond a mere "adult problem," so answer choice D does not have enough support in the passage.

14. A: Nowhere in the passage does the author mention deaths in the United States as a result of chicken pox. The author does, however, note that shingles develops from the same virus as chicken pox. The author states quite clearly that some researchers and doctors believe *not* getting chicken pox might cause problems later on. And the author points out that shingles is a far more serious disease than chicken pox, in part because it attacks elderly adults whose health is already frail.

15. B: The author makes the connection between chicken pox and avoiding shingles: people who contract chicken pox in childhood develop a built-in immunity to shingles later in life. While chicken pox is inconvenient and it might be better to get it over with during childhood, the author says nothing to suggest this as a reason in favor of contracting chicken pox. Answer choice C gets part of the way there, but it does not offer the real reason for contracting chicken pox during childhood: the dormant virus helps *avoid contacting shingles*. And answer choice D is fairly absurd; one should not be in favor of contracting a disease just for the purpose of demonstrating the body's ability to develop a natural immunity to something else.

16. C: The author notes that contracting chicken pox means the individual always has the virus in his or her body. Being around others who have or have had chicken pox creates a kind of booster shot against the disease—just without the actual vaccine. It is a natural immunity boost against the virus, even as it remains in the body. Answer choice A presents a fairly backward way of looking at the issue. What is more, it does not identify the real reason for *being around others who have or have had the disease*, as explained in the correct answer choice, C. Answer choice B provides the desired side effect of catching chicken pox but does not answer the question that is posed. And answer choice D is the preferred result, but again it does not answer the specific question.

17. D: While the author explains that doctors and researchers are concerned about the long-term effects of the vaccine and continue to debate it, there is nothing in the passage to suggest that anyone is advising against it. The author says quite clearly that chicken pox is usually seen as a childhood disease, so it can be inferred that most people contract it during childhood. The author mentions that shingles affects adults over 60, and many of them already have weakened health. This would suggest that their age and state of health increases the problems that shingles brings with it. Finally, the author points out in the first paragraph that vaccines have been invaluable for ridding society of many serious diseases.

18. D: Question 18 requires a little analytical thinking. Avoiding the shingles has two primary parts to it: contracting chicken pox (preferably in childhood) and then being around those who have or have had chicken pox. Extensive vaccinations might not prevent some from catching chicken pox (primarily if they were not vaccinated), but this might mean that people are not around enough people who have had the disease to boost the immunity to it. Answer choice D, therefore, is correct. The author states that the amount of disease in the vaccine is not enough for those who have had chicken pox to boost their immunity to it (among those who have had the vaccine). The author does not, however, mention that the amount in the vaccine is not enough to prevent the shingles later on. Answer choice A cannot be correct. Answer choice B makes little sense. The fears of researchers should not be based on whether there are enough people to use for the study of a disease. Answer choice C has little connection to the question that is posed, so it too cannot be correct.

19. B: The author notes that epidemiologists project the possibility for over 20 million cases of shingles and about 5,000 deaths from the disease. Nothing is mentioned, however, about the time period over which this could occur. One year? Five years? Ten years? Without this information, it is difficult to know how serious of a problem this really is. (In reality, these numbers are projected over the course of fifty years, something that would greatly aid the reader in appreciating the information better.) The names of the researchers would make no difference to the reader's appreciation of the information. The detail about the countries where the vaccine is currently in use has little value for the reader, since these cases/deaths are projected in the United States. The information about the number of people currently vaccinated against chicken pox might be useful elsewhere in the essay, but it does very little to make the author's point stronger in the sentence that is mentioned.

20. C: As noted before, the author does not take a stand but rather focuses on providing information. As a result, the only valid inference from the final statement—when taken in the context of the entire essay—is that the ongoing debate means that researchers continue to evaluate and consider the long-term effects of the chicken pox vaccine. Nothing is said about researchers who advise against the vaccine; the only mention is that there is concern and debate. The final sentence notes only "ongoing debate," so there is not enough here (or in the rest of the essay) to infer that researchers believe the vaccine to cause more harm than good. The author says nothing about the number of people who have received or plan to receive the vaccine, so the reader cannot infer that the number of chicken pox vaccinations has decreased.

21. C: An expository composition *exposes* a subject matter by looking at it more closely and analyzing its significance. Additionally, the reader can determine the author's purpose through a process of elimination. As the author takes no clear stand on the issue and does not attempt to convince the reader to assume one side or the other, the passage cannot be persuasive. An investigative piece would require the subject matter to be a mystery that needs to be solved or a problem that needs to be revealed to the public. The author explores the topic and analyzes it more closely, but there is no major reveal within the passage. Finally, an advisory passage would be similar to a persuasive passage in that the author would encourage the reader to take a stand on the issue. As the author does not do that, the only possible answer choice is C.

22. D: The final two sentences of the passage present its main point. The World Health Organization agrees that the remaining samples of the smallpox vaccine should be destroyed, but those within the organization cannot agree about whether all of the samples should be destroyed and when the destruction should occur. Answer choice A cannot be correct because it suggests a persuasive tone that is not within the passage; the author presents information but does not take a stand on the issue. In the same way, answer choice B is incorrect; it offers the polar opposite view that is in answer choice A, but it is still persuasive in tone. And while the author suggests that the United States and Russia cannot agree about whether to destroy the samples, this small part of the passage cannot represent the main point.

Writing

1. A: The sentence refers to reindeer as a collective group, so the word *the* is not necessary. The words in choices B, C, and D are necessary for the meanings of the sentences.

2. D: No apostrophe is necessary because *hundreds* is plural, not possessive in this sentence. In choice A, *child's* is possessive of the word *home*, so the apostrophe is correct. In choice B, *its* is possessive, referring to the reindeer's antlers. *It's* is a contraction meaning "it is." Choice C refers to a plural possessive referring to many reindeer; therefore, *reindeers'* is correct.

3. B: *Because* is the best coordinating conjunction to connect the two independent clauses; the second explains the first. In choice A, although *since* can be used as a causal conjunction in place of *because*, it should not have a comma before it when joining two clauses. Choices C and D do not flow as well in the passage. The lichen should be mentioned first because that connects this sentence with the one before it. Marker

4. C: While it is true that animals roam to find food during the winter, sentence 10 halts the flow of the paragraph. Sentence 9 and sentence 11 both speak on the birth and rearing of caribou calves. Choices A, B, and D are appropriate to the topic and flow of the passage.

5. A: The instrument has been used for many *millennia*, the plural version of *millennium*. The words in choices B and C are correct as singular. The word in choice D is already plural.

6. C: The addition of the word *reeds* would correctly show that the cane has been used to create reeds for the oboes, not the oboes themselves. In choice A, the comma is correct after the introductory phrase. In choice B, no comma is needed after *create*. In choice D, the word *many* is unnecessary.

7. C: Sentence 16 begins with a participial phrase, "customizing them," so the subject of the next clause needs to be the one doing the customizing. This is not the case. The reeds are customized; they do not do the customizing. Choices A, B, and D are all grammatically correct sentences.

8. D: The second clause contrasts with the first, so the word *but* is the correct conjunction. Choices A, B, and C do not indicate that contrast between the two clauses.

9. B: In sentence 14, the clause that follows *but also* is dependent, so no comma is needed. The words referred to in choices A and C are essential to the sentence meaning, so no comma is needed. In choice D, the comma sets off an introductory phrase, so it is correct.

10. A: Sentence 1 provides the same information as sentence 2 but with less detail. The sentences in choices B, C, and D are relevant to the meaning of the passage.

11. C: The use of the word *have* here indicates the present perfect tense of "to go," which is *gone*, not *went*. The tenses of the verbs in choices A, B, and D are all incorrect.

12. C: The comma after the introductory word *thus* is correct. No comma is necessary before *and* because the clause that follows is a dependent clause. Choice A includes an incorrect comma before *and*. Choices B and C both lack the comma after *thus* and include an incorrect comma and semicolon, respectively, before the word *and*.

13. A: The art is less familiar to people today, so it is less *known*. The words in choices B, C, and D are used correctly.

14. B: The passage is informative about types of fabrics and how they have changed over time. Sentence 9 presents and opinion that does not relate to the other topics in the passage. Choices A, C, and D have meaning that is relevant to the passage.

15. B: Choice B reduces redundancy and includes a comma before the nonessential phrase starting with "which." Choice A is redundant in that it repeats "China," and it lacks a comma before *and*. Choice C is incorrect because there is no causality between the two clauses. Therefore, the use of *because* is incorrect. Choice D is incorrect, because it lacks a comma after China to set off the nonessential phrase.

The earliest known example was in China, and China is still the world's top producer by far.

16. C: The word *Despite* does not make sense in sentence 19. It should be replaced with *Like* or a similar word. The words in choices A, B, and D are all used correctly.

17. B: Following sentence 9, which mentions both animals and plants, it is unclear what the subject of sentence 10 is. The introductory phrase in the question would clarify that at the beginning of sentence 10. The phrase would not be appropriate in the sentences in choices A, C, or D.

18. A: The word *its* is the correct form for the possessive pronoun in this sentence; the contraction *it's* means "it is," which is not correct in this sentence. Choice B is not a word. Choice C is a plural pronoun, which is not correct for the singular subject *organism* in this sentence. Choice D is a contraction meaning "they are," which is not correct in this sentence.

19. B: The subject of this verb is *classification*, a singular noun that would take the verb *was*. The words in choices A, C, and D are all used correctly.

20. D: The information after the comma is essential to the meaning of the sentence, so the comma is an error. In choices A and B, a semicolon cannot be used, because it would not create two independent clauses. In choice C, the comma is necessary before the nonrestrictive information that follows. Marker

21. D: The information in sentence 25 is in a discussion of classification, and it does not fit in with the flow of the passage as it progresses toward a general conclusion. The sentences in choices A, B, and C are all relevant to the passage.

Mathematics

1. B: A percentage is a number of hundredths; in this case $75\% = \frac{75}{100}$. To find a percentage of a number you multiply the number by the percentage in fraction or decimal form. So 75% of 500 = $500 \times \frac{75}{100} = \frac{37500}{100} = 375$.

There is an alternative way to solve this problem. 75% is a common enough percentage that it's worth committing to memory its equivalent fraction: 75% is $\frac{3}{4}$ (which $\frac{75}{100}$ reduces to). So we're really looking for $\frac{3}{4}$ of 500. One quarter of 500 is $500 \div 4 = 125$, so three quarters of 500 is $125 \times 3 = 375$.

2. A: When performing a series of operations, we always perform the operations in parentheses first. We also always perform multiplications and divisions before additions and subtractions, so in this case even without the parentheses the order of operations would be the same. In any case, we first carry out the multiplications in the parentheses: $(7 \times 5) + (8 \times 2) = 35 + 16$. Now we carry out the addition: $35 + 16 = 51$.

3. D: When performing a series of operations, we always perform the operations in parentheses first. So we'll start with the divisions in parentheses: $(8 \div 2) \times (12 \div 3) = 4 \times 4$. Now we carry out the multiplication: $4 \times 4 = 16$. In this case, the parentheses didn't really matter; if we had just carried out the operations left to right we would have obtained the same answer. But that isn't always true: for instance, $(12 \div 2) \times 3 = 6 \times 3 = 18$, but $12 \div (2 \times 3) = 12 \div 6 = 2$.

4. D: A number is a **factor** of another number if the first number can be multiplied by some integer to get the second number. Equivalently, a number is a factor of another number if a division of the second number by the first number does not leave a remainder (or in other words leaves a remainder of zero). In this case, there is no integer we can multiply by 5 to get 36, and dividing 36 by 5 leaves a remainder of one. Either of these facts tells us that 5 is not a factor of 36. Neither 7 nor 8 can be multiplied by another number to get 36; dividing 36 by 7 leaves a remainder of 1, and dividing 36 by 8 leaves a remainder of 4. So 7 and 8 aren't factors of 36 either. However, we *can* multiply 9 by another number to get 36: $9 \times 4 = 36$. And so dividing 36 by 9 does not leave a remainder. So 9 is a factor of 36.

5. C: We can, of course, easily solve this problem by typing the operation into a calculator. But we can do it without a calculator as well. We write the numbers one above the other, and then start by multiplying 75 by 4: $5 \times 4 = 20$, write down the 0 and carry the 2, $7 \times 4 = 28$, plus 2 = 30:

$$\begin{array}{r} \overset{2}{7}5 \\ \times\ 34 \\ \hline 300 \end{array}$$

Now we multiply 75 by 3, writing this result one space to the left: $5 \times 3 = 15$, write down the 5 and carry the 1, $7 \times 3 = 21$, plus 1 = 22:

$$\begin{array}{r} \overset{1}{7}5 \\ \times\ 34 \\ \hline 300 \\ 225 \end{array}$$

Finally, we add the two lines together:

$$\begin{array}{r} 75 \\ \times\ 34 \\ \hline 300 \\ 225 \\ \hline 2550 \end{array}$$

6. B: To solve for a variable in an algebraic equation, we can isolate the variable on one side by reversing any operations done to it, carrying out the reverse operation on both sides. In this case, 372 is added to x; the reverse operation is *subtracting* 372: we can get rid of the 372 on the left side of the equation by subtracting 372 from both sides:

$$x + 372 = 853$$
$$x + 372 - 372 = 853 - 372$$
$$x = 481$$

7. A: 0.25 is a decimal that comes up often enough it's worth committing to memory, so you may know the answer to this without having to work anything out. Even if you don't, however, it's still possible to solve for it. The second space after the decimal is the hundredths space, so 0.25, with two digits after the decimal point, is equal to $\frac{25}{100}$. This can be simplified: $\frac{25 \div 25}{100 \div 25} = \frac{1}{4}$.

8. B: To convert a decimal into a fraction, we first note the place value of the rightmost digit in the decimal. In this case, 0.85 has two digits after the decimal point, and the space of the second digit after the decimal point is the hundredths space. Now, we take the digits after the decimal, and make them the numerator of a fraction with that denominator: in this case that gives us $\frac{85}{100}$. Finally, we simplify if possible. In this case, both the numerator and denominator are divisible by 5, so we can write $\frac{85}{100} = \frac{85 \div 5}{100 \div 5} = \frac{17}{20}$.

9. B: Perhaps the quickest way to solve this problem is to use a calculator to convert each fraction to a decimal, by dividing the numerator by the denominator. $6 \div 13 = 0.4615 \ldots$, $7 \div 12 = 0.5833 \ldots$, $11 \div 16 = 0.6875$, and $9 \div 12 = 0.75$. We want to compare those with $2 \div 3 = 0.6666 \ldots$. It is evident that 0.6875 and 0.75 are greater than 0.6666..., and of the remaining two numbers, the larger is 0.5833..., or $\frac{7}{12}$.

It is possible to solve this problem without a calculator and without converting the fractions to decimals, but it is more involved. There are some shortcuts we can use if we're familiar with fractions to make some estimates that will help us, but without those shortcuts we'll have to compare each fraction to $\frac{2}{3}$, finding which ones are less than $\frac{2}{3}$ and what the difference is. To find the difference between $\frac{2}{3}$ and $\frac{6}{13}$, we can rewrite both fractions with the same denominator, $\frac{2 \times 13}{3 \times 13} = \frac{26}{39}$ and $\frac{6 \times 3}{13 \times 3} = \frac{18}{39}$. $26 > 18$, so $\frac{6}{13} < \frac{2}{3}$... so far so good. The difference is $\frac{26-18}{39} = \frac{8}{39}$. Proceeding similarly with the other numbers, we find that the difference between $\frac{2}{3}$ and $\frac{7}{12}$ is $\frac{1}{12}$, and that both $\frac{11}{16}$ and $\frac{9}{12}$ are greater than $\frac{2}{3}$, ruling these last two out as answers. So the answer must be A or B; it only remains to find which is closer to $\frac{2}{3}$—i.e. which difference is smaller. Converting them, again, to the same denominator, we get $\frac{8}{39} = \frac{8\times 4}{39\times 4} = \frac{32}{156}$, and $\frac{1}{12} = \frac{1\times 13}{12\times 13} = \frac{13}{156}$. Clearly $13 < 32$, so $\frac{1}{12} < \frac{8}{39}$, and so it is $\frac{7}{12}$ which is closer to $\frac{2}{3}$.

10. B: If $\frac{1}{3}$ of the patients seen are pediatric patients, then $\frac{1}{3}$ of the circle should indicate pediatric. The full circle contains 360 degrees, so $\frac{1}{3}$ of the circle is $\frac{1}{3}$ of 360 = 120 degrees.

11. C: The average of a series of values is equal to the total sum of the values divided by the number of values. In this case, then, to find the average weekly food expenditure we divide the total food expenditure times the number of weeks. From the given information, the total food expenditure is $25 + $52 + $52 + $34 = $163. This was over four weeks, so the average weekly food expenditure was $163 ÷ 4 = $40.75.

12. A: We can easily solve this problem by typing the operation into a calculator. However, it's not difficult to do without a calculator, either. We just write the numbers one over the other, lining them up at the decimal point and padding the top number with zeroes on the right until it goes out to the same number of places as the bottom number:

$$437.650$$
$$-325.752$$

Now, we subtract the two exactly as we would subtract ordinary integers, putting the decimal point in our answer in the same place as it is in the numbers above:

$$\begin{array}{r} 6^15^14 \\ 437.6\cancel{5}\cancel{0} \\ -\ 325.752 \\ \hline 111.898 \end{array}$$

13. A: Again, we can solve this problem simply by just typing the expression into a calculator. However, it can also be done without a calculator. We can multiply these numbers just as if they were integers, ignoring the decimal points at first:

$$\begin{array}{r} 43.3 \\ \times\ 23.03 \\ \hline 1299 \\ 0 \\ 1299 \\ 866 \\ \hline 997199 \end{array}$$

Now, we count the total number of digits after the decimal points in the factors, and place the decimal point in the product so that it has that same number of digits after it. In this case, 43.3 has one digit after the decimal point, and 23.03 has two, so our product should have three digits after the decimal point. The answer is 997.199.

14. D: To find out how much the patient lost, we need to calculate 6% of 157. A percentage is a number of hundredths, so we can express 6% as either a fraction, $\frac{6}{100}$, or a decimal, 0.06. Either way, to find 6% of 157, we can multiply this fraction or decimal by 157: $0.06 \times 157 = 9.42$, or, rounded to the nearest pound, 9. That's the amount of weight *lost*, so to find the final weight we subtract that from the initial weight, 157: $157 - 9 = 148$.

Alternatively, we could have done the subtraction first: if the patient lost 6% of their original body weight, then their final weight was 100% − 6% = 94% of their body weight. We then can multiply that by 157: 94% × 157 = 0.94 × 157 = 147.58, which rounds to 148.

15. B: 65% of the school's 650 students must request the vending machine. To determine how many students that is, we just multiply 65% by 650. 65% means 65 hundredths, so we can express the percentage as a fraction, $\frac{65}{100}$, or as a decimal, 0.65, and then carry out the multiplication: 0.65 × 650 = 422.5, which we can round up to 423.

So, we know that 423 students must request the vending machine. We are told that 340 students have already requested it. To find out how many *more* students must request the vending machine, then, we just subtract the number of students who have already requested it from the total number of students required: 423 − 340 = 83.

16. C: The digit just before the decimal point is in the unit (ones) space, and each space right from there represents $\frac{1}{10}$ the amount of the previous space. The digit just after the decimal place is the tenths place, and the digit after that—the second digit after the decimal place—is the hundredths. This, then, is the digit we want to round to: the second digit after the decimal place, which in this case is 4. Because the next digit after that, 6, is greater than 5, we round up, so the 4 becomes a 5 and we remove all the following digits. So we're left with 390.25.

17. A: One way to solve this problem is as follows: We're asked, effectively, to solve the equation $\frac{4}{5}x = 1$. We can get the x by itself by dividing both sides by $\frac{4}{5}$: so $x = 1 \div \frac{4}{5}$. Dividing by a fraction is equivalent to multiplying by its reciprocal—the same fraction with the numerator and denominator swapped—so this is equivalent to $1 \times \frac{5}{4}$, which of course is just $\frac{5}{4}$.

However, we don't have to go to that much trouble, if we just recall that a fraction times its reciprocal is always 1. So if we want to know what number times $\frac{4}{5}$ will equal 1, the answer must be just the reciprocal of $\frac{4}{5}$, which is $\frac{5}{4}$.

18. C: The average of a series of values is equal to the total sum of the values divided by the number of values. In this case, the sum is 300 mg + 1240 mg + 900 mg + 1500 mg + 900 mg = 4840 mg. This is the total over five days, so to find the average we divide this total by five: 4840 mg ÷ 5 = 968 mg.

19. C: The tenth is the first digit after the decimal point. This rules out A, which leaves *two* digits after the decimal point, which means it's rounded to the nearest hundredth. When rounding, we round *down*—leaving the last digit as it is—if the next digit is less than 5, and we round *up*—increasing the last digit by 1—if it is 5 or greater. In choice B, the digit after the tenths digit is a 6, so the number should be rounded up: the tenths digit should be increased. But it isn't—the 5 remains a 5 rather than being changed to a 6. Conversely, in choice D, the digit after the tenths digit is a 2, so the number should be rounded down: the tenths digit should stay the same. But instead, it's incorrectly increased to 4. Choices B and D are therefore incorrect.

In choice C, the digit after the tenths digit is 8. This means we round up, the 9 changes to a 10. The 1 carries over to the next digit to the left, increasing it as well. This is exactly what we see in the answer: the 9 changes to a 0 and the 6 increases to a 7. Choice C is therefore the correct answer. As for the other answers, the number in choice A should be rounded to 3.8; choice B should be rounded to 4.6; and choice D should be rounded to 54.3.

20. C: There are several ways to approach this problem. One is to express the decimal as a fraction. Since there are three digits after the decimal point, the decimal represents a number of thousandths; the equivalent fraction is $\frac{625}{1000}$. Since both 625 and 1000 are divisible by 5, this fraction can be reduced to $\frac{625 \div 5}{1000 \div 5} = \frac{125}{200}$. Since 125 and 200 are also both divisible by 5, we can further reduce the fraction to $\frac{125 \div 5}{200 \div 5} = \frac{25}{40}$. We can still repeat the process one more time: $\frac{25 \div 5}{40 \div 5} = \frac{5}{8}$.

While this is the most straightforward way to solve the problem, we could also have done it the other way around, converting each fraction to a decimal and seeing which one matched. We can convert a fraction to a decimal by just dividing the numerator by the denominator (a calculator makes this easier, but isn't required). $\frac{3}{4} = 3 \div 4 = 0.75$, $\frac{5}{6} = 5 \div 6 = 0.8333...$, $\frac{5}{8} = 0.625$ (as desired), and $\frac{2}{3} = 0.6666...$

21. A: We can call the volume of the solution that can be made x. We know 6% of the solution is pure bleach. We can therefore express the amount of bleach as $6\% \times x$—or, converting the 6% into a decimal, $0.06x$. (A percentage is a number of hundredths, so we can convert a percentage to a decimal by dividing by 100—or, equivalently, by moving the decimal point two spaces to the left.) Now, the amount of pure bleach that we have is 50 mL. That means $0.06x = 50$ mL. To solve for x, we can divide both sides by 0.06: $\frac{0.06x}{0.06} = \frac{50 \text{ mL}}{0.06}$, so $x = 50$ mL $\div$ 0.06 $= 833.333...$ mL, which rounds to 833 mL.

We could also have expressed the percentage as a fraction instead of a decimal: $6\% = \frac{6}{100}$, so $\frac{6}{100}x = 50$ mL, and $x = 50$ mL $\div \frac{6}{100} = 50$ mL $\times \frac{100}{6} = \frac{5000 \text{ mL}}{6} = 833.333...$ mL, again rounding to 833 mL.

22. A: While we could solve this problem easily using a calculator, it's also not that hard to solve by hand. To multiply two decimal numbers, follow the same procedure as if you were multiplying two ordinary integers, ignoring the decimal point until the last step:

```
      8.7
   × 23.3
    26 1
    261
    174
   2027 1
```

Then, count the total number of digits after the decimal points in the two factors. The product should have that same number of digits after the decimal point. 8.7 has one digit after the decimal point, and 23.3 has one, so between them they have a total of two digits after the decimal points. So the product should also have two digits after the decimal point, and the correct answer is 202.71.

23. A: This is another problem that we could solve with a calculator, but that we could also do without a calculator if necessary. To divide a decimal number, we can perform a long division the same way as we would if we were dividing integers, placing the decimal point in the quotient directly above the decimal point in the dividend.

$$\begin{array}{r} 26.9 \\ 5\overline{)134.5} \\ \underline{10} \\ 34 \\ \underline{30} \\ 4\,5 \\ \underline{4\,5} \\ 0 \end{array}$$

If there had also been a decimal point in the divisor, we would have to eliminate it by moving the decimal point to the right the same number of spaces in the dividend as the number of digits after the decimal point in the divisor. In this case, however, the divisor was an integer, so that wasn't necessary.

24. C: A fraction is essentially a way to express a quotient: it's equal to the numerator divided by the denominator. So $23 \div 3$ can be written as $\frac{23}{3}$. However, this is an improper fraction—a fraction with a numerator larger than the denominator—while all the answer choices are mixed numbers—numbers consisting of an integer and a (proper) fraction.

We therefore have to convert this improper fraction into a mixed number. We do that by dividing the numerator by the denominator, making note of both the quotient and the remainder. $23 \div 3 = 7$, with a remainder of 2. The quotient is the integer in the mixed number, and the remainder is the numerator of the fraction part. So the correct answer is $7\frac{2}{3}$.

25. C: Once again, we could add these numbers with a calculator, but we could also do it by hand. We place the numbers in a column and add one place value at a time, carrying the tens digit of the sum as necessary. For example, $0 + 2 + 9 = 11$, so the rightmost digit of the answer is 1 and we carry a 1 to the next column, giving us $1 + 0 + 2 + 0 = 3$, and so on:

$$\begin{array}{r} 4500 \\ 3422 \\ +3909 \\ \hline 11831 \end{array}$$

26. C: This is a simple addition problem involving the process of carrying. Start with the ones column and add 4+7. Write down the 1 and add the 1 to the digits in the tens column: Now add 3+7+1. Write down the 1 and add the 1 to the digits in the hundreds column. Add 6+3+1 and write down 0. Add the 1 to the digits in the thousands column. Add 4+7+1 and write down the 1. Add the 1 to the digits in the ten-thousands column. Add 1+1 and write down 2 to get the answer 22,011.

27. D: This is a simple subtraction problem. Start with the ones column and subtract 5-2, then 4-3, then 6-1, then 9-6 to get 3,513.

28. D: This is a multiplication problem with carrying. Start with the ones column. Multiply 4 by each digit in above it beginning with the ones column. Write down each product: going across it will read 3572. Now multiply 6 by each of the digits above it. Write down each product: going across it will read 5358. Ensure that the 8 is in the tens column and the other numbers fall evenly to the right. Now add the numbers like a regular addition problem to get 57,152

Science

1. A: Sodium and potassium are the two key ingredients needed to transmit a message down the nerve cell. The ions move in and out of the cell to generate an action potential to convey the impulse. Once the impulse reaches the end of the neuron, calcium channels open to allow calcium to rush into the synaptic space. Actin and myosin are the two proteins that cause contraction of muscle fibers.

2. B: The answer is translocation. Nondisjunction is a genetic mutation where the chromosomes fail to separate after replication. This results in two cells with an abnormal number of chromosomes (one with too many, one with too few). Deletion is when a section of the chromosome is erased. Crossing over occurs when the two chromosomes are joined by the centromere and two of the legs cross over and switch places on the two chromosomes.

3. A: Our skin and mucus membranes are the first line of defense against potentially invading bacteria. Their purpose is to keep the bacteria from getting into the body in the first place. Any break or tear in the skin or mucus membranes can allow harmful bacteria or viruses to attack the body. Once inside, macrophages, T-cells, and lymphocytes will be summoned to attack infected body cells and the invading pathogens.

4. C: Capping the end of a mRNA strand protects the strand from degradation and "wear and tear." Such damage to a strand of mRNA could be catastrophic, as it directs the synthesis of proteins that are vital for life.

5. A: A clue here is that chlorophyll is involved, meaning this is a photosynthesis reaction. The light-dependent reaction involves a hydrolysis reaction to provide electrons to chlorophyll, and the release of oxygen molecules. During the light-independent reaction, the energy produced from the dependent reaction is stored in the form of chemical bonds in glucose molecules.

6. D: Photosynthesis is the process that plant cells use to obtain energy from the sun. Diffusion and active transport are both methods of ionic movement, but transpiration occurs when water moves up a plant's conduction tubes against the force of gravity.

7. C: Ethylene is the plant hormone that causes ripening of fruit. Auxins and cytokinins both promote cell growth. Auxins specifically encourage stem elongation and can also inhibit growth of lateral branches. Abscisic acid inhibits cell growth and seed germination.

8. D: Thigmotropism is the growth of plant structures in response to physical contact, similar to how vines will change their direction of growth to stay in contact with a wall or other item. Growth towards light is called phototropism, and gravitropism is growth of leaves and stems opposite to the force of gravity.

9. A: The stigma is a long tube that extends from the center of a flower whose function it is to gather pollen and transport it down the carpel toward the ovum. The bright colored petals of a flower help attract pollinators like birds, bees, and butterflies. Pollen is made in the stamen and anther, which protrude from the flower to make it easier for the pollinators to gather pollen as they fly from flower to flower. The ovary of the flower provides nourishment for the developing seeds.

10. B: Think of the mnemonic "Dear King Philip Came Over For Good Soup." This stands for domain, kingdom, phylum, class, order, family, genus, species. It relates the classification system for every species organism in the world. The further down the line that two species are similar, the more closely related they are. Genus is the most specific taxonomic category listed in the given answer choices, and so organisms with the same genus are most closely related.

11. A: The triceps reflex forces the triceps to contract, which in turn extends the arm. Eliciting the deep tendon reflexes is an important indication of neural functioning. Without them, it can be a clue to serious spinal cord or other neurological injury. The physician should be notified immediately if a patient loses deep tendon reflexes.

12. C: The acoustic nerve, or CN VIII, is responsible for hearing and balance. To test this nerve, the practitioner could test the patient's hearing in each ear and use a tuning fork to determine the patient's ability to hear and feel the vibrations.

13. A: The parathyroid glands are four small glands that sit on top of the thyroid gland and regulate calcium levels by secreting parathyroid hormone. The hormone regulates the amount of calcium and magnesium that is excreted by the kidneys into the urine.

14. D: The empty egg follicle (once the egg was ovulated) is now called the corpus luteum and secretes large amounts of progesterone. Progesterone is the primary hormone responsible for maintaining a pregnancy. Follicle stimulating hormone and luteinizing hormone have already stopped production, and estrogen decreased right before ovulation.

15. B: Insulin and glucagon are the two main options here. Insulin is produced during periods of high blood sugar and promotes glucose absorption into the cells and the storage of glucose as glycogen and lipids in the liver. Glucagon has the opposite effect; when blood sugar is low, glucagon production promotes the breakdown of glycogen into glucose.

16. C: The SA node in the right atrium generates the impulse that travels through the heart tissue and to the AV node. The AV node sits in the wall of the right atrium and coordinates atrial and ventricular contraction of the heart. The impulse then travels down to the bundle of His, the two main (left and right) branches of conduction fibers and to the Purkinje fibers which spread the impulse throughout the rest of the heart.

17. A: This is a tricky question; most of the time, veins carry deoxygenated blood and arteries carry oxygenated blood. However, in this case, the pulmonary veins carry oxygenated blood from the lungs to the heart and the pulmonary arteries carry deoxygenated blood from the heart to the lungs.

18. B: Vitamin K is stored by the liver and is essential for the synthesis and conversion of several clotting factors, including Factor II, Factor VII, Factor IX, and Factor X. Without adequate amounts of this vitamin, the clotting factors will not be able to function properly.

19. C: Afferent vessels carry fluid toward a structure; efferent vessels carry fluid away from the structure. So afferent lymph vessels carry lymph towards the node, and efferent vessels carry lymph away from the node.

20. A: The mediastinum is found in the middle of the thorax, right between the lungs. It contains many structures, including the heart, the upper part of the aorta, pulmonary blood vessels, the superior and inferior vena cava, the thymus, the trachea, the esophagus, and large nerves, such as the phrenic, vagus, and cardiac. The xiphoid process lies below the mediastinum.

How to Overcome Test Anxiety

Just the thought of taking a test is enough to make most people a little nervous. A test is an important event that can have a long-term impact on your future, so it's important to take it seriously and it's natural to feel anxious about performing well. But just because anxiety is normal, that doesn't mean that it's helpful in test taking, or that you should simply accept it as part of your life. Anxiety can have a variety of effects. These effects can be mild, like making you feel slightly nervous, or severe, like blocking your ability to focus or remember even a simple detail.

If you experience test anxiety—whether severe or mild—it's important to know how to beat it. To discover this, first you need to understand what causes test anxiety.

Causes of Test Anxiety

While we often think of anxiety as an uncontrollable emotional state, it can actually be caused by simple, practical things. One of the most common causes of test anxiety is that a person does not feel adequately prepared for their test. This feeling can be the result of many different issues such as poor study habits or lack of organization, but the most common culprit is time management. Starting to study too late, failing to organize your study time to cover all of the material, or being distracted while you study will mean that you're not well prepared for the test. This may lead to cramming the night before, which will cause you to be physically and mentally exhausted for the test. Poor time management also contributes to feelings of stress, fear, and hopelessness as you realize you are not well prepared but don't know what to do about it.

Other times, test anxiety is not related to your preparation for the test but comes from unresolved fear. This may be a past failure on a test, or poor performance on tests in general. It may come from comparing yourself to others who seem to be performing better or from the stress of living up to expectations. Anxiety may be driven by fears of the future—how failure on this test would affect your educational and career goals. These fears are often completely irrational, but they can still negatively impact your test performance.

Review Video: 3 Reasons You Have Test Anxiety
Visit mometrix.com/academy and enter code: 428468

Elements of Test Anxiety

As mentioned earlier, test anxiety is considered to be an emotional state, but it has physical and mental components as well. Sometimes you may not even realize that you are suffering from test anxiety until you notice the physical symptoms. These can include trembling hands, rapid heartbeat, sweating, nausea, and tense muscles. Extreme anxiety may lead to fainting or vomiting. Obviously, any of these symptoms can have a negative impact on testing. It is important to recognize them as soon as they begin to occur so that you can address the problem before it damages your performance.

> **Review Video: 3 Ways to Tell You Have Test Anxiety**
> Visit mometrix.com/academy and enter code: 927847

The mental components of test anxiety include trouble focusing and inability to remember learned information. During a test, your mind is on high alert, which can help you recall information and stay focused for an extended period of time. However, anxiety interferes with your mind's natural processes, causing you to blank out, even on the questions you know well. The strain of testing during anxiety makes it difficult to stay focused, especially on a test that may take several hours. Extreme anxiety can take a huge mental toll, making it difficult not only to recall test information but even to understand the test questions or pull your thoughts together.

> **Review Video: How Test Anxiety Affects Memory**
> Visit mometrix.com/academy and enter code: 609003

Effects of Test Anxiety

Test anxiety is like a disease—if left untreated, it will get progressively worse. Anxiety leads to poor performance, and this reinforces the feelings of fear and failure, which in turn lead to poor performances on subsequent tests. It can grow from a mild nervousness to a crippling condition. If allowed to progress, test anxiety can have a big impact on your schooling, and consequently on your future.

Test anxiety can spread to other parts of your life. Anxiety on tests can become anxiety in any stressful situation, and blanking on a test can turn into panicking in a job situation. But fortunately, you don't have to let anxiety rule your testing and determine your grades. There are a number of relatively simple steps you can take to move past anxiety and function normally on a test and in the rest of life.

> **Review Video: How Test Anxiety Impacts Your Grades**
> Visit mometrix.com/academy and enter code: 939819

Physical Steps for Beating Test Anxiety

While test anxiety is a serious problem, the good news is that it can be overcome. It doesn't have to control your ability to think and remember information. While it may take time, you can begin taking steps today to beat anxiety.

Just as your first hint that you may be struggling with anxiety comes from the physical symptoms, the first step to treating it is also physical. Rest is crucial for having a clear, strong mind. If you are tired, it is much easier to give in to anxiety. But if you establish good sleep habits, your body and mind will be ready to perform optimally, without the strain of exhaustion. Additionally, sleeping well helps you to retain information better, so you're more likely to recall the answers when you see the test questions.

Getting good sleep means more than going to bed on time. It's important to allow your brain time to relax. Take study breaks from time to time so it doesn't get overworked, and don't study right before bed. Take time to rest your mind before trying to rest your body, or you may find it difficult to fall asleep.

> **Review Video: The Importance of Sleep for Your Brain**
> Visit mometrix.com/academy and enter code: 319338

Along with sleep, other aspects of physical health are important in preparing for a test. Good nutrition is vital for good brain function. Sugary foods and drinks may give a burst of energy but this burst is followed by a crash, both physically and emotionally. Instead, fuel your body with protein and vitamin-rich foods.

Also, drink plenty of water. Dehydration can lead to headaches and exhaustion, especially if your brain is already under stress from the rigors of the test. Particularly if your test is a long one, drink water during the breaks. And if possible, take an energy-boosting snack to eat between sections.

> **Review Video: How Diet Can Affect your Mood**
> Visit mometrix.com/academy and enter code: 624317

Along with sleep and diet, a third important part of physical health is exercise. Maintaining a steady workout schedule is helpful, but even taking 5-minute study breaks to walk can help get your blood pumping faster and clear your head. Exercise also releases endorphins, which contribute to a positive feeling and can help combat test anxiety.

When you nurture your physical health, you are also contributing to your mental health. If your body is healthy, your mind is much more likely to be healthy as well. So take time to rest, nourish your body with healthy food and water, and get moving as much as possible. Taking these physical steps will make you stronger and more able to take the mental steps necessary to overcome test anxiety.

Mental Steps for Beating Test Anxiety

Working on the mental side of test anxiety can be more challenging, but as with the physical side, there are clear steps you can take to overcome it. As mentioned earlier, test anxiety often stems from lack of preparation, so the obvious solution is to prepare for the test. Effective studying may be the most important weapon you have for beating test anxiety, but you can and should employ several other mental tools to combat fear.

First, boost your confidence by reminding yourself of past success—tests or projects that you aced. If you're putting as much effort into preparing for this test as you did for those, there's no reason you should expect to fail here. Work hard to prepare; then trust your preparation.

Second, surround yourself with encouraging people. It can be helpful to find a study group, but be sure that the people you're around will encourage a positive attitude. If you spend time with others who are anxious or cynical, this will only contribute to your own anxiety. Look for others who are motivated to study hard from a desire to succeed, not from a fear of failure.

Third, reward yourself. A test is physically and mentally tiring, even without anxiety, and it can be helpful to have something to look forward to. Plan an activity following the test, regardless of the outcome, such as going to a movie or getting ice cream.

When you are taking the test, if you find yourself beginning to feel anxious, remind yourself that you know the material. Visualize successfully completing the test. Then take a few deep, relaxing breaths and return to it. Work through the questions carefully but with confidence, knowing that you are capable of succeeding.

Developing a healthy mental approach to test taking will also aid in other areas of life. Test anxiety affects more than just the actual test—it can be damaging to your mental health and even contribute to depression. It's important to beat test anxiety before it becomes a problem for more than testing.

> **Review Video: Test Anxiety and Depression**
> Visit mometrix.com/academy and enter code: 904704

Study Strategy

Being prepared for the test is necessary to combat anxiety, but what does being prepared look like? You may study for hours on end and still not feel prepared. What you need is a strategy for test prep. The next few pages outline our recommended steps to help you plan out and conquer the challenge of preparation.

STEP 1: SCOPE OUT THE TEST

Learn everything you can about the format (multiple choice, essay, etc.) and what will be on the test. Gather any study materials, course outlines, or sample exams that may be available. Not only will this help you to prepare, but knowing what to expect can help to alleviate test anxiety.

STEP 2: MAP OUT THE MATERIAL

Look through the textbook or study guide and make note of how many chapters or sections it has. Then divide these over the time you have. For example, if a book has 15 chapters and you have five days to study, you need to cover three chapters each day. Even better, if you have the time, leave an extra day at the end for overall review after you have gone through the material in depth.

If time is limited, you may need to prioritize the material. Look through it and make note of which sections you think you already have a good grasp on, and which need review. While you are studying, skim quickly through the familiar sections and take more time on the challenging parts. Write out your plan so you don't get lost as you go. Having a written plan also helps you feel more in control of the study, so anxiety is less likely to arise from feeling overwhelmed at the amount to cover.

STEP 3: GATHER YOUR TOOLS

Decide what study method works best for you. Do you prefer to highlight in the book as you study and then go back over the highlighted portions? Or do you type out notes of the important information? Or is it helpful to make flashcards that you can carry with you? Assemble the pens, index cards, highlighters, post-it notes, and any other materials you may need so you won't be distracted by getting up to find things while you study.

If you're having a hard time retaining the information or organizing your notes, experiment with different methods. For example, try color-coding by subject with colored pens, highlighters, or post-it notes. If you learn better by hearing, try recording yourself reading your notes so you can listen while in the car, working out, or simply sitting at your desk. Ask a friend to quiz you from your flashcards, or try teaching someone the material to solidify it in your mind.

STEP 4: CREATE YOUR ENVIRONMENT

It's important to avoid distractions while you study. This includes both the obvious distractions like visitors and the subtle distractions like an uncomfortable chair (or a too-comfortable couch that makes you want to fall asleep). Set up the best study environment possible: good lighting and a comfortable work area. If background music helps you focus, you may want to turn it on, but otherwise keep the room quiet. If you are using a computer to take notes, be sure you don't have any other windows open, especially applications like social media, games, or anything else that could distract you. Silence your phone and turn off notifications. Be sure to keep water close by so you stay hydrated while you study (but avoid unhealthy drinks and snacks).

Also, take into account the best time of day to study. Are you freshest first thing in the morning? Try to set aside some time then to work through the material. Is your mind clearer in the afternoon or evening? Schedule your study session then. Another method is to study at the same time of day that you will take the test, so that your brain gets used to working on the material at that time and will be ready to focus at test time.

STEP 5: STUDY!

Once you have done all the study preparation, it's time to settle into the actual studying. Sit down, take a few moments to settle your mind so you can focus, and begin to follow your study plan. Don't give in to distractions or let yourself procrastinate. This is your time to prepare so you'll be ready to fearlessly approach the test. Make the most of the time and stay focused.

Of course, you don't want to burn out. If you study too long you may find that you're not retaining the information very well. Take regular study breaks. For example, taking five minutes out of every hour to walk briskly, breathing deeply and swinging your arms, can help your mind stay fresh.

As you get to the end of each chapter or section, it's a good idea to do a quick review. Remind yourself of what you learned and work on any difficult parts. When you feel that you've mastered the material, move on to the next part. At the end of your study session, briefly skim through your notes again.

But while review is helpful, cramming last minute is NOT. If at all possible, work ahead so that you won't need to fit all your study into the last day. Cramming overloads your brain with more information than it can process and retain, and your tired mind may struggle to recall even previously learned information when it is overwhelmed with last-minute study. Also, the urgent nature of cramming and the stress placed on your brain contribute to anxiety. You'll be more likely to go to the test feeling unprepared and having trouble thinking clearly.

So don't cram, and don't stay up late before the test, even just to review your notes at a leisurely pace. Your brain needs rest more than it needs to go over the information again. In fact, plan to finish your studies by noon or early afternoon the day before the test. Give your brain the rest of the day to relax or focus on other things, and get a good night's sleep. Then you will be fresh for the test and better able to recall what you've studied.

STEP 6: TAKE A PRACTICE TEST

Many courses offer sample tests, either online or in the study materials. This is an excellent resource to check whether you have mastered the material, as well as to prepare for the test format and environment.

Check the test format ahead of time: the number of questions, the type (multiple choice, free response, etc.), and the time limit. Then create a plan for working through them. For example, if you have 30 minutes to take a 60-question test, your limit is 30 seconds per question. Spend less time on the questions you know well so that you can take more time on the difficult ones.

If you have time to take several practice tests, take the first one open book, with no time limit. Work through the questions at your own pace and make sure you fully understand them. Gradually work up to taking a test under test conditions: sit at a desk with all study materials put away and set a timer. Pace yourself to make sure you finish the test with time to spare and go back to check your answers if you have time.

After each test, check your answers. On the questions you missed, be sure you understand why you missed them. Did you misread the question (tests can use tricky wording)? Did you forget the information? Or was it something you hadn't learned? Go back and study any shaky areas that the practice tests reveal.

Taking these tests not only helps with your grade, but also aids in combating test anxiety. If you're already used to the test conditions, you're less likely to worry about it, and working through tests until you're scoring well gives you a confidence boost. Go through the practice tests until you feel comfortable, and then you can go into the test knowing that you're ready for it.

Test Tips

On test day, you should be confident, knowing that you've prepared well and are ready to answer the questions. But aside from preparation, there are several test day strategies you can employ to maximize your performance.

First, as stated before, get a good night's sleep the night before the test (and for several nights before that, if possible). Go into the test with a fresh, alert mind rather than staying up late to study.

Try not to change too much about your normal routine on the day of the test. It's important to eat a nutritious breakfast, but if you normally don't eat breakfast at all, consider eating just a protein bar. If you're a coffee drinker, go ahead and have your normal coffee. Just make sure you time it so that the caffeine doesn't wear off right in the middle of your test. Avoid sugary beverages, and drink enough water to stay hydrated but not so much that you need a restroom break 10 minutes into the test. If your test isn't first thing in the morning, consider going for a walk or doing a light workout before the test to get your blood flowing.

Allow yourself enough time to get ready, and leave for the test with plenty of time to spare so you won't have the anxiety of scrambling to arrive in time. Another reason to be early is to select a good seat. It's helpful to sit away from doors and windows, which can be distracting. Find a good seat, get out your supplies, and settle your mind before the test begins.

When the test begins, start by going over the instructions carefully, even if you already know what to expect. Make sure you avoid any careless mistakes by following the directions.

Then begin working through the questions, pacing yourself as you've practiced. If you're not sure on an answer, don't spend too much time on it, and don't let it shake your confidence. Either skip it and come back later, or eliminate as many wrong answers as possible and guess among the remaining ones. Don't dwell on these questions as you continue—put them out of your mind and focus on what lies ahead.

Be sure to read all of the answer choices, even if you're sure the first one is the right answer. Sometimes you'll find a better one if you keep reading. But don't second-guess yourself if you do immediately know the answer. Your gut instinct is usually right. Don't let test anxiety rob you of the information you know.

If you have time at the end of the test (and if the test format allows), go back and review your answers. Be cautious about changing any, since your first instinct tends to be correct, but make sure you didn't misread any of the questions or accidentally mark the wrong answer choice. Look over any you skipped and make an educated guess.

At the end, leave the test feeling confident. You've done your best, so don't waste time worrying about your performance or wishing you could change anything. Instead, celebrate the successful completion of this test. And finally, use this test to learn how to deal with anxiety even better next time.

> **Review Video: 5 Tips to Beat Test Anxiety**
> Visit mometrix.com/academy and enter code: 570656

Important Qualification

Not all anxiety is created equal. If your test anxiety is causing major issues in your life beyond the classroom or testing center, or if you are experiencing troubling physical symptoms related to your anxiety, it may be a sign of a serious physiological or psychological condition. If this sounds like your situation, we strongly encourage you to seek professional help.

Tell Us Your Story

We at Mometrix would like to extend our heartfelt thanks to you for letting us be a part of your journey. It is an honor to serve people from all walks of life, people like you, who are committed to building the best future they can for themselves.

We know that each person's situation is unique. But we also know that, whether you are a young student or a mother of four, you care about working to make your own life and the lives of those around you better.

That's why we want to hear your story.

We want to know why you're taking this test. We want to know about the trials you've gone through to get here. And we want to know about the successes you've experienced after taking and passing your test.

In addition to your story, which can be an inspiration both to us and to others, we value your feedback. We want to know both what you loved about our book and what you think we can improve on.

The team at Mometrix would be absolutely thrilled to hear from you! So please, send us an email at tellusyourstory@mometrix.com or visit us at mometrix.com/tellusyourstory.php and let's stay in touch.

Additional Bonus Material

Due to our efforts to try to keep this book to a manageable length, we've created a link that will give you access to all of your additional bonus material.

> **Please visit**
> <u>http://www.mometrix.com/bonus948/kaplannursing</u> **to access the information.**

Made in the USA
Coppell, TX
15 April 2022